"I DON'T
    SEE COLOR"

Edited by

Bettina Bergo *and*

Tracey Nicholls

"I DON'T SEE COLOR"

Personal *and*
Critical Perspectives
on White Privilege

The Pennsylvania State University Press
University Park, Pennsylvania

On the cover: Rachel Echenberg, *Blind Spots*, performance, 2011.
Photo: Sebastien Worsnip.

The performance was visible through a translucent screen covered in
round holes that separated the audience from the action. The screen
flattened the live performance space into an image so that only
certain details could be focused on at once. In doing this, the piece
attempted to portray the blind spots of perception, forcing attention
to shift between the visible and the experiential.

Variations on a repetitive action of filling a tall glass with water,
drinking only half of it, and allowing the glass to slowly slip and
crash to the ground, repeated for forty minutes.

Library of Congress Cataloging-in-Publication Data

I don't see color : personal and critical perspectives on white
privilege / edited by Bettina Bergo and Tracey Nicholls.
    pages   cm
Summary: "A collection of essays weaving together theoretical
insights from philosophy, sociology, economics, psychology,
literature, and history, as well as the authors' personal narratives,
to examine the forms and persistence of white privilege"—
Provided by publisher.
Includes bibliographical references and index.
ISBN 978-0-271-06499-4 (cloth : alk. paper)
  1. Whites—Race identity.
  2. Racism.
  3. Race relations.
  I. Bergo, Bettina, editor.
  II. Nicholls, Tracey, editor.

HT1575.I22   2015
305.809—dc23
2014027258

The Pennsylvania State University Press is a member of the
Association of American University Presses.

It is the policy of The Pennsylvania State University Press to use
acid-free paper. Publications on uncoated stock satisfy the minimum
requirements of American National Standard for Information
Sciences—Permanence of Paper for Printed Library Material,
ANSI Z39.48–1992.

This book is printed on paper that contains 30%
post-consumer waste.

Contents

Foreword

Eula Biss

Having worked under the relentless command of an infant, I am convinced that one of the most curious cruelties of babies is the way they compel us to mercy. This mercy they draw from us may be beautiful, like all mercies, but it is not effortless.

"For black people," Hilton Als writes, "being around white people is sometimes like taking care of babies you don't like, babies who throw up on you again and again, but whom you cannot punish, because they're babies." What a burden this mercy is. And what a tender metaphor Als offers for the burden our privilege imposes on others. Babies are made powerful, when we allow them power, only through their helplessness. It is one thing to understand one's privilege as a kind of power, but quite another to understand that power as a kind of helplessness.

"That's the life," old men used to joke with me as I pushed my baby in his carriage. They meant, I suppose, being constantly cared for and tended to by a woman. But neither the baby nor I believed that this was the life. We had both seen enough of helplessness to want something else for ourselves.

Babies, by nature, are not aware that they are babies. Once they can point at other babies and say "baby," they aren't really babies any more. So, too, with those of us who believe ourselves to be educators or executives or public servants—until we can point at each other and say "baby," the humiliating truth remains evident only to those who serve us our pacifiers.

Privilege does not exalt us so much as it diminishes us, though we like to imagine otherwise. We like to imagine that it is a privilege to be privileged. Strange, that our fantasies would be such perfect inversions of what we live that they read like code or encryption. The powerful feel vulnerable and are plagued by fear, and those of us who live our lives as babies like to imagine others as infantile even as they care for us.

When a conference on whiteness was held at the university where a friend of mine teaches, she asked me, "Why should we dedicate a weekend to study whiteness when it's all whiteness studies all the time everywhere?" What

she meant, of course, was that when we study art history or anthropology or poetry we are very often taught in terms of whiteness, bounded within the limits of whiteness. But what happens to whiteness there is the opposite of study—whiteness isn't being looked at so much as looked through.

Looking at something we've been trained all our lives to look through can be like grasping water or examining glass. There may seem to be an artifact in the lens, but then we find that the artifact is our eye and that the lens is a mirror. Even language betrays us: "earn" no longer means "earn" and "deserve" means nothing at all.

"Don't be a baby" is something you can say to a baby who knows he is a baby, but until he understands exactly what it means to be a baby, that command is useless. We can grow old and go to our graves still babies, all the while imposing our infancy, and the demands of our care, on everyone around us. But we do not have to remain babies. I believe in the power of study to offer us some existential maturity. This book harnesses the power of study, and invites us to look at, rather than through, whiteness. By including works that are not just scholarly but also narrative, that deal not just in theory but also in lived experience, the editors make the bold proposition that the insights offered here might not be simply absorbed but also applied.

My baby never learned the word "diaper"; he preferred to ask for "change." One day, I brought him a new diaper when he asked for change and it made him cry, because, as I finally understood, what he really wanted in that moment was to change into something new, like a butterfly. "Transform" was the word he was looking for. That baby's ambition might well be applied to our study here. Yes, this book may change our thinking, replacing worn analysis with something fresher, but will we allow it to transform us?

Reference

Als, Hilton. 1999. A Pryor love. *New Yorker*, 13 September. http://www.newyorker.com/archive/1999/09/13/1999_09_13_068_TNY\LIBRY_000019041.

Introduction: A Focus on White Privilege Through Personal Narratives

Bettina Bergo and Tracey Nicholls

This volume is a collection in critical white studies with a specific focus on privilege. We come from the academic field of philosophy, but we are aware that the subject of white privilege has emerged from a host of disciplines, including philosophy, literature, sociology, psychology, and intellectual history. We have invited our contributors to adopt an expository style called "braided narrative," which links the authors' critical analyses to events and values that they identify as formative within their own lives. Our hope is that this stylistic innovation will provide students and readers with useful pedagogical tool, motivating them to inquire into their own experience of privilege. Our aim here is to map out relations between conscious perception, self-evaluation, and the ideas and images of white privilege tied to cultural and social institutions. It is in the service of this mapping that the personal narratives, which our expository choice "braids into" scholarly analysis, emerge as a crucial feature of critical white studies, as we understand it.

A critical white studies with a focus on privilege confronts the difficulty of the multiple meanings and interpretations of privilege. It raises the question of how to begin to study privilege in a synthetic way, a way that investigates the mutually reinforcing tendencies of privileges without obscuring the ways that each of them, as a distinct claim, enacts its own logic of entitlement. Privilege has a thick interpretive component, in that the identification of privilege carries a critical awareness of its presence and its impact, and this is invariably a matter of comparisons—among types of privilege but also among

bearers of privilege. One need only point out a privilege to elicit responses as varied as recognition and resignation, or indeed the conviction that the privilege in question is an earned right. Within a supposedly neutral framework, we discover that one person's privilege is frequently another's just deserts. Part of the difficulty lies in the absence of an overarching point of comparison: if one compares oneself to persons belonging to social or cultural groups, or to economic classes of people who have limited access to education, financial resources, or practical goods, one might say that one has privilege. Frequently, however, the response is to challenge that comparison with the claim that it is every bit as legitimate to compare oneself only with the members of one's own socioeconomic or cultural or educational group. A number of authors (George Yancy and Ernest-Marie Mbonda, among others) have pointed to this claim as salient to the invisibility, especially to whites, of whiteness as race and symbol.[1] And the presupposition of the universality or normalcy of one's racial or ethnic position may indeed influence the choice to compare oneself with members of one's primary reference group.

An interesting feature of this process lies in the close relationship between certain affects, like resentment or victimization, and the ability to perceive privilege at all. We see this in the protest, "But I worked for everything that I have; I have given back to my community; I pay taxes." In chapter 7 in this volume, George Yancy notes that a white student in his class on slavery and racism remarked, incongruously, "that she did not understand how her whiteness could possibly be a site of terror as she did not own any black people as slaves and was not violent toward black people." Moreover, the insistence that responses like these refuse to acknowledge privilege is similarly deflected as "liberal guilt," "ideology," or, worse, third-party "resentment." This has the effect of reducing the debate to parochialism, in that from a fictive, overarching viewpoint, differences in perspective are judged irreconcilable and in some sense equal; or again, that the critical, privilege-confronting perspective suffers as much from "ideology" as the perspective of the taxpayer who has harmed no one deliberately. In other words, the defensive reflex adopts a view from nowhere as a defense against what it perceives as a false "transcendentalism," whereby the critic or questioner forces his or her interlocutor to adopt—against his or her interests—a meta-class or metarace perspective. The contest here is for the "right" to assert the metaposition, which, in presenting comparative discourse as a competition for rhetorical hegemony, weakens all interclass and interracial comparison. Hence the terrible problem of identifying "privilege." How do we get past this conundrum?

If we consider the etymology of the word "privilege"—its formulation out of the verb *legere* (to bind), itself related to *lex, legis* (law)—then *privi-legere* looks like a contradiction.[2] What would a private law mean? The first etymological definition is suggestive: "An exceptional law that concerns a specific individual" could either elevate or diminish that individual's freedom of action or status within the community. In practice, however, social privileges—working as if they were "private laws"—typically elevate those persons they target. In critical white studies, a focus on privilege, understood minimally as the examination of the governing norms and symbols within given communities, entails grasping the history and dynamics through which persons or groups are constituted within a larger community as *differently* subject to precisely what holds the larger community together—i.e., the shared laws. In this regard, "privilege" as *privum-lex* frequently undermines the solidarity of the community, restructuring it in a vertical sense such that, practically and juridically, certain laws apply principally to the unprivileged while other laws relate to the privileged. Privilege is thus hostile to a system of social organization built upon concepts of equality and fairness—for example, a rule of law dedicated to the provision of common, even universal, human rights.

To be sure, discussions of the meaning of privilege in light of *privum lex* and its negative impact on communities will go on. In effect, this may be an "ideological" interpretation of *privilegere* (as though a private law could exist without a system of ideas supporting it), one that we are reading back into the complexities of the Roman law from a contemporary critical approach to white privilege. According to that objection, the critical perspective starts from a conception of implicit unearned advantages, setting those who have them outside an undetermined larger community in which some people are denied comparable privileges. But that debate remains within the stalemate of abstraction, like the competition for metapositions mentioned above.

The object of this volume is the *operation* of segregating and sanctioning that underlies the privilege reflex. As Peggy McIntosh, one of the earliest analysts of white privilege, observes, "though 'privilege' may confer power, it does not confer moral strength," and therefore it is crucial "to distinguish between earned strength [often on the part of the dominated] and unearned power conferred systemically" (1986, 296). The systemic bestowal of privilege as unearned power is perpetuated through its connection with mystifications and symbolic strategies that sacralize or give a timeless, universal character to the entitlements of privilege. Having admitted the difficulties, and above all the artificiality, of the polemics staking out metapositions, we

approach the concept from the perspective of the application of laws and norms. If this volume operates on a presupposition, it is the desirability of promoting equality, but also equity, in a society based on democratic values.

Following McIntosh in examining the function of segregation and sanction that underlie the privilege reflex, we would emphasize that the isolated identification of privilege may entail three negative consequences. First, it may produce a recursive essentialization whereby the holder of privilege employs a naturalist argument to justify the discrimination it promotes, using anecdotes and sometimes science to insist that people are only "differentially equal," and that in fact some are better able than others to procure social advantage or other goods. Second, the isolated identification of privilege may elicit quietism or despair: even if the power of a group set apart is not natural, little can be done to dismantle it. Indeed, there are so many privilege structures to be dismantled that one scarcely knows where to begin. Third, and perhaps most pernicious, the isolated identification of privilege may create the impression of a greater activism and engagement than mere identification can nourish. More is required—namely, extensive dialogue and interaction with social, legal, and political groups outside the "ivory tower." Given the mechanisms of self-legitimation that accompany and promote privilege, instituting and perpetuating its hegemony, we cannot in good conscience assume that social change will naturally follow from academic debate about privilege.

In short, we submit that there is an irresponsible attitude toward privilege that encourages the exculpatory view that "everyone has *some* form of privilege," or that "what is earned (or unearned) is ultimately indeterminable." On this view, we are all "equal," and we are all complicit in the systems of privilege within which we operate. The diversity of forms of privilege cannot and *must not* be allowed to follow George Orwell's famously ironic dictum in *Animal Farm* that "all animals are equal, but some animals are more equal than others" (1951, 114). No doubt, the curious "private rights and benefits" implicit in the concept are many; they vary over time and place. Yet we must not turn away from the reality that—using McIntosh's analogy of privilege as a bank account—a person whose privilege takes the form of white skin has more "income" to spend, and certainly more places to spend it, than the nonwhite person whose privilege conforms to a different model of the socially constructed "normal" citizen (including simply being able-bodied or heterosexual). So, while it is true—and necessary to acknowledge—that privileges come in many forms, we, the current social actors in a society still shaped by its history of racism against black people and white supremacist

dogma, must become conscious of the particular perniciousness of white privilege. This, in essence, is why we feel the need at this time to contribute a volume in the area of critical white studies that challenges our readers to attend to the braiding of personal comforts into a broader economy of privilege.

White privilege can be empirically demonstrated: sociologists and anthropologists examine it as a process, for example, that takes shape in education, in the evolution of neighborhoods, in political representation, and in cultural creation. In these areas, privilege entails obstacles to and foreclosures of participation and presence in what is defined as common space. However, when proponents of the concept of privilege confront accusations that they are ideologically motivated, or pursuing restricted, parochial interests, and that they cannot prove that they are pursuing an authentically good life of a political community—or indeed, when they are accused of bad faith and resentment—*this* use of privilege opens onto what the philosopher Jean-François Lyotard calls "a differend."

A differend is what takes place when a group voices a complaint or a demand, say, as a plaintiff in a lawsuit. In voicing its demand, the group must use a language impervious to its experience; sometimes this is the language of the court itself, or of empirical science, or indeed of statistics. The language that must be heard and evaluated silences the demand or complaint; neither seen nor heard, the claimants discover that their lived experience cannot reach the legal or political status of that against which they are speaking. Thus, a differend is a communicative impasse. Practically speaking, it may be the death of the plaintiffs. Lyotard gives the example of plaintiffs bringing suit against the revisionist historian Robert Faurisson, a Holocaust denier in France (1988, 3–14). The claim they contest is one of existence itself: there were no gas chambers in Poland; therefore, there were no camps of "death." If there had been, then those in the death camps would have been exterminated. But if the plaintiffs are alive to contest the Holocaust denier, then either they really do not know that the camps "killed" people (they could have been worked to death), or they would have to be dead themselves. Prove to us, then, you who are alive, that there were actual gassings. Many deniers resort to "scientific" arguments, objecting that they have sampled the stone in the structures remaining from the gas chambers and find no trace of gas. Thus the process, and even the question of proof, is stymied in a differend; in the language of chemistry and law, the plaintiffs can only adduce the numbers of the dead, perhaps in studies but above all of witnesses. Whether we have direct eyewitness accounts of lethal situations or not—in the case of the Holocaust, they exist in the journals

of kapos and in transcripts of the trials of SS members, among others—the possibility of witnessing remains. One can bear witness to a differend by attempting to give voice to those whose voices do not qualify, that fail to reach the metaphorical radar screen of the dominant or reference group and its language. Precisely because analyses of privilege confront this accusation of ideological motivation, and are thereby reduced to relativistic and opportunistic claims for the authority of the metaposition—because the question of proof is stymied within this rhetorical contest of "competing ideologies"—we need to use braided narrative to produce the possibility of witnessing. In this volume, we present direct witnesses, frequently using braided narrative to that end. These witnesses examine their privilege and present examples of the denial of rights and benefits that they have witnessed. This is no longer "science"; it is an essential restoration of voice. Without a voice, confrontation and dialogue are impossible.

For all of these reasons, a focus on white privilege must be multiperspectival. It must assemble a variety of disciplines and discourses, that is, if it is to decompartmentalize "studies" and unite voices from poetry, literature, philosophy, anthropology, and sociology. From the vast contributions of women's studies, critical race theory, and critical white studies, we draw the lines that intersect around white privilege itself, as an idea and as a multiplicity of lived realities.

This focus leads to a kind of epistemic crossroads at which the critical, comparative approaches to over- and underprivileged groups, to strategies of privilege conferral, and to the social outcomes of privilege distinctions can be examined from the perspective of a variety of academic disciplines. The decisive advantage of such a focus is the possibility of an expanded basis for *comparison*. Through a comparative approach, we can discern parallels and distinctions in strategic exclusions, and the institution of norms and myths that perpetuate them. Critical comparison brings to light the "factitious" quality of the social, psychological, and legal categories mobilized to maintain or increase privilege. It shows that these categories are neither inherent nor immutable. It brings to light the dynamic variety of external references—from language, to clothing, to social codes—and to what are deemed the "internal" aspects of privilege, understood here as gender, color, and physiognomy, to name a few. As an exercise in demystification, such an approach is useful for decompartmentalizing the important insights and analytic advances made by gender studies, critical race theory, critical white studies, and other class and gender analyses.

From a historical perspective, such a demystification project might ask, with respect to racial privilege, who is white, and why should we care today? There was a time when the immigrants of New York City's Lower East Side—the Irish, Poles, Italians, and Russian and eastern European Jews—were not considered white. But today, it appears, they are. There was a time when the French-speaking working classes of Quebec were told to "speak white," that is, to speak English. Whiteness is a mythological category—denoting sameness, purity, and an internally changing yet fixed "transcendental"—even before it is ethnic or demographic. It might be surprising to hear whiteness described as mythological, but the research of many disciplines over the past several decades suggests that this is precisely how we should understand both race and privilege.[3] When the question of white privilege was first raised, isolated attempts were made to theorize it within specific disciplines, occasionally broadening into interdisciplinary efforts. Today, however, analyses of white privilege are spilling over disciplinary boundaries, and we are beginning to see the formation of multidisciplinary discourse on the subject. This more encompassing way of conceptualizing privilege has many styles.

The collection of essays presented here encourages this transgression of disciplinary boundaries by bringing together the finest creative nonfiction, statistical analysis, and clinical and cross-cultural research in the philosophical framework of critical white studies. We have attempted to collect a representative cross-section of research by some of the most prominent scholars of white privilege and marginalization in the fields of philosophy, sociology, psychology, and literature, including some intriguing new voices. Our approach to white privilege is an intentional act of subversion of the so-called silos that academic disciplines often are, each holding itself out as *the* site at which reality is being critically investigated within the academy. These diverse interrogations, taking place in parallel and without sufficient reference to one another, sometimes create what the philosopher Lewis Gordon calls "disciplinary decadence": the territoriality and self-imposed isolation of academic discourses. While it must be acknowledged that each of the disciplines studying privilege, how it functions, and its consequences is producing valuable and exciting research, we think that the findings are more valuable when the disciplines cross-fertilize one another. When we arrive at a crossroads at which we can see disciplinary convergences and divergences, we confront the possibility of a more critical discourse—because better informed by interdisciplinary insights—and more coherent strategies for building socially just communities. Our hope in marking this crossroads is

precisely to illuminate the commonalities and interconnections of apparently discrete interrogations by placing them side by side.

Thus our approach to privilege is grounded in attention to equity and solidarity. Perhaps the best way to describe what is at stake is to highlight the discussion of one of our contributors, the philosopher Marilyn Nissim-Sabat. Nissim-Sabat recounts Lewis Gordon's argument for abandoning the trope of white privilege: "A privilege is something that not everyone needs, but a right is the opposite. Given this distinction, an insidious dimension of the white privilege argument emerges. It requires condemning whites for possessing, in the concrete, features of contemporary life that should be available to all, and if this is correct, how can whites be expected to give up such things?" (quoted in Nissim-Sabat's chapter in this volume). Opposing rights to privileges in this way suggests two important aspects of our inquiry: first, whether either discursive community realizes it or not, discourse on privilege is linked conceptually to discourse on human rights. Second, scholarly attention to white privilege should be the academic counterpart to the public policy of affirmative action. That is, it should be a broad-based initiative that aims to bring about its own eventual demise. The critiques of white privilege being produced in different disciplinary domains these days—a diversity reflected in this volume—will ultimately (or *should* ultimately) bring about a recognition that privilege, as *privilegere*, must be abolished if we are to create a world in which "necessities for a decent life" (Gordon's phrase) are acknowledged as everybody's basic human right.

A crossroads is a place at which people can, by definition, arrive by different paths. In identifying interdisciplinary investigation into white privilege as a crossroads, it is our hope to trace the origins of our journey to this point modestly and contingently, noting our multiple starting points. One such journey was Eula Biss's collection of essays *Notes from No Man's Land*, which won the National Book Critics Circle Award in 2009. Part of the power of this book is precisely its use of "braided narrative" in autobiographical essays that provide historical and social analysis of racism in the United States. Moved by her fresh and incisive analysis, we invited some of the most creative writers in critical race theory and critical white studies to contribute an essay to this volume. In adopting an approach that seeks to combine disciplines and well-structured personal narratives, we look at privilege as an experiential reality in the lives of philosophers, sociologists, psychologists, and poets—whether African American, African, Caribbean, Latino/Latina, or white.

In the pages that follow, the insights of personal experience ground the chapters in individual lives, even as they destabilize any academic claim that

this discourse belongs to a specific discipline or disciplines that could have the final, authoritative word. Our conception of braided narrative encompasses both first-person-singular and first-person-plural voices—speaking into the scholarly record of the lived realities of groups and nationalities, as well as individuals, on the matter of white privilege. Some of our contributors have taken up this methodology, as invitation or as challenge, and have woven deeply personal memoirs and anecdotes into their analyses of privilege. Other chapters provide a metadiscussion; see, for instance, Lilia Moritz Schwarcz's discussion of the social and statistical array of colors along the color line in Brazil; Eduardo Bonilla-Silva, Victor Ray, and Louise Seamster's meditation on global racialized practices in the age of Obama; and Paget Henry's account of the interwoven history of Africana phenomenology and political economy with European history. Their contributions model forms of cultural hybridity that expand our conception of "braiding" as a narrative synthesis of theory and practice.

Notes

1. To be sure, this is much less the case among persons claiming whiteness as a sovereign or hegemonic identity and aesthetic object of pride. That is, if one *is* persuaded that European culture represents the highest realization of all human cultures, then one already has a legitimation mechanism so powerful that one will be impervious to the question of "privilege." Privilege per se will flow by definition from cultural and social Darwinism.

2. The *Dictionnaire latin français*, known as the "Gaffiot," defines "privilegium" as the synthesis of *privus* and *lex*, thus "an exceptional law that especially concerns a particular person or group, and is passed against him or them." It refers to Cicero, *De legibus* (*On the laws*), 3.44. At its inception, "private law" circumscribed particular persons or groups with a view to social or legal exclusion. Later, it took on an expanded sense, moving from circumscription to the normalization of unearned entitlements. See Gaffiot 1934.

3. See, for example, Yancy 2003; Bonilla-Silva 2010. A comprehensive list would be impossible here, but Bhabha 1998, Feagin 1995, Ignatiev and Garvey 1996, Guess 2006, Kincheloe 1999, Omi and Winant 1986, Perea 1997, and Stanfield 1985, among others, discuss this question.

References

Bhabha, Homi. 1998. The white stuff (political aspects of whiteness). *Artforum International* 36, no. 9: 21–23.

Bonilla-Silva, Eduardo. 2010. *Anything but racism: How social scientists limit the significance of racism.* New York: Routledge.

Feagin, Joe. 2000. *Racist America: Roots, current realities, and future reparations.* New York: Routledge.

Feagin, Joe, Hernán Vera, and Pinar Batur. 1995. *White racism.* New York: Routledge.

Gaffiot, Félix. 1934. *Dictionnaire latin français.* Paris: Hachette. http://www.lexilogos .com/latin/gaffiot.php.

Guess, Teresa. 2006. The sociological construction of whiteness: Racism by intent, racism by consequence. *Critical Sociology* 32, no. 4: 649–73.

Ignatiev, Noel, and John Garvey, eds. 1996. *Race traitor.* New York: Routledge.

Kincheloe, Joe L. 1999. The struggle to define and reinvent whiteness: A pedagogical analysis. *College Literature* 26, no. 3: 162–94.

Lyotard, Jean-François. 1988. *The differend: Phrases in dispute.* Trans. Georges van den Abbeele. Minneapolis: University of Minnesota Press.

McIntosh, Peggy. 1988. White privilege and male privilege: A personal account of coming to see correspondences through work in women's studies. Working Paper #189, Wellesley Centers for Women, Wellesley College, Massachusetts.

Omi, Michael, and Howard Winant. 1986. *Racial formation in the United States from the 1960s to the 1980s.* New York: Routledge and Kegan Paul.

Orwell, George. 1951. *Animal farm.* Harmondsworth, UK: Penguin.

Perea, Juan. 1997. The black/white binary paradigm of race: The "normal science" of American racial thought. *California Law Review* 85, no. 5: 1213–58.

Stanfield, John H. 1985. Theoretical and ideological barriers to the study of race-making. *Research in Race and Ethnic Relations* 4:161–81.

Yancy, George. 2003. *Who is white? Latinos, Asians, and the new black/nonblack divide.* Boulder, Colo.: Lynne Rienner.

1

Approaching White Privilege

1

Deprivileging Philosophy

Peggy McIntosh

I was very pleased when two philosophers, Bettina Bergo and Tracey Nicholls, asked me to write a chapter for this book. I was happy that the field of philosophy might entertain some commentary on privilege in the field itself, and I welcomed the chance to write narratively. So I will start with some narrative of my own story in philosophy. It is a relief to be able to tell this story in print, indeed, to be *authorized* to tell it.

When I was a little girl, I thought of myself as a philosopher. I enjoyed living in a haze of thought. What my teachers might have called "wool gathering" I thought of as philosophizing. I liked to look out the tall windows of Kenilworth School in Ridgewood, New Jersey, and think of nothing. That is, nothing school-like. So I thought I had found my calling—to think, and ramble mentally, out into the world.

But in college I learned that to be a philosopher one had to think about the themes and topics that famous philosophers of the past had thought about. I learned that if you were going to be a philosopher, you had to think about "free will," to have opinions about it, to argue about it, and to defend your opinions. I was scared of this method, but I also thought it was ludicrous. Argumentation did not allow us to have mixed feelings and to defend paradoxes. I was also incredulous that free will was considered such an important subject—out of all of the thousands of things we could have been thinking about! Philosophy was a boot camp for learning to argue about free will. We were not allowed to follow our own trains of thought into whatever else was out there. It seemed that famous philosophers had already made all

the necessary trails through thinking itself. Students were not meant to bushwhack and make new trails. Almost immediately, I gave up on the idea that I was a philosopher.

Quite significant to me now is remembering how quickly I learned (i.e., internalized the idea) that I *could not be* a philosopher; philosophers were "other" than and "higher" than me, a seventeen-year-old girl born in Brooklyn. Therefore, when a young French student at a youth hostel in Sweden declared to me, "Je suis philosophe," I scorned him. At that point, I had not heard of the French *philosophes* of the Enlightenment, so I thought he was declaring that he was a philosopher rather than describing his philosophical vantage point. In any case, I felt he was crazy to presume that he was a philosopher. He was too young, and too human. After he had followed me around for a couple of days, saying, "Je suis philosophe," I finally answered him, in Brooklyn Franglais, "Depuis quand vous êtes philosophe?" For the next two days, he persisted in assuring me that he was a philosophe, and I just avoided him. How could *he* feel that he was welcome in philosophy?

Time passed. I taught English, American studies, women's studies, multicultural women's studies, and gradually, as I followed my own trains of thought and found that they affected others' perceptions, I came to think that I was in some sense a philosopher. The editors of this volume expanded philosophy enough to include me and my kind of conceptualizing. I am grateful and pleased, because they have seen that my conceptions have moved and influenced many people and have, for some, transformed their worldviews. Perhaps my conceptions and testimonies have affected more lives than most modern philosophy does because my narrative testimonies have evoked others' daily experiences, and in many cases have helped people who thought they had no use for philosophy to relocate themselves in the universe and respect their lives and thoughts as having coherence.

At first, when I saw that my ideas were influential for some people, I was embarrassed and felt like a fraud. But then I explored my reactions and wrote a Moebius-strip theory on self-silencing and self-doubt in the first of three papers (McIntosh, 1985, 1989a, 2000) called "Feeling Like a Fraud." When it was well received, the responses gave me courage to ask, "If I don't take my ideas more seriously, who will?" And when I began to take my ideas more seriously, I felt the usefulness of them. William James described his test for an idea as being how many different places it could take him. I saw that some of my ideas had taken me and others to many places.

Now I encourage all students—all people, really—to follow their own trains of thought, to delve deeply into their own numerous trains of thought,

and even to dream on their essential perceptions and memories, tapping into their subconscious knowledge, in order to develop coherence and meaning. Now I feel that all students are scattered but potential philosophers, and I feel that they deserve the support to think that they are. My definitions of philosophy have become elastic, and this is a matter of principle, not, I think, a matter of incomprehension. I think that not only would William James have understood the kind of philosophy I do, but that Emerson, Dewey, Santayana, and Peirce would too, along with the authors in this volume who are aware of the limiting cultural whiteness of philosophy. I respect James's pragmatism— judging an idea's validity by how many places it can take one, what now would be called its explanatory power—and I also respect pluralism, both within the world and within the psyches of people. And I respect multicultural dimensions of philosophy—the fact that philosophical traditions are so many, all over the world.

So when Bettina Bergo and Tracey Nicholls invited me into this volume, they made me feel encouraged about philosophy as a field. They opened its doors and widened its reach by inviting many "nonphilosophers" into the volume, thereby reflecting the diversity of scholars who in colleges and universities today reflect philosophically and otherwise on privilege systems, from many perspectives. Their invitation to those of us who are not Canadian also fills me with admiration for their collaborative spirit and their willingness to be border crossers, truly putting our shared pursuits and avowed love of wisdom over national comparisons and potential competitiveness.

In addition, the editors' invitation to authors to use narrative thrilled me. Personal narratives usually do not surface in philosophy's modes of abstraction, definition, generalization, and argumentation. Narratives like mine, here, come from a "sample of one." But my feeling is that the deeper each of us goes into our own remembered experience, the more useful our thoughts may become to ourselves and to others. This is a paradox and a mystery. I think of Emily Dickinson (a sample of one if ever there was one), going so daringly into her own thoughts, sensations, perspectives, and guesses that her words resonate with millions of people who read her, all over the world. I'm not comparing my gifts or influence to hers, just noting that private, quirky, unexpected utterances may connect with and speak to the experience, or the thirst, of large numbers of people. And I have seen this happen in local, academic ways with my work on privilege, on fraudulence, and on Phases of Curricular and Personal Re-vision, all of which are testimonies from a sample of one.

Another aspect of my pleasure in contributing to this volume is that it focuses on privilege and privilege systems through the lenses of many different disciplines. In this it is, even now, ahead of its time. Despite the attention paid to privilege in academic teaching and scholarship over the past twenty-five years, I feel that privilege is still a new and difficult subject. Understanding privilege systems requires leaps of thinking and feeling that most of us were not prepared for by our own education, which evaded matters of both social injustice and unearned dominance. Even if we had careful and conscientious training in seeing discrimination, we were probably not taught to see its upside, privilege, which is exemption or protection from discrimination. In general, we were not taught to see society systemically, or to see knowledge itself as a social construction carrying and reinforcing systemic inequities.

The editors have asked that I address the question of how the fact of and the understanding of white privilege have changed (or not) since I started articulating the concept in 1988. I was not the first, and I give credit especially to W. E. B. Du Bois and to James Baldwin for writing about whiteness, and to David Wellman, who, unbeknownst to me when I wrote my articles, had already in 1977 written about white privilege as "a system of advantage based on race," in his book *Portraits of White Racism*.

But my forty-six autobiographical examples of my white privilege, seen in contrast to the circumstances of my African American colleagues, and my analysis of what I saw as the consequences for my own comparative comfort in life, gave so much detail on one white woman's daily experience of skin color privilege that it immediately spoke to people of many races and ethnicities, sexual orientations, religions, nations, and social classes who had known that there was something "going on out there" besides discrimination, working against them, but had not known how to name or track it. I named privilege as "unearned advantage," and contrasted it with "unearned disadvantage."

Now, the good news is that on thousands of college and university campuses in the United States and around the world, the idea of privilege is known and taken seriously by many faculty and students. It is also seriously used in scholarship in virtually all academic fields. It is a strong analytical tool that carries people to many different places. On some campuses, the effort to lessen unearned advantage, or privilege, has brought about changes in curriculum, teaching methods, programming, and campus climate. Though I am personally plagued by plagiarism of my work and by overgeneralization by people who, for example, imply that I wrote about all whites' privileges everywhere, I am very glad and grateful that my metaphors and ideas about privilege have found such a welcome in the academic world, despite right-

wing reactions and the need for courage for us to withstand them. The invisible knapsack is the best known of my metaphors, but privilege as a "bank account to spend" and the image of the "hypothetical line of justice" have also been taken up and used by others. In a major development that actually began with the black women's Combahee River Collective Statement of 1977, many kinds of oppression and privilege are now recognized and seen as interwoven. The Matrix Center at the University of Colorado in Colorado Springs is wholly devoted to the study of the intersecting systems of privilege and oppression with regard to race, ethnicity, gender, class, sexual orientation, nation, religion, and age. The center's yearly Knapsack Institute includes all of these dimensions and more. Whereas twenty years ago, those who tried to widen discussions of race into discussions of class, gender, or sexual orientation were often acrimoniously silenced, it is now generally understood that all of the oppressions are interrelated, and all lives uniquely located in relation, moment by moment, to myriad kinds of power. The whole picture matters. The discussion must not get too simple to allow us to explore complexly what Adrienne Rich calls "the politics of location" (1986, 225).

I often feel doubts when following my own trains of thought, but I encourage all students to follow their trains of thought, while building their capacity to see systemically and historically. I have felt blessed when my trains of thought turned out to be useful to others in many other places and kinds of life, and I trust that theirs will be too. When I exhort college students to take themselves seriously and use their ability to think deeply, they look at me with disbelief. But I feel that their trains of thought, if they come from open, pluralized sensibilities that can tolerate mixed feelings and complex overlapping realities, will help to make and mend the social fabric of their time and place.

Outside the academic world, I feel that in the United States (I cannot speak for other countries), the understanding of privilege has not done much to change society. Though the word "privilege" has entered into the general public vocabulary, and not a day goes by without my hearing it or reading about it in some source, the word is most often used casually and does not show any particular systemic understanding on the part of the writer or speaker. Frequently, it is used to describe an individual's good luck. Or it is yoked with power in the phrase "power and privilege," usually to express a dislike of those who have power. The good news is that the word "privilege" is now in the air. But outside the academy, when it comes down to actual discussion and framing of an issue in terms of privilege, there is a general resistance by white U.S. citizens to the idea that they have any unearned

advantage and that systems of advantage exist. This reaction is not surprising. It rests on centuries of top-down individualistic ideology in which the individual is seen as the only unit of society, ending up with whatever he or she wanted, worked for, earned, and deserved. This ideology is at odds with the concepts of unearned disadvantage and unearned advantage, as two aspects of people's arbitrary placement in systems of power that they did not invent but that bear significantly on their life outcomes. To describe unearned advantage and disadvantage is to challenge at least five major elements of white and male U.S. capitalist ideology: the idea of meritocracy, the idea of manifest destiny, the myth of monoculture, the idea of white racelessness, and the idea of white moral superiority. I have written about these five myths as frameworks that keep racism in place (McIntosh 2009). I feel that to "get" the idea of privilege, people in dominant groups need to look critically at the history of these mythical beliefs that are taught to us and that justify U.S. institutional structures, values, and foreign policies. This would require exercising intellectual and emotional muscles that are as yet untrained, and it would require a willingness to see social reality in new, uncomfortable ways—ways that will never in our lifetimes stop feeling very uncomfortable.

How can willingness to see privilege become more widespread? It is discouraging for me to consider the question—especially in 2014, with the disappearance or destruction of so many liberal writers, newspapers, and radio and TV stations that helped people look critically at myths that no longer serve the United States or the world well. The myths die hard because they reflect positively on U.S. people in power and have nearly convinced all citizens that power must be so inequitably distributed, and that the powerful deserve all of their power. The twenty-first century so far is a time of worldwide political upheaval in many countries, with people calling for freedom from dictatorship, answered in the United States by ruthless force following populist resistance and uproar on behalf of workers in the state of Wisconsin, there were nonviolent, populist occupy protests on Wall Street in New York and in many other U.S. cities. It seemed as though more and more people in the United States, especially young people, were questioning the governing myths out loud and in public, not just in college and university classrooms. Until this happened, the colleges and universities and some liberal media were our best hope of keeping alive the ideas of privilege, patriarchy, and white supremacy. Now popular culture and social media are more usefully contributing to the spread of passive resistance, awareness, and resolve to set "the I percent and 99 percent" in a new relation to each other—to change the ratio of rich to poor. But recently, there is a sharp backlash against

the idea of privilege from right-wing media pundits. Through thick and thin, I hope that we can keep depending on the academy to sustain the analysis of privilege systems.

I honor all in the academic world who have been teaching about privilege. They are bravely taking a kind of action. I disagree with those who say that mere thinking is not activism. It takes activist work to understand and teach about how privilege works in the society at large. It takes mental and emotional effort to turn that understanding back on the academic institutions that house our departments and faculties, with their particular histories. It requires still greater mental and emotional activism to recognize how the thinking and teaching methods in one's chosen academic field were most probably formed on the basis of privilege. Once we realize that the traditional canons and framing dimensions of the disciplines are built on exclusion, it takes an activist commitment to revise what and how we teach—to redesign content and teaching methods so that the existing systems of privilege are not simply replicated in course content and pedagogy. And further, it takes active imagination and courageous action to elicit our students' thinking and invite their trains of thought into the process of knowledge making is, in any discipline. All of this takes bravery, and in the midst of the complex matters of tenure and promotion and partisan politics in the academy, I feel that it took courage to write any of the essays in this volume.

I want to comment briefly on the field of philosophy itself, and first to honor its potential for dealing with privilege or any other multiconsequential set of ideas. Its claim as a field for intellectual exploration gives it permission and opportunity to link a new conception with what has gone before and to create new world pictures. But white and male privilege have severely limited the field's self-conception in the past. There is for me great hope in the self-critique of the field by all of the unflinching contributors to George Yancy's book *The Center Must Not Hold: White Women Philosophers on the Whiteness of Philosophy* (2010).

Greek philosophy has given us the idea of balance as a golden mean between extremes. I believe that a balance is desirable in philosophy classes between what Emily Style calls "windows and mirrors" in philosophy classes (1988). Style imagines that a course curriculum is like a structure built around students' minds. She thinks that ideally the curriculum will give each student a balance of windows onto the experience of others, and mirrors of their own reality and validity. In this regard, reading philosophers can serve as windows out, into the thoughts and explorations of others. Assignments that invite students to relate their own experience (not their opinions) to

what they are reading provide mirrors so that they can recognize themselves as potential philosophers. Encouraging students' trains of thought, giving them space to engage their own philosophical minds, is a demonstration of philosophy itself, cultivating a balanced "love of wisdom" that comes from within themselves and from other philosophers. Serious trains of thought are on a path to somewhere, but helping students to make more sense of their own thoughts may need to be a labor of love for faculty. It's also potentially part of their own ongoing education.

Another of Emily Style's visions for education is a balance of "the scholarship on the shelves and the scholarship in the selves" (1981). Philosophers on reading lists can be balanced with students' developing self-knowledge. "Know thyself" is quoted as Socrates's sage advice and passed on to students as an exhortation. But I notice that almost never do classroom assignments draw on students' close observation and experience rather than on their opinions. And it is equally rare for university personnel to do deep self-study to know themselves and develop institutional self-awareness, disciplinary self-awareness, pedagogical self-awareness, and awareness of the deep-seated assumptions that keep privilege systems in place within our teaching and students' learning. I think that philosophy departments frequently choose not to "know themselves." Many teachers have let the field of philosophy remain unselfconscious about its origins, its assumptions, and pedagogical distance from their own and students' experiences. The editors of this book understand that it is time for all of the academic disciplines, including philosophy, to study the role of all kinds of privilege in their founding, their development, and their practices.

Outside the Parthenon, downhill from its crowning temples and somewhat to the side, is a rock outcropping called the Areopagus. It is documented that it is here, in the "golden age" of Greece, that Plato and Aristotle met with others to talk. I am deeply moved by the thought of people taking so seriously the act of speaking together. Taking this act seriously is for me a hallmark of both education and civilization. But there were tremendous constraints put on the question of who was allowed to sit on those rocks and engage in the discourse. In the same way that the U.S. Constitution left out all but white men who owned property, the discussions on the Areopagus left out all but "citizens," as against females, "barbarian" men, and slaves. In both cases, inheritors of these discourses and also descendants of those excluded from participation are now analyzing the long-term effects of these exclusions. They are feeling the need to mend the institutions and norms that derive from the Areopagus, the Constitution, and other foundational exclusions.

My contribution to the discourse is not so much focused on the exclusions as on the corresponding overinclusion of those who were allowed onto those heights and into those enclaves. In other words, I focus on making clearer the "upside" of exclusion, which is privilege. When work on social inclusion began to be formulated and framed, I wrote to a colleague that I was interested in overinclusion. She wrote back to say that there is no such thing as overinclusion. "You're in or you're out." I said, no, the outcome of seeing privilege is seeing that some are allowed "in" regardless of whether they merit being there; they have unearned inclusion. A "good" liberal arts education can still leave students completely unequipped to understand this idea.

I hope that as time goes on, philosophy will become more attuned to what is plural and relational, and far less reverential about its singular famous texts. What were the social, political, sexual, ethnic, and class circumstances of the famous philosophers? How did their contexts affect their ideas? How do our contexts relate to theirs, or not relate to theirs? And something I have often wondered is how did "I think; therefore I am" become such a revered text? How about setting it beside "I was born; therefore I am"? Or "I was conceived by two and I was born as one; therefore I am." One might say this is biology, not philosophy. But why shouldn't it be seen as philosophy? Students could be asked about the social consequences of any of these three frames, and could be asked to supply further alternatives. Both of the latter frames are more relational than "I think; therefore I am." Neither posits the aloneness of the thinker in the universe. "I feel; therefore I am" could be added to the alternatives. Or "My body incarnates my spirit; therefore I am. . . ." Philosophy could invite students to think more plurally about how they substantiate their own sense of existence within the universe.

The chronological imperative built into many courses of philosophical study, the focus on other people's thinking, the abstract language, the lofty discourse, the even loftier self-image of philosophy, together with the neglect of students' own trains of thought, can dampen the confidence of the student in considering her- or himself a practicing philosopher. This discouragement can feed into political inertia and downheartedness, or else create dependent clinging onto the founding fathers of philosophy or, for that matter, of a church or nation. Yet when I meet seventeen-year-olds who have not yet entered college, I often hear that they have an eager interest in philosophy, as I thought I did at their age. I would like our philosophy departments to meet that interest and empower them along democratic lines of pluralized thinking and reflection, rather than battling for dominance. If they are going to go to battle for something, I hope they will battle for the wisdom of having

mixed feelings in the midst of philosophical thought, and for having plural understandings, multiple lenses, and conceptions of power that include daily experience. I recently attended a symposium on the thinking of John Dewey and Daisaku Ikeda. A person in the audience said, "I'm a professor of philosophy and I've never heard of John Dewey until today." This showed me how disrespected daily experience is in the kinds of philosophy this woman was taught. I want to rescue John Dewey for the liberal arts curriculum.

I envision a horizontal line of hypothetical justice. Below it, through force of circumstances beyond their control, individuals or groups are pushed down, doubted, victimized, ignored, dehumanized, and persecuted. Above it, through force of circumstances beyond their control, individuals or groups are pushed up, aided, given the benefit of the doubt, enriched, exempted, allowed to feel entitled to more than most people have. There are myriad factors that can push one above or below the line at any moment, depending on circumstances. It is very encouraging to me that some philosophers are teaching students to understand the arbitrary nature of distributions of power. Some also creatively team-teach with colleagues in the social sciences and in other humanities fields without feeling that they are above those in other fields. I hold out a hope that professors who are teaching about privilege are also encouraging students to practice philosophy relationally rather than simply to read and argue about famous philosophers.

I would like philosophy to mean much more to humankind than it does at present. Unlike sectarian religion, in the name of which people kill one another, philosophy can keep us thinking. It can help us follow trains of thought rather than wage ideological and literal wars. It has less of a propensity to incite and justify war and much more potential to knit and connect us than sectarian religion has.

But to be of such use, philosophy must expand its views of what philosophy is and who is a philosopher. It must greatly expand its repertoire of thinkable thoughts. It must invite us to join. There are great holes in the fabric of what could be thought. We need people who see the omissions and feel that they can propose ways of filling them. George Lakoff has defined as a cultural disability "hypocognition," which is the absence of a critical idea that the society hasn't developed, but needs (2004, 24). I think that the field of philosophy is crippled by hypocognition and needs help.

Philosophy can decolonize itself as well as the minds of its students, encouraging them to both recognize and analyze their trains of thought. In discussing the ways by which she came to write the pathbreaking *Diet for a Small Planet*, Frances Moore Lappé wrote about the period after she dropped

out of graduate school at the age of twenty-eight and began to "follow her nose": "To discover my own questions required wandering in a self-created void, allowing each question to push me to the next. The process permitted me to see what the experts had missed, not because I was smarter or had more data but because I listened to my own questions and let them take me wherever they would. I had the advantage of starting at square one, whereas those more advanced in the field had long ago leapt over it" (Lappé and Perkins 2004, 48). Having seen the grip of privilege systems on the construction of philosophy, teachers can support and free thinkers like Lappé to listen to their own questions, "follow their noses," and begin filling some of the vacancies with ideas that are "as yet undreamt of" in our philosophy.

The authors in this volume work to expand the uses and understandings of philosophy, and for this I am deeply grateful. They are aware of the politics embedded in ways of thinking, and have made many fields more sophisticated than before with regard to the operations of power in and around us. In choosing to take on the conception and editing of this book, Bergo and Nicholls are helping to deprivilege philosophy itself. I am grateful for this.

References

Combahee River Collective. 1981. A black feminist statement. In *This bridge called my back: Writings by radical women of color*, ed. Cherríe Moraga and Gloria Anzaldúa, 210–18. Watertown, Mass.: Persephone Press.

Lakoff, George. 2004. *Don't think of an elephant! Know your values and frame the debate: The essential guide for progressives*. White River Junction, Vt.: Chelsea Green.

Lappé, Frances Moore. 2002. *Diet for a small planet*. New York: Random House.

Lappé, Frances Moore, and Jeffrey Perkins. 2004. *You have the power: Choosing courage in a culture of fear*. New York: Jeremy P. Tarcher/Penguin.

McIntosh, Peggy. 1985. Feeling like a fraud. Wellesley College, Stone Center for Developmental Services and Studies.

———. 1988. White privilege and male privilege: A personal account of coming to see correspondences through work in women's studies. Working Paper no. 189. Wellesley College, Wellesley Centers for Women.

———. 1989a. Feeling like a fraud part II. Wellesley College, Stone Center for Developmental Services and Studies.

———. 1989b. White privilege: Unpacking the invisible knapsack. *Peace and Freedom*, July–August, 10–12.

———. 2000. Feeling like a fraud part III: Finding authentic ways of coming into conflict. Wellesley College, Stone Center for Developmental Services and Studies.

———. 2009. White people facing race: Uncovering the myths that keep racism in place. Saint Paul Foundation, Saint Paul, Minnesota.

———. 2009. White Privilege: An Account to Spend. Saint Paul Foundation, Saint Paul, Minnesota.

Rich, Adrienne. 1986. Notes towards a politics of location. In Rich, *Blood, bread, and poetry: Selected prose, 1979–1985*, 210–31. New York: W. W. Norton.

Style, Emily. 1981. *Multicultural education and me: The philosophy and the process, putting product in its place*. Madison: University of Wisconsin Teacher Corps Associates.

———. 1988. Curriculum as window and mirror. In *Listening for all voices: Gender balancing the school curriculum*, 6–12. Summit, N.J.: Oak Knoll School.

Wellman, David T. 1977. *Portraits of white racism*. Cambridge: Cambridge University Press.

Yancy, George. 2010. *The center must not hold: White women philosophers on the whiteness of philosophy*. Lanham, Md.: Lexington Books.

2

White Privilege and the Problem with Affirmative Action

Lewis R. Gordon

Henry Louis Gates Jr., the famed African American literary scholar and director of the Du Bois Institute at Harvard University, told an interviewer on National Public Radio that if it weren't for affirmative action, he would not have been admitted to Yale University, regardless of how strong his credentials were, and he would not have had the opportunities to demonstrate his talent, which far surpassed that of many of his white colleagues, over the past four decades (Gates 2011).

Gates's admission reflects a fundamental problem with affirmative action that poses a great threat to white privilege: it works.

I had the opportunity to reflect on that fact out loud in a discussion at the Race and Higher Education conference in Grahamstown, South Africa, which was part of the Rethinking Africa Series, in 2011, when I asked, "Are there no mediocre white people in South Africa? Is every white person hired, every white person offered admission to institutions of higher learning, excellent?"

My rhetorical question was premised upon what Gates and many other high-achieving blacks know, and that is that the myth of white supremacy is the subtext of the "qualifications" narrative that accompanies debates on affirmative action.

When I was tenured at an Ivy League university, that institution's process required evaluations of my work from five referees. Expected performance was a published monograph, several articles, satisfactory teaching, service, and signs of international recognition. My dossier included three monographs

(one of which won a book award for outstanding work on human rights in North America), an edited book, a co-edited book, forty articles (several of which were reprinted in international journals and anthologies), two teaching awards, and service that included heading a committee that recruited twenty-three scholars of color to the university. The process for my promotion and tenure was dragged out because of repeated requests for more referees. The number grew to seventeen.

There was an allegedly comparable white candidate in the Philosophy Department. He also claimed to specialize in existentialism, one of my areas of expertise. His dossier? A publication contract for his dissertation and a few articles. His case was successful. His contracted dissertation was published several years later. He has not published a second book since then. As this book goes to press, he is a full professor and chair of the Philosophy Department at that institution. Over the years, I have met only one person in his field who knew and spoke well of that scholar's work. That person was a classmate of his in graduate school. Additionally, and this is perhaps a reflection of the scale of racism in professional philosophy, he is also on the advisory board of the Leiter Report (a.k.a. the Philosophical Gourmet Report), an annual conservative ranking and misrepresentation of philosophy departments in the English-speaking world that demonstrates much antipathy to the work of people of color.

Was affirmative action necessary for my promotion and tenure? Yes. This is because racism makes excellence irrelevant. As should be evident in this example, and no doubt in Gates's and many others, there is another truth. Was investment in white supremacy necessary for less than stellar whites to be promoted? Absolutely.

Affirmative action, which brought people of color to the table to learn firsthand about the level of performance of their white predecessors and contemporaries, stimulated a reflection on standards in many institutions, not only in the United States but also across the globe.[1] As more people of color were forced to meet inflated standards, what were being concealed were the low standards available to the whites who preceded them (think of the days of Harvard's "gentleman's C"), and no doubt to many whites who continue to join them as presumed agents of excellence (see Katznelson 2006). Most elite institutions of higher education, which almost by definition mean primarily white ones, are places in which student consumers receive inflated grades as receipts for their parents' investments. The institutions simply cannot afford to admit, through accurate grading, the truth.

So what is the truth about the qualifications narrative, the claim that standards had to be lowered for the admission of people of color, especially blacks, to institutions of higher learning? This claim masks racial hegemonic mediocrity, which we shall call the first premise of white privilege: the ability to be mediocre with impunity and without social stigma. One would think that for blacks and others, the opposite would apply—that is, that mediocrity would meet with deserved disdain—but this is not the case. The situation for other groups, especially blacks (because treated as at the furthest distance from whites), is the catch-22, as Frantz Fanon observed more than half a century ago, of degraded excellence through *presumed mediocrity*. Thus achievement (often in the form of being proverbially twice as good) and failure (which, unfortunately, also includes simply being equally good, in addition to being below average) both amount to a form of failure, that of being black in the first place (Fanon 1967).[2]

There is another truth. Few social systems depend on excellence in order to function. Most of the services we rely on to get through our lives depend on average levels of performance. And that's pretty much it. The norm, by definition, is not the exception, whether by that we mean excellence (above the norm) or wanting (below the norm). Nearly a decade ago I wrote an essay entitled "Critical Reflections on Three Popular Tropes in the Study of Whiteness," in which I argued against a dimension of the discourse on white privilege in cases of what could properly be called entitlements or basic human needs (Gordon 2004a). One reason for white defensiveness regarding that conception of privilege is white guilt about having access to things that most, if not presumably all, other human beings need—namely, security, health, education, shelter, and a society encouraging one's self-esteem and basic dignity. Privilege, I argued, pertains more to luxuries or simply undeserved rewards without social objection. The general advantages available to whites as a function of white supremacy and antiblack racism properly belong to those basic social goods and needs. Privilege, however, pertains to those benefits beyond basic goods and expectations of justice. The rewards lavished on many whites in the modern world have not been based on merit. What many people of color discovered upon entering previously closed corridors was not white superiority but, for the most part, white mediocrity.[3] What also baffled them was the seeming inability of many, including some people of color, to admit what was right before their eyes. It's as if there is a cognitive incapacity to see white mediocrity. I have elsewhere described this as institutional bad faith,

a phenomenon in which a social world facilitates believing (and seeing) what one prefers to believe (Gordon 1995).

Now, in order to preserve a system of white supremacy, there must be investment in the notion that blacks and other groups of color who enter fall short. While it is unlikely that every member of a group exemplifies excellence in her or his vocation, what is not brought up is the group of black and brown people who were excluded on the basis of their excellence. The prevailing view in predominantly white institutions about such candidates is fear of whether such candidates are "controllable." Although I mentioned blacks and other people of color, this concern about controllability is almost exclusively reserved for blacks, and especially for black males.[4] Women fall under the rubric of affirmative action as well. The success of affirmative action is evident in the case of gender, but primarily for white women.[5] Black and brown women are harder cases to discuss in terms of controllability, but in recent times the logic of controllability, with all its sexist connotations, has found a home with gender, where it remains dormant until women seek leadership. There are exceptions, but *real power*, which means not what is seen in public but what takes place behind closed doors, the *power behind power*, remains categorically male and white.

Keeping institutions white and predominantly male isn't only about tests and evaluating dossiers. It's also about creating unnecessary obstacles that are rationalized as important criteria. Consider the story of James Weldon Johnson, the famed novelist and songwriter of, among other great works, "Lift Every Voice and Sing," known as the black national anthem. Johnson was also a lawyer. How he became one is indicative of what changed the criteria for the American bar admissions. He became a lawyer the way Abraham Lincoln became a lawyer: he took the bar examination. In the past, one did not need a law degree in order to become a lawyer. One did not even need a bachelor's degree. All that was required was passing the examination. A passing score meant that one had mastered the required understanding of the law and could practice it.

Johnson, the principal at the time of the now famous Stanton College Preparatory School in Jacksonville, Florida, showed up to take the Florida bar exam in 1897.[6] Because there was no rule stating that blacks couldn't take the exam (it was presumed that no black person either would dare show up to take it or could take it and pass), Johnson was permitted to undergo examination. As it became clear that he knew the law, his examiners inflated the standards and tested him at several times the expectation of white candidates. One of the examiners left the room in protest of the possibility that a

black man might meet the criteria. Reluctantly, the others capitulated, and Johnson was sworn in as a member of the Florida bar (Johnson 2008, 143). Other blacks followed in droves.

We know what happened next. Although law degrees had been awarded at various institutions of higher learning for nearly a millennium, their recipients were not required to achieve such a degree in order to sit before the bar. That changed. First came the bachelor of law degree. Since many blacks couldn't afford to go to college, that reduced significantly the number of prospective black candidates for the bar. But since there was a growing black middle class, even with American apartheid, more began to meet that criterion. So the American Bar Association imposed the additional requirement of postbaccalaureate study. To sit for the bar exam, a candidate now had to have completed law school, which normally consists of three years of study *after completing an undergraduate degree*. In effect, seven or more years of investment in higher education were now required of candidates who wanted to sit before the bar. The stratagem was effective: the number of blacks qualified to take the bar examination plummeted.[7]

This story of increased obstacles is also one of great social costs. If one considers the damage to institutions of legalized white supremacy done by the small cadre of blacks who met the additional criteria, imagine what would have happened if their ranks were larger. Nelson Mandela studied law, but what might have happened if he had been joined by a large number of comrades who were not only armed with the knowledge of law but also with the credentials to act on it?

Law is but one example; there are many cases across a variety of professions, disciplines, and activities ranging from political participation to sports. The resources devoted to excelling in many fields are invariably stacked in favor of whites, often from childhood through adolescence and early adulthood. The demise of investment in the public infrastructures of North America and Europe, a model that nations such as Canada and South Africa are following, pretty much assures the demographic elimination of many groups of color, especially blacks. A stark example is the impact of unearned white advantages on jazz music. Although jazz was originally an African American art form, the elimination of music programs in predominantly black public schools has led, in effect, to the privatization of music education. The result is an increased whitening of the face of jazz (and, for that matter, of those who actually play musical instruments) and, additionally, a decline in the black audience for jazz music, an art form that requires some ongoing relationship with its performance, which increasingly prices out many black

populations. We've seen a similar decline in public investments in other areas of the arts, in the sciences, and even in physical education, in spite of the stereotype of the superior black athlete. Although some blacks manage to achieve access to the limited resources available, the overwhelming reality is one of abrogated societal responsibility for developed infrastructures in favor of *disaffirmative* action, in the form of a punishing state and civil society, as the prison-industrial complex attests (see Alexander 2010; Comaroff and Comaroff 2006; and Gordon and Gordon 2009).

A genuine commitment to affirmative action, under circumstances such as the ones outlined here, would demand not only insistence on inclusion but also critical reflection on the purposes of articulated criteria and a commitment to the material, social, and cognitive conditions conducive to more just arrangements. Such requirements should be created for the healthy functioning of a society's institutions, which will entail just practices of inclusion. But, as we know, in a society committed to injustice, it is very easy to create unjust practices of distinction and elimination. In the words of Boaventura de Sousa Santos, "This much is expressed in the idea, widely shared by activists, that there will be no global social justice without global cognitive justice" (2007, xviii).

So we come to another problem with affirmative action for beneficiaries of white privilege who seek further comforting about their condition. Its very existence is proof of continued racism and sexism.

In the United States, the bad-faith language of denial has hijacked the language of affirmative action. For instance, the expression "past discrimination" dominates debates on the subject.

Past discrimination? If racial and gender discrimination were aberrations of the past, that would mean that no overseer of criteria is any longer motivated by racist and sexist goals. It would mean that there is no racial or gender discrimination today, which would make the use of race or gender as a criterion for access prejudicial and thus unjust. Yet, as we know, the language of "reverse discrimination" emerged in the United States in the 1970s.[8] Such language turned the tables on affirmative action. In effect, it stimulated a reactionary movement that treated discrimination as a reality ultimately faced only by white males, precisely by denying the continued existence of racism and sexism in unmonitored processes of selection.

We come, then, to an observation made by Frantz Fanon. Although he detested violence, as his former student and friend Alice Cherki reminds us in her poignant portrait of his life and thought, he did not shy away from speaking the truth about how violence is tolerated under colonial regimes

and the strange logic of what he called the "Greco-Latin pedestal" of sup-posed moral objections to anticolonialist efforts (Fanon 1963; Cherki 2006, 172). If colonialists regarded colonialism as just, how could they be expected to see decolonization as anything but unjust? If the efforts to maintain colo-nialism were considered just, how could they be considered violent? This became a charge against efforts to dismantle colonialism. Likewise, if the exclusion of colonized people was just, then would not their inclusion be unjust? Even worse, the appearance of such people was considered more than unjust. It was considered violent.[9]

Fanon argued that the effort to demonstrate nonviolent change was futile. By this he did not mean that one should aim to be as violent as possible. His point was a sobering one: the only way to satisfy the expectations of nonvio-lence was to be ineffective at practices of social change. We forget that Martin Luther King Jr., one of the apostles of nonviolence, was considered violent in his day. When he and his fellow protestors marched against American apart-heid, it was not the police officers who set German shepherds on them, the hordes of whites who stoned them, the firefighters who sprayed them with water at a force capable of stripping skin, the gangs who lynched many of them—it was not those people and agents of state power who were consid-ered violent. What supporters of the status quo "saw" was violent black peo-ple from whom the society was being protected.[10]

The situation is familiar to many South Africans. There are those who praise South Africa for making the transformation to a supposedly post-apartheid society nonviolently. Yet the many blacks (in the black conscious-ness conception)[11] and their supporters who were killed, tortured, and imprisoned, the many protestors who were harmed, the tanks, the guns, the dogs, the 3:00 A.M. knock on the door, the many instances of trauma make such an assessment mystifying; do none of those people count? What is hid-den in this misguided notion, just as what is suppressed about racism and sexism in the anti–affirmative action rhetoric of reverse discrimination and qualifications, is this: in a white supremacist state, violence is recognized only when it is waged against whites (see Alexander, Gibson, and Mngxi-tama 2008; Gibson 2011).

So the hysteria about crime, about insecurity, in South Africa is no doubt similar to the hysteria we see in the United States and a growing number of other countries gripped by growing states of insecurity. Even when the actual number of violent crimes declined, incarceration of blacks remained high in South Africa and the United States because there was in effect the crim-inalization of a people (see Davis 2003; Comaroff and Comaroff 2006; and

Alexander 2010). As violent appearance, black visibility was criminalized (see Gordon 2004b).

An odd feature of postcolonial states is that criminalization of black populations doesn't require white institutional leadership. The phenomenon also occurs in so-called black countries, and it is color-dependent, in that darker-skinned blacks are more criminalized than lighter-skinned blacks. The reasons for this are manifold, but most boil down to the close relationship between closed social options and skin color, a legacy of racial slavery and colonialism in postcolonial environments that are heavily invested in keeping capital in the hands of the former governing population.[12]

The correlation between anti–affirmative action attitudes and the preservation of colonial institutions of exclusion and violence emerges because both rely on the same things—namely, racist states and civil societies. In fact, "uncivil society" becomes the *inclusion* of the black masses (see Mamdani 1996; Comaroff and Comaroff 2000).

Stacking the deck in favor of whites is a consequence of two prevailing ideologies of state function (or dysfunction) in recent times—namely, neoconservatism and neoliberalism. Together, these twins move to the right of center (neoconservatism) and slightly right of center (neoliberalism) on rationalizations of reality devoid of verification and rigorous analysis. Particularly with regard to race, their proponents rely more on fictional and often mythical tropes than on empirical evidence. Although the income of whites is typically twelve times that of blacks (and ironically even more than that in many predominantly black countries), whites complain that they are at a disadvantage, and point to the miniscule number of affluent blacks in their countries as an indication of black privilege. If there are no impediments to black progress, then there must be something inherent *in most blacks* that curtails their success. The neoconservatives thus offer portraits of blacks as depraved, diseased, deviant, delinquent, and intellectually deficient. The correlated disciplinary rationalizations of these tropes are black people as problems of judicial and criminal justice studies, health, and education. The specific correlates are studies of crime, AIDS, and intellectual deficiency. The effect is manifold. It is theodicean, where the society or the nation is idolized as a god without responsibility for good and evil. The United States and the entire modern Western tradition are exempted from blame, and the plight of the many whose labor and lives were fodder for their emergence are characterized not only by their own supposed inherent deficiencies but also by their apparent lack of gratitude for the privilege of having played a part in this self-congratulatory history. This process of historical misrepresentation

of socially produced disadvantage is thus also an attempt at what Boaventura de Sousa Santos calls "epistemicide," which he describes as the cognitive side of genocide, in an effort to achieve what Michael Tillotson recently called "resistance to resistance," a form of political nihilism in which the will to fight is beaten out of a people (de Sousa Santos 2007, xviii; de Sousa Santos 2008, xix; Tillotson 2011, 106).

There are many contradictions and double standards in the neoconservative position, including its proponents' amnesia about the role they played in creating the very circumstances they criticize. The decimation of public institutions from the Reagan and Thatcher administrations onward, for instance, created dysfunction on a scale that made it appear foolish to seek public solutions to problems of the commonweal (see Handler 1995, 2004). At the same time, the bloated military budgets of the United States and some of its allies are premised upon the use of public funds to advance private interests. We could call this what it is: welfare for the rich. That black interests tend to be linked to a viable public infrastructure made blacks a marked enemy of privatization. In some instances, blacks were collateral damage, but in most cases they were quite deliberately in the direct line of fire.

The neoliberal position is not as blatant as the neoconservative. While neoliberals share the neoconservative fetishizing of privatization, they would like to preserve some semblance of human rights and democracy in the process. They are thus compelled to offer an alternative to the neoconservative mantra that blackness is inherently pathological. Instead, they present a conception of democratic life premised upon individualism, which makes the collective needs of disenfranchised black, brown, and other disadvantaged populations illegitimate. Privatization demanded an engagement with these groups, as neoliberals continued the neoconservative attacks on public infrastructure. For neoliberals, such populations were at first more collateral damage. As it became clear that disenfranchised groups' interests rested on a model of democracy premised on group or collective rights, neoliberal critics waged war on them in the insidious language of being concerned about their ultimate interests *as individuals*. That assault, ironically, received its greatest support from what at first appeared to be perhaps the most paradoxical effect of previous struggles, namely, the changed hue of leadership in countries such as South Africa and the United States.[13]

With respect to the question of white privilege and affirmative action, this new leadership presents us with a stark contradiction: white people who love Nelson Mandela and Barack Obama are not required to love black people. White normativity and privilege can be preserved through making such

leaders "exceptions" to the norm of black failure. Their existence can thus be subverted, ironically, for the preservation of a racist system, however noble their individual intentions may be. This has been a difficult problem for black high achievers from the moment antiblack racism emerged. Such blacks face the pressure to succeed, even while their success is undermined by being depicted as an exception to the rule. Mandela and Obama did not get rid of white supremacy, as the overwhelming evidence of decline in black communities attests, but we have a sense that the world would be much worse off without them (see Alexander 2010; Tillotson 2011).

There is also the irony of the situation of each black person who manages to scrape through and rise in a system premised on black suppression. There will always be objections to the presence of such people, as the uproar over the emergence of a paltry black middle class across the globe reveals.[14] Whereas the existence of millions of affluent whites doesn't so much as raise an eyebrow, the fact that there are fewer than a million rich blacks in countries with populations exceeding forty million people, such as South Africa, Brazil, or Colombia, in addition to the United States, leads to often hypocritical concerns about class. There are even objections about where such affluent blacks live. A recent Brown University study found that most affluent blacks live in predominantly black and brown neighborhoods with lower overall opportunities (see Logan 2011). And why is this so? In the end, affluent whites, although they pay lip service to the ideal of integrated neighborhoods, prefer to live in segregated neighborhoods. Even lower-middle-class and working-class whites have greater access to neighborhoods with more resources and a greater possibility of accruing wealth than many blacks with higher incomes. None of this comes as news to middle-class black people. As in the debate over affirmative action, this truth can be denied only through closing one's eyes to the continued practice of institutional racism.

This is not to say that every reward that white people receive is unmerited. History offers ample evidence to the contrary.[15] It is to say, however, that, as with every group, high performance is by definition a virtue of those who are devoted and talented. The odds that a *people* will manifest such characteristics without an extraordinary cultural investment are very low. But, as Anna Julia Cooper has shown in her provocative essay "What Are We Worth?," far too much is invested in those who fail to demonstrate such qualities in white supremacist societies. Very little is invested in those who, even with few incentives, produce more. Imagine the results if proper social investments were made in the people who are resourceful enough to survive in the shacks of South Africa, the *favelas* of Brazil, the slums of India, and the ghettoes and

reservations of the United States. What could such investment mean for the future of humankind?

To make some headway on these matters demands, then, bringing to the fore the truth about affirmative action and the so-called postapartheid world in which we now live. It requires admitting that the onus of past victories is the next stage of struggle, a reality that, unfortunately, never quite arrives but a battle that must be waged, however weary we may feel in our souls. Because, as many of us in higher education know, and as those who sacrificed their lives for social justice knew, what is at stake is no less than humanity's most precious resource, and that resource is demeaned by such a logic and speaks, in the end, to the future of all.

Notes

1. See, e.g., Darity 2005, which offers empirical data and analysis of affirmative action in the contexts of England, Ireland, India, Malaysia, South Africa, and the United States.

2. For discussion of this problem, see Gordon 2005.

3. A previous version of this chapter appeared in *Truthout* (15 August 2011), www .truth-out.org/problem-affirmative-action/1313170677, and was reprinted in *Pambazuka News* at http://pambazuka.org/en/category/features/75787, and, in shortened form, in *Thinking Africa: Special Supplement to the Mail & Guardian* (26 August–1 September 2011); it stimulated a series of e-mail messages and postings to the author, most of which were admissions of the shocking scale of white mediocrity the writers discovered when they gained access to white-dominated institutions. After working twice as hard, sometimes four times as hard, as whites to achieve the same employment status and credentials, people of color found that they were in the company of white people who worked at minimum levels or less while receiving several times the rewards.

4. This is so for many reasons in this stage of global capitalism and its investment in the production of vulnerable populations. The empirical data regarding black males are overwhelming. For lucid and frank discussion of the data, see Alexander 2010 and King and Smith 2011.

5. For discussion, see, e.g., American Bar Association 1998.

6. This once all-black and now predominantly black high school is the only public school in the United States to have been in the top five U.S. high schools in the *Newsweek* rankings since 2000, a ranking it has achieved four times since that year. The presumption that large numbers of black students are disastrous for school performance persists, however. See Saltman 2007.

7. Although I focus on blacks here, the presence of people of color, such as Native Americans and Latinos, in the American Bar Association has a history with a similar logic. For many discussions, see various issues of *La Raza Law Journal*, especially volume 12, no. 2 (2001), which features, among many illuminating articles, Valdes 2001.

8. Principally through the U.S. Supreme Court case *Regents of the University of California v. Bakke* (1978).

9. A visit to the Civil Rights Museum in Memphis, Tennessee, or the Slavery Museum in Liverpool, England, should dispel any doubts about the veracity of this observation.

Nearly every serious study of slavery and various systems of apartheid also attests to this double standard. See not only Gutman 1976 but also Guthrie 2003, a prescient history in which the author examines how black resistance and struggles for freedom have been treated as forms of mental illness.

10. For discussion of civil rights activists as, in effect, monsters, see Gordon and Gordon 2009, chapter 4.

11. Blacks were simply enemies of the apartheid state. Blackness, then, was a political identity. The most influential formulation of this conception of black consciousness is Biko 2002; for discussion, see Alexander, Gibson, and Mngxitama 2008.

12. The phenomenon in black postcolonial states is so rampant that Fela Kuti and Bob Marley even wrote songs about it (Fela Kuti's "Sorrow, Tears, & Blood" [1977] and Marley's "Burnin' and Lootin'" [1973]). The situation is well chronicled in the literature on criminalization in predominantly black countries; see, e.g., Comaroff and Comaroff 2006 and Mbembe 2001. For a recent study of criminalization of dark-skinned people and police brutality in Jamaica, see Bell 2011.

13. For more on this point, see Gordon and Gordon 2009, chapter 4.

14. Much of this uproar is based on the disingenuous rhetoric about socioeconomic class through which such expressions as "truly disadvantaged" and "underclass" emerged. In spite of the claim that poverty is a function of class rather than race, it continues to be highly correlated with skin color, as nearly every recent study on poverty has shown. For more discussion, see Darity 2005, Handler 1995, and Handler 2004.

15. In a radio interview on this topic, I was asked to name an institution that functions according to the thesis of excellence in diversity that I put forth here. The National Aeronautics and Space Administration (NASA) is an excellent example. Given the high stakes, NASA has genuinely sought the most capable people it could find, and this extraordinary institution was and continues to be racially diverse. It is unfortunate that it is among the institutions targeted for reduced federal funding in spite of its representing a fragment of federal spending (0.6 percent as of 2008).

References

Alexander, Amanda, Nigel Gibson, and Andile Mngxitama, eds. 2008. *Biko lives! Contestations and conversations*. New York: Palgrave.

Alexander, Michelle. 2010. *The new Jim Crow: Mass incarceration in the age of colorblindness*. New York: Free Press.

American Bar Association. 1998. Affirmative action: A dialogue on race, gender, equality, and law in America. *Focus on Law Studies* 13, no. 2. http://www.americanbar.org/publications/focus_on_law_studies_home/publiced_focus_spr98gender.html.

Bell, Deanne. 2011. Ode to the downpressor: A psychological portrait of racism, classism, and denial in (post)colonial Jamaica. PhD diss., Pacifica Graduate Institute.

Biko, Steve Bantu. 2002. *I write what I like: A selection of his writings*. Chicago: University of Chicago Press.

Cherki, Alice. 2006. *Fanon: A portrait*. Trans. Nadia Benabid. Ithaca: Cornell University Press.

Comaroff, Jean, and John Comaroff, eds. 2000. *Civil society and the political imagination in Africa: Critical perspectives*. Chicago: University of Chicago Press.

———. 2006. *Law and disorder in the postcolony*. Chicago: University of Chicago Press.

Cooper, Anna Julia. 1998. What are we worth? In *The voice of Anna Julia Cooper: Including "A voice from the South" and other important essays, papers, and letters*, ed. Charles Lemert, 161–87. Lanham, Md.: Rowman & Littlefield.

Darity, William A., Jr. 2005. Affirmative action in comparative perspective: Strategies to combat ethnic and racial exclusion internationally. Durham: Sanford Institute of Public Policy, Duke University.

Davis, Angela Y. 2003. *Are prisons obsolete?* New York: Seven Stories Press.

de Sousa Santos, Boaventura, ed. 2007. *Democratizing democracy: Beyond the liberal democratic canon.* London: Verso.

———. 2008. *Another knowledge is possible: Beyond northern epistemologies.* London: Verso.

Fanon, Frantz. 1963. *The wretched of the earth.* Trans. Constance Farrington. New York: Grove Press.

———. 1967. *Black skin, white masks.* Trans. Charles Lam Markmann. New York: Grove Press.

Gates, Henry Louis, Jr. 2011. What it means to be "black in Latin America." National Public Radio, *Fresh Air*, 27 July. http://www.npr.org/2011/07/27/138601410/what-it-means-to-be-black-in-latin-america.

Gibson, Nigel, ed. 2011. *Living Fanon: Global perspectives.* New York: Palgrave.

Gordon, Jane Anna, and Lewis R. Gordon. 2009. *Of divine warning: Reading disaster in the modern age.* Boulder, Colo.: Paradigm.

Gordon, Lewis R. 1995. *Bad faith and antiblack racism.* Atlantic Highlands, N.J.: Humanity Books.

———. 2004a. Critical reflections on three popular tropes in the study of whiteness. In *What white looks like: African-American philosophers on the whiteness question*, ed. George Yancy, 173–94. New York: Routledge.

———. 2004b. Philosophical anthropology, race, and the political economy of disenfranchisement. *Columbia Human Rights Law Review* 36, no. 1: 145–72.

———. 2005. Through the zone of nonbeing: A reading of *Black skin, white masks* in celebration of Fanon's eightieth birthday. *C. L. R. James Journal* 11, no. 1: 1–43. Available online in Post-continental philosophy, ed. Nelson Maldonado-Torres, special issue, *Worlds & Knowledges Otherwise: A Web Dossier* 1, dossier 3 (Fall 2006). https://globalstudies.trinity.duke.edu/wp-content/themes/cgsh/materials/WKO/v1d3_LGordon.pdf.

Guthrie, Robert V. 2003. *Even the rat was white: A historical view of psychology.* 2nd ed. Boston: Allyn & Bacon.

Gutman, Herbert G. 1976. *The black family in slavery and freedom, 1750–1925.* New York: Pantheon Books.

Handler, Joel F. 1995. *The poverty of welfare reform.* New Haven: Yale University Press.

———. 2004. *Social citizenship and workfare in the United States and Western Europe: The paradox of inclusion.* Cambridge: Cambridge University Press.

Johnson, James Weldon. 2008. *Along this way: The autobiography of James Weldon Johnson.* New York: Penguin Classics.

Katznelson, Ira. 2006. *When affirmative action was white: An untold history of racial inequality in America.* New York: W. W. Norton.

King, Desmond S., and Rogers Smith. 2011. *Still a house divided: Race and politics in Obama's America.* Princeton: Princeton University Press.

Logan, John. 2011. Separate and unequal: The neighborhood gap for blacks, Hispanics, and Asians in metropolitan America. *US 2010 Project* (July). http://www.s4.brown.edu/us2010/Data/Report/report0727.pdf.

Mamdani, Mahmood. 1996. *Citizen and subject: Contemporary Africa and the legacy of late colonialism.* Princeton: Princeton University Press.

Mbembe, Achille. 2001. *On the postcolony.* Berkeley: University of California Press.

Saltman, Kenneth J. 2007. *Schooling and the politics of disaster.* New York: Routledge.

Tillotson, Michael. 2011. *Invisible Jim Crow.* Trenton, N.J.: Africa World Press.

Valdes, Francisco. 2001. Insisting on critical theory in legal education: Making do while making waves. *La Raza Law Journal* 12, no. 2: 137–58.

3

Revisioning "White Privilege"

Marilyn Nissim-Sabat

As soon as I desire I am asking to be considered. I am not merely here-and-now, sealed into thingness. I am for somewhere else and something else. I demand that notice be taken of my negating activity insofar as I pursue something other than life; insofar as I do battle for the creation of a human world—that is, of a world of reciprocal recognition.
—FANON 1967, 218

A few years ago, I attended a send-off party for two friends who were leaving Chicago to live abroad for an extended period. I had never met their other friends and was invited to the party by the departing couple. There were about twenty people there, all African American, except myself. I was delighted to have been invited and found everyone to be friendly and warm. At the same time, there was, in the proverbial phrase, an elephant in the room: I was the only white person present. It was, of course, impossible not to notice and wonder about this (but this is not to say that one shouldn't notice and wonder about it). Though I had been invited by mutual friends, the other guests could not be sure whether or not I experience my whiteness, consciously or unconsciously, as conferring a deserved advantage, a privileged status, on me vis-à-vis black people. Thus there was in the room an undercurrent of some, albeit mild, tension. After a while, we formed a circle around the departing couple so that each guest could express his or her sentiments. Everyone spoke fondly of the couple and wished them a wonderful stay abroad. I presented my own version of the same; however, quite spontaneously, "in the

moment," so to speak, I added a remark I first heard stated by Lewis Gordon (the author of the previous chapter and of the article discussed below): since *Homo sapiens* first appeared in Africa and was undoubtedly dark-skinned, it follows that we are all "different shades of black." After the party resumed, I noticed, in the reciprocal give-and-take of my interactions with others, that the tension had receded: the elephant had left the room.

Situations in which white privilege is a factor occur frequently, of course. Nor are efforts like mine unique. I refer to efforts to reframe the situation in order to counteract the power of "white privilege," which I believe compromises what is in my, and everyone's, best interest: human relations unfettered by ideological distortions. The aim of this chapter is to pursue a new critical approach, one that opens up dimensions of the meaning of white privilege that are often marginalized, and shows thereby the continuing usefulness of the trope in the face of potent critiques of it. I am not indissolubly wedded to "white privilege" as either term, notion, or trope; rather, I wish to bring out what I take to be a dimension of liberatory struggle that is too often left by the wayside.

What is, it seems to me, too often left by the wayside in discussions of "white privilege" is any effort to show or to raise consciousness regarding the role in critical thinking and liberatory action that is played by an implicit vision of the nature of human relations "unfettered by ideological distortions." My contention is that such a vision is more or less abstractly constitutive of all efforts to work against white supremacy, but that such a vision can be concretized in and through the praxis of everyday life. Since the enactment of "white privilege" often occurs in everyday intersubjective interactions, like the one that occurred at the party described above, the critical trope of "white privilege" allows us to assess such interactions critically, rather than leave them by the wayside. Most important, however, such an analysis allows us to encounter experientially the concrete vision of new human relations that—beyond our constant and necessary awareness of the incalculable human suffering produced by racism and sexism in all dimensions of our existence—can, it seems to me, motivate liberatory praxis.

Before embarking on the analysis, it is helpful to frame the issue historically and globally: the current existential situation vis-à-vis race relations in the United States of America will, I believe, either remain in an entirely unacceptable status quo, improve marginally and with glacial slowness, or suffer regression—unless, that is, new ideas and new practices emerge. New ideas about race, racism, and liberatory practices are doubtless germinating in many areas of this world. In offering an interpretation of the event

described above, I am at the same time suggesting one possible direction that may, and perhaps must, be part of a revitalization of the struggle for a human and humane world.

Lewis Gordon's Critique of the Trope of White Privilege

In the concluding paragraph of his incisive essay "Critical Reflections on Three Popular Tropes in the Study of Whiteness" (2004), Lewis R. Gordon writes, "In the end, a key reminder in whiteness studies should also be bringing out the humanity of white people. It is absurd for us to expect people to argue against the value of their own survival. But with such critical engagements should also, always, be an understanding that our liberating pleas for common ground bring along with them an underlying optimism not only of what is to be done, but also what *can* be done" (Gordon 2004, 190). The "liberating pleas for common ground" in play here are those that Gordon elaborates in his essay. One of these is that the notion of "white privilege" should be abandoned as a trope, or preoccupying theme, of critical white studies because it obstructs the realization of common ground that is essential for progressive change. Those who deploy the trope may seek to establish a common ground in the sense of greater equality by eliminating white privilege, or racial inequality. For Gordon, however, this attempt is misguided in that the term itself instantiates the division between the privileged whites and the nonprivileged blacks. Put another way, Gordon points out that since the claim is that such necessities for a decent life as, for example, safety, food, clothing, shelter, education, and positive self-regard—in short, all of those factors that enable "the transformation of a human world into a humane one" (175)—are what whites are privileged to have, the term "white privilege" is a misleading misnomer because these are not privileges but rights common to all human beings. And so designating them as privileges simply cedes too much to the status quo and its perpetuators.

Gordon further elaborates the disadvantages for critical white studies of the notion of white privilege by pointing out that "a privilege is something that not everyone needs, but a right is the opposite. Given this distinction, an insidious dimension of the white privilege argument emerges. It requires condemning whites for possessing, in the concrete, features of contemporary life that should be available to all, and if this is correct, how can whites be expected to give up such things?" (176). This is the point that Gordon invokes in his closing paragraph, quoted above, as marking the "humanity"

of white people, who, as human beings, cannot be expected "to argue against the value of their own survival." These are among the considerations that Gordon refers to when he suggests that an underlying optimism (regarding the struggle for liberation) requires that we focus not only on "what is to be done, but also what *can* be done." His point, then, is that attempting to persuade whites to give up their advantages where those advantages are actually prerequisites for a "humane," i.e., decent, life is to court failure, with its resultant pessimism.

There is, however, another side to this coin. Certainly, Gordon believes that those fighting for real equality must aim to dismantle institutional racism; indeed, it is doubtful that many, if any, of the theorists of critical white studies would disagree. On the other hand, this struggle has not been a source of unmitigated optimism, either. After the civil rights movement of the 1950s and '60s, progress in dismantling institutional racism has been painfully and unacceptably slow, with generations of blacks and other minorities still condemned to less than "humane," and therefore less than human, lives, and there have been setbacks as well. Witness the ferocious resurgence of racism, still intensifying, that followed the election of President Barack Obama, and the ongoing attacks on the 1965 Voting Rights Act and the wave of voter-suppression legislation in the states.[1] The point is that it is one thing to say that refusing to attempt to change that which as such cannot be changed will allow us to maintain our optimism; it is quite another thing to point to or reveal factors that will nurture optimism about creating a society founded, as it should be, on the common ground of the human condition, human needs, and human capacities. Thus we must ask: what can motivate such optimism? In the lengthiest and most intense section of his essay, in which he critiques the white studies trope of the social construction of race, Gordon does offer a source or agent of optimism: science and fact, which both clear up notorious areas of confusion in the critical white studies literature and can dispel some of the principal arguments that have given racism legitimacy. After discussing Gordon's analysis of social constructionism, I will propose what I take to be a necessary supplement to his incisive and necessary critique, a supplement that restores, on different grounds, the usefulness of white privilege as a trope of critical white studies.

Gordon begins his critique of social constructionism as a trope of white studies by pointing out that "the social world, like normality, is an *achievement,* and although we are all born into this achievement, the achievement of its continuity and adaptation is a function of our participation in this world, a world of selves and others. Whiteness, then, as a system of meaning and

identity is an achievement . . . it is a social construction" (Gordon 2004, 182–83, emphasis in original). Following this, citing discussions with students, Gordon notes their fact- and experience-based claims that would contravene the claim that race is a social construction: children of same-race parents don't produce children of other races; medical treatments must be adjusted along racial lines to avoid iatrogenic deaths; why do we see races (183–84)? Gordon then clarifies that his point is not that race is not a social construction; his point is, rather, that it is a mistake fostered by disciplinary decadence[2] to infer that race is *only* a social construction, for one must consider "intervening forces of reality" (184). What Gordon means is that if one were to infer that race is only a social construction, then one implies that prior to its social construction, for example, one hundred thousand years ago, "there is no material historical difference" (185). In point of fact, however, one hundred thousand years ago "there were no people whom we would today upon observation consider to be white people. Such people are relative newcomers on the scene" (184). He writes further that "in spite of white normativity's depiction, the reality is that early human beings were very dark beings with tightly curled hair and all the other features necessary to protect them from the sun's radiation and enable the release of heat" (186).

Gordon concludes his critique of the trope of social constructionism with these poignant and telling remarks: "The upshot of this story, which is the prevailing story of human evolution and subsequent morphological differentiation, is that the physical features that we have come to associate with whiteness were not always apparent in our species . . . [and] have been around for only 20,000 years or less. What this means is that the operative conditions of identity in historic inquiry that have dominated our studies of human beings should be radically changed, for those are built upon the question, 'How did black people come about?' when in fact they should pose the opposite question: How did white and other light-skinned peoples come about?" (Gordon 2004, 188). The next section of Gordon's essay is his conclusion, in which he makes clear that posing the new question can and should recast the struggle against white privilege into the struggle against white supremacy (on which white privilege depends), and against white manifest destiny (i.e., the notion that the future of humanity is destined to be white). For Gordon, the consciousness that is aware of the historical-genetic priority of black people will be more radical, and, I think this implies, more revolutionary, in its aims than the consciousness constituted by critiques of or attacks on white privilege, white normativity, and the social construction of race. That is, this scientifically demonstrated historical-genetic priority of blacks drastically

undercuts the demoralizing cultural baggage according to which blacks are historically and genetically secondary and, by implication, inferior offshoots of the original white, i.e., master, race. For Gordon, the demise of such demoralizing cultural tropes has the potential to radicalize those who seek progressive change in a way that the tropes of white studies—particularly the trope of "white privilege"—cannot. Thus the true story of human evolutionary and genetic development is, it seems, Gordon's candidate, so to speak, for a motivating factor that can energize radical action by clearing away pseudoscientific, incorrect, and oppressive notions that, where accepted, severely damage the image of black people. Moreover, that Gordon insists on making these facts clear and working toward a very wide provenance for them so as to constitute a motivating force is made clear by the recognition that the fact that the original colonists, slavers, and other purveyors of white supremacy did not have access to these facts in no way exonerates them for dehumanizing persons of different hues and cultures. In fact, as Gordon notes, it was the passionate commitment to white supremacy and white manifest destiny, the very things that gave rise to white privilege, that perpetuates pseudoscientific distortions today—for example, the demand for ever more "proof" [sic!] of Obama's birth in the United States or the denial of climate change. The knowledge we have today will motivate us today.

White Privilege as the Nexus of Critical White Studies

Though he rejects it as a trope of critical white studies, Gordon does not deny the actuality of white privilege; he only points out that it is dependent on white supremacy and that therefore white supremacy is what must be addressed, i.e., the cause, not the symptom. White supremacy is ensconced in law, economics, social stratification, institutions, civil society, and so on, and these therefore are the sites for conceptualizing and acting for change. My point is that, necessary as it is to wage war against institutional racism, this way of conceiving the problem and the path to a solution needs supplementation. Gordon points out that self-interest will deter whites from surrendering their "privileges," especially since they are, as he rightly emphasizes, not privileges of the few but rights, conditions for the possibility of a human, that is, humane, life for any and all. However, viewed from the perspective of one who is aware of the transmogrification of rights into privileges that is one of the perduring hallmarks of racial injustice, and wishes to undo such inequality, we see that we must wait for the permanent revolution, the total

transformation of society, in order fully to experience the humanity of others, and, for that matter, our own humanity. We must wait, in Marx's terms, until we bring about the end of the "realm of necessity" and enter the "realm of freedom."[3] No matter how I cherish and am cherished by my loved ones, no matter how creative and rich my life, and so on, I know, with Eugene Victor Debs, that "while there is a soul in prison, I am not free."[4] As long as gross injustice, with its many abominations, characterizes my society and my world—to that extent is my humanity compromised.

Gordon poses the question for us: what *can* be done? Is there not, however, a prior question: if I do not already have a vision of new human relations, of what encounters with others can be when we are free, then how will I conceive the work of transformation, of what can be done, let alone do it? What vision of new human relations can animate my struggle to bring about transformation? What epiphanic experience, what glimpses of a better world to come, can preclude pessimism and despair? Such a vision is the supplement that I referred to above. It is a supplement that, coming on the heels, so to speak, of the relentless critique that philosophical responsibility alone demands, is, in the terms of Husserlian phenomenology, awareness that consciousness, subjectivity, always already does and must have a protended lifeworld and world horizon of future possibilities; or—in the words of the revolutionary pamphleteer and philosopher-poet Percy Shelley—it is a pre-sentiment of "the gigantic shadows that futurity casts upon the present" (Shelley 1966, 297). In order to develop further the theme of the necessity for this supplement, I return to the discussion initiated in Gordon's critique of the role of self-interest in sustaining white privilege.

Gordon emphasizes that it is not in the self-interest of whites to surrender their "privileges," especially since those privileges are actually human rights. What is not made explicit in his formulation is the way in which white privilege as *belief* (belief that what are in fact human rights nevertheless ought to be distributed to a few) is fostered by societies that artificially generate the chronic state of exigency reflected in the politics and economics of scarcity. The intended result is that whites fear that if blacks and other minorities obtain the same "privileges," then they—the whites—will lose out because there is not enough to go around. This artificial exigency is evident today in the United States in the way that the issue of rationing health care has entered the debate on health care. Moreover, it is abundantly clear at this point that the underlying fear is that the undeserving minorities, blacks in particular, may siphon off health care from whites. Among the rationalizations for thus justifying gross inequity is the notion that the poor, the elderly,

blacks, gays, and women are deficient (perhaps even "subhuman") and that that is why they do not, and should not, have the "privileges." In other words, the current socioeconomic system fosters the sense that the privileged whites are privileged because, in a situation of scarcity (largely manufactured for this purpose) wherein a principle of distribution must be constituted, they, the whites, are more deserving. So, then, how, from a liberatory perspective, can we appeal to the common ground of universal humanity, even in the face of the facts of human evolution and dispersal, as a liberatory motif when it is just this common ground that is powerfully, in a fight literally to the death, obscured? Indeed, powerful social forces pressing on us all insist that we view the necessities of a human and humane life as privileges and thus as things that can be (and have been) taken from us. Marx's writings are replete with passionate attempts to convey just this to his readers, to expose and get beyond their false consciousness, which is the product of alienation, and to show that the level of alienation in capitalist societies dehumanizes all, work-ers and capitalists, rich and poor alike, and does so by obscuring, even ren-dering unthinkable, a common ground.

From the point of view of Marx's theory of alienation, I define "white privilege" as a critical trope denoting not the status quo as such, for if that is all that it denotes, then Gordon's rebuttal that it simply duplicates the status quo that sets blacks against whites would be enough to convince us to abandon it. Rather than, or better, in addition to this, the trope of white privilege denotes as well the alienation of consciousness in the specific context of race relations, the very alienation of consciousness that gener-ates white-black animosity and injustice. Moreover, as Marx showed, alien-ation is just that deformation of consciousness that is manifest when people act on what they mistakenly take to be their own best self-interest. When Gordon avers that whites see their "privileges" (because the privi-leges are not, as they should be, universally available) as what must be defended and protected, and certainly not surrendered, he does not make explicit whether the whites only *believe* that such actions are in their own best interest, or whether such actions are *actually* in their own best inter-est; nor does Gordon suggest that *ideally* whites, rather than surrender their "privileges," should recognize them as rights, not privileges, and therefore should fight to have those privileges—i.e., rights—universalized. But if they are ensconced in their privileges, what would motivate them to join the struggle? What could motivate them, I aver, is the understanding that what they believe is in their own best interest, i.e., maintaining their privileged access to the means for a meaningful life, is not actually in their

best interest.[5] This means that they lose more than they gain, as I explain below.

Conclusion

My act, at the party, of raising the issue of the blackness of the first human beings was motivated by self-interest. An important factor here is, of course, that I have been involved both intellectually and actively in the struggle for liberation all of my life. Nevertheless, my action, though it was a culmination of my personal history and beliefs, at the same time transcended, I think, all of that. My motivating vision was one that flowed from a deeply desired imagined future in which all human relations were transformed into just that: nonalienated human relations. Moreover, in acting thus I sought just that epiphanic moment, reaching beyond myself, of connection with concrete individuals, who, in the Hegelian-Marxist view, are subjects, and thus can never lose their universality.

Returning to the party, the question of self-interest looms large. In the first place, I could not just stand there in the circle and expect people to assume that I was not a racist of one variety or another, beyond what afflicts everyone, living as we do in a racist society. Such an assumption could be dangerous, and those present were under no obligation to make such an assumption. But, most important, and here is the nub of my meaning: I wanted to have a good time at the party! I did not want to miss out on one iota of the experience of getting to know the people who were there through conversation and through the kind of pop-up intimacies that occur when one is in party mode. In short, it was *myself* I was thinking of; I wanted to cut my losses, and that meant doing whatever I could to contribute to the happening of a great evening. What I am saying, then, is that the notion of white privilege as denoting an attitude of mind can help us to bring out the fact that in a racist society everyone suffers, and suffers big-time. For myself, barriers that prevent me from becoming known to others as the person I am entail suffering. Insofar as I am imbued with the ideology of white privilege and the attitude of mind that ideology engenders, there is a barrier to communication, sociality, self-development, and so on, and I am artificially limited in the range of people with whom I can have intersubjective communion. This is an immense loss and a price I am not willing to pay.

My larger point is to convey that a meaningful strategy for change that uses the notion of white privilege is an investigation of the intersubjective

costs of white privilege to whites and nonwhites alike, the personal losses that it imposes on us, beyond material losses and the kinds of losses that stem from institutional racism, sexism, classism, though these are very great, and also personal losses. Whites may not want to give up their privileges if they base their identity on those racial privileges and thus base their survival on their whiteness, in the white-privilege sense of whiteness (this is the reason why we have a field called white studies), but they might be more willing to consider doing so if they became aware that their losses are greater than their gains, indeed, that their gains pale (pun intended) beside their losses. In short, people whose attitude is that of white privilege may believe that their attitude and consequent actions are in their own best interest, but they are mistaken in this belief, and I would suggest, further, that developing a vision of a new society can uncover the source of this mistaken belief.

Notes

1. In June 2013 the U.S. Supreme Court nullified a key portion of the Voting Rights Act that had forced southern states (and some northern communities) with a history of restricting access to the voting booth on the grounds of race to obtain federal approval for any new voting legislation. Since then, many southern states have passed legislation—for example, requiring state identification cards for eligibility to vote—that effectively makes it much more difficult for the large African American populations in those states to vote.

2. "*Disciplinary decadence* is the anthologizing or reification of a discipline. In such an attitude, we treat our discipline as though it was never born and has always existed and will never change or, in some cases, die. . . . Its assertion as absolute eventually leads to no room for other disciplinary perspectives" (Gordon 2006, 4–5).

3. "The realm of freedom only begins where labour determined by necessity and external expediency ends; it lies by its very nature beyond the sphere of material production proper." The true realm of freedom is the realm of "the development of human powers as an end in itself" (Marx [1894] 1981, 959).

4. "Your Honor, years ago I recognized my kinship with all living beings, and I made up my mind that I was not one bit better than the meanest on earth. I said then, and I say now, that while there is a lower class, I am in it, and while there is a criminal element I am of it, and while there is a soul in prison, I am not free" (Debs 1918).

5. The *locus classicus* for analysis of beliefs regarding what is and is not in one's own best interest is Plato's dialogue *Protagoras*. I discuss *Protagoras* at length in Nissim-Sabat 2009.

References

Debs, Eugene V. 1918. Statement to the court upon being convicted of violating the Sedition Act. http://www.marxists.org/archive/debs/works/1918/court.htm.

Fanon, Frantz. 1967. *Black skin, white masks.* Trans. Charles Lam Markmann. New York: Grove Press.

Gordon, Lewis R. 2004. Critical reflections on three popular tropes in the study of whiteness. In *What white looks like: African-American philosophers on the whiteness question*, ed. George Yancy, 173–94. New York: Routledge.

———. 2006. *Disciplinary decadence: Living thought in trying times.* Boulder, Colo.: Paradigm.

Marx, Karl. [1894] 1981. *Capital: A critique of political economy III.* Trans. David Fernbach. London: Penguin.

Nissim-Sabat, Marilyn. 2009. Addictions, *akrasia*, and self psychology: A Socratic and psychoanalytic view of *akrasia* as victim-blaming. In Nissim-Sabat, *Neither victim nor survivor: Thinking toward a new humanity*, 81–96. Lanham, Md.: Lexington Books.

Shelley, Percy Bysshe. 1966. *A defense of poetry.* In *Shelley's prose: Or, the trumpet of a prophecy.* Ed. David Lee Clark. Albuquerque: University of New Mexico Press.

2

The Images and Rhetoric of
White Privilege

4

The Very Image of Privilege: Film Creation of White Transcendentals in Vienna and Hollywood

Bettina Bergo

This essay works from three initial hypotheses. First, the persistence of privilege and "coded" forms of racism is due in part to the way in which images and affects intertwine and become sedimented, often unbeknownst to us (Bergner 1995; cf. Winnubst 2004, 37–38). Second, the presence of images is not available to conscious scrutiny in the precise way that words or texts are. Sedimented images have an "organization" close to that of dreams, condensing into one another, becoming displaced from original events and concentrating affective weight, which resurfaces in situations that evoke comparable images and behaviors, including unconsciously retained ones. This is the shared discovery of psychoanalysis and phenomenology (cf. Husserl 2001, 162–220). It helps account for the persistence of largely unconscious biases and prejudices. Third, film plays a significant role in influencing the sedimentation of images and affects. If it occasionally questions stereotypes, it also modifies and updates them. I will show how images from pre–World War II Viennese cinema contributed to conceptions of whiteness (and white privilege) in both Austria and the United States. It is my working thesis that confronting a racist heritage means taking responsibility—in this case, my own—for images and types that we insist we have not personally created.

A number of studies have examined the role of images in behavior—notably, images in contemporary mass media (Adorno 1974; Winnubst 2004, 27–28). The persistence of racism certainly goes beyond the role of unconscious images. Nevertheless, the role of such images is not negligible; George

Yancy's example of the "elevator effect," in which a white woman clutches her purse to her chest when a black man enters the elevator, clearly shows the impact on bodies "of color" of acts that are understood or interpreted by the white body as innocent, as moments of mere distraction. In this chapter, I tarry with the persistence of racism, as Yancy puts it, by pursuing such phenomenological dimensions of racism through a brief look at the accumulation and diversification of images in cultural imaginations. I hope to demonstrate just how racist they can be.

There are a number of ways to study the buildup of images in a culture. I focus on the 1930s because during the rise of fascism—which represents a paroxysm of privilege and racism—films, cartoons, and photographs played a central role in creating a dense topography in which whiteness represented transcendent purity, a motivating ideal and untouchable form that polarized everything around it, depicting everything else not just as subservient but as ultimately eliminable. I would like to push Yancy's concept of "false transcendence," which he locates for today's African American community in *hope*, idealized and overinvested in an unrealized justice whose outcome paralyzes critique. Because the political unfolding of fascism is one of the clearest recent illustrations of the exploitation of false transcendentals, from escapism to mass racist scapegoating, I take up the fascist rhetoric of types and focus on the creation of two white transcendentals, one masculine, the other feminine. At the end of the chapter, I explain my personal motivations for this study. As the student of Nazi propaganda Klaus Theweleit has shown, these types depended on the iconic motors of white fantasies of transcendence, the false transcendence of the oppressor's positions. Further, because cinematic techniques forged by Austrian and German cinematographers evolved through ongoing exchanges with Hollywood in the 1920s and '30s (Munby 1999), I address the question of what happens when images and types framed in one culture migrate into another.

"How Dare You Say Such a Thing!": Interactions of Image, Affect, and Myth

When George Yancy argues that "whiteness is precisely the *historical* metanarrative that affects [white people's] sense of themselves as atomic individuals, *and as sites of exclusive transcendence*,"[1] he refers to the construction and reconstruction of a *myth*. The myth of whiteness has taken different forms in Europe and the Americas, but a false transcendental inhabits it, polarizing

around it concepts such as purity, beauty, truth, right. Sander Gilman reminds us that within the metanarrative of whiteness, black is not first a color or even a race; "the very concept of color," he argues, "is a quality of Otherness, *not* of reality" (Gilman 1986, 6; see also Brown et al. 2003, 42–43). This statement echoes Althusser's description of ideology as "an *illusion* considered to be a truthful representation of reality that at the same time makes an *allusion* to reality" (quoted in Semmerling 2006, 4).

But what is reality? Is it absurd to argue that in the defense of privileges—especially when they are perceived as under threat—there are factors at play that prove as important as "reality"? Forging a metanarrative generally entails creating a myth (cf. Mosse 1975, 100–107); the latter may be protean and flexible, and it may be disavowed or oblivious to the bodies and spaces it excludes from legitimacy or basic rights. However, the creation of myth should not be understood as mere "fabrication" or traffic in falsehood. Rather, it contributes to that complex logic that grounds individuals' reasons for living and allows them to find "kindred spirits." Myth mobilizes something more important than cognitive claims and fully conscious perceptions. Indeed, myths *become* "reality" when their constituent beliefs are put into action (Lacoue-Labarthe and Nancy 2005, 68). Cultures have a variety of myths that serve political ends, from legitimation to "the myth of normalcy" (Semmerling 2006, 214–47), from solidarity to motivations for aggression (Theweleit 1989, 170–91). In lieu of arguments, a myth has "for its nature and its end to incarnate itself in a *figure*, or in a *type*" (Lacoue-Labarthe and Nancy 2005, 55). We find examples of these types in German and Austrian cinema, where a masculine and a feminine white transcendental are staged. Analyzing the Nazi myth, Philippe Lacoue-Labarthe and Jean-Luc Nancy argue that the "types" on which it depends formed structures and worked at both a conceptual level and an iconic-symbolic one. This was a powerful combination because the iconic-symbolic level is never free of affects and the sentiments we call "liking" and "disliking."

The unremarked presence of types conditions our selection of rational arguments, and the buildup of images and symbols in unconscious memory contributes to the return of prejudices even when they are challenged by arguments. Phenomenology has proved adept at showing the mechanism of the sedimentation of images in the ongoing flow of consciousness. Edmund Husserl analyzed the flow of consciousness as it moved from now-moments to "the past," where distant but retained experiences may resist being recollected but nevertheless exert emotional force and can sometimes be sequentially reconstituted. He argued that this sedimentation creates "fusion

phenomena" (Husserl 2001, 185–86), and he demonstrated that these, and not some inborn concepts, were the sources of our perceptual categories. Through elaborate examples, Husserl showed how consciousness identifies images, cognitively and affectively, as either matching, correspondent, or divergent from one another. Language need not be central to this process. For example, when identifying triangles in a series of mental pictures, we experience the triangular images as fusing with similar, previously perceived phenomena (177–78). When an image of a circle is introduced, a spontaneous contrariety is experienced—that is, *an affect is evoked* as "This does not fit; this *is not right!*" Husserl's argument starts from simple images entering consciousness dynamically and surreptitiously, creating a ground as dense as verbal discourse and charged with affect (180–81). This happens in all experience, but preeminently in cinema.

Husserl's fusion phenomena also clarify how a certain hiatus can exist between our retained linguistic memories and our retained images. The distinction turns again around *types* and the affects awakened when they are activated by a new perception. Similarly, psychologists have encountered acute instances of the separability of affects and images from discourse when they proposed interpretations of patients' verbal accounts. Separated from its emotions, the account may *suggest* anger or fear, while the images are evoked with little awareness of their interrelationships or emotional charge. It is thus common to hear responses such as "How dare you say such a thing? I'm not afraid of . . . !" or "I never meant that I hated . . . !" Beyond the well-known displacement of unacceptable affect, the extralinguistic dimension of accumulated images runs as if *beneath* language (Husserl 2001, 32). Sometimes it overruns it entirely, and fusion phenomena can persist independently of discourse.

Thus, whatever we make of psychology's intuitions concerning the separation of affect and ideation, we find in Husserl's phenomenology bona fide descriptions of the formation of fusion phenomena. These phenomena thereby offer the student of aesthetics and privilege an advantage that psychological intuitions lack, because phenomenology, like cinema (but unlike psychology), describes lived experience before it is parsed into subjective and objective dimensions. Phenomenology, like cinema, focuses on visuality and hearing, thereby undercutting the formal theorizations of psychology. This makes the findings of phenomenology particularly valuable to our understanding of the formation of types from the sedimentation of images.

The Aesthetics of Escapism and Freedom: From Berlin and Vienna to Hollywood

The sedimentation of images within the flow of consciousness, which Husserl called fusion phenomena, is precisely what Nazi propaganda produced to support white privilege on an affective level. In this respect, one of the best laboratories for studying the construction of types and myths is German-language cinema, because this construction was carried out and extensively theorized by Nazi "intellectuals." Alfred Rosenberg's *The Myth of the Twentieth Century* (1930), for example, drew parallels between races and souls, urging the creation of new types to shape the "race" in order to raise the "souls" of Aryan Germans. Citing the anti-Semitic Orientalist Paul de Lagarde (1827–1891), Rosenberg argued that nations, when purified of degenerate peoples, reflect "the thoughts of God" himself (Lacoue-Labarthe and Nancy 2005, 56–57). Elaborating a romantic conception of race that presented itself as mysticism *and* science, the Nazi myth exploited a host of nineteenth-century polygeneticists' racial hierarchies, adding on newer cultural elements.

Cultural creation became the laboratory for political hegemony. German and Austrian films, while not strictly identical, forged striking transcendentals of whiteness. In the German case, responding to and fostering the increasing militarization of society in the 1930s, the masculine transcendental required a machinelike, desexualized aesthetic that would protect the members of the SA and the SS from anxieties about Others and from their own fears of fragility, fluidity, and effeminacy. Many German images of the masculine transcendental stemmed from World War I literature, like that of Ernst Jünger, who celebrated the German soldier: "This was a whole new race, energy incarnate . . . supple bodies, lean and sinewy . . . stony eyes petrified in a thousand terrors beneath their helmets" (quoted in Theweleit 1989, 159). Comparable themes run through German literature of the 1920s.

The Austrian case was more complex because it was hybrid. Despite class and regional segregation, Austria remained a multiethnic country. Moreover, in the wake of the 1933 German elections, artists of all sorts—including "some 900 members of the German film industry [who became] unemployable in Germany and ultimately stateless" (Dassanowsky 2008, 162)— swelled the ranks of artistic talent in Vienna, and later in Hollywood. They created the influential *Emigranten* film industry in Vienna as well as the system of B films in Hollywood. In the wake of the civil war that broke out in 1934 with the Nazis' assassination of Engelbert Dollfuss, Austria's chancellor,

Austrian film itself gravitated powerfully toward the creation of a "false transcendental" distinct from the German ideals, notably through the *Heimat-*
film (homeland film). This nostalgic pastoral genre indulged spectators in
dreams of hope and escape into a *féerie* version of Austria far from the city,
where music and the art of the old empire were the primary values. The
Austrian cinematographer Arthur Maria Rabenalt characterized these productions as strictly "unpolitische Filme" and divided them into "musical
comedies," "society films," and "homeland idylls" (Rabenalt 1978, 43). The
strikingly apolitical nature of these films made sense in the context of the
Schuschnigg regime, which, while clearly engaged in a fascist *process* (Mann
2004, 13; Thorpe 2010, 326), understood itself as distinct from German mil-
itarism and as motivated by a "corporatism [that] could transcend class conflict [via] Catholicism and idealized notions of a national front" (Dassanowsky
2008, 169). The illusion of unity grew out of adept manipulation of the
myths of musical genius, self-sacrifice, homeland, and religious solidarity.

Collaboration between Vienna and Hollywood had begun in the 1920s
with U.S. film studios like Warner Brothers and Universal working with Austrian studios like Tobis-Sascha. I discuss below the impact of Viennese artists on American cinema. For now, note that the "film agreement" of 1934
put a Nazi clamp on the Austrian film industry, outlawing the presence of
"non-Aryans" and encouraging Austrian immigration to the United States
(Dassanowsky 2008, 160). But it was the Rome-Berlin Axis agreement of
1936 that threatened Italian and Austrian solidarity, spurring further Austrian flight to Hollywood (161).[2] The immigrants included Otto Preminger,
Josef von Sternberg, Erich von Stroheim, Edgar Ulmer, Joe Pasternak, Billy
Wilder, and many others. In the 1930s, they brought with them to the United
States escapist dreams of transcending city life, violence, and terror, as well
as white transcendentals of purity and elegance, which they assimilated to
the American myths of self-creation, freedom, and popular mobility. By the
1940s, however, exiles who had experienced their own disillusionment with
the American master narrative became the prime movers behind film noir,
as they began to stage the violence underlying the American myth (Munby
1999, 154–59).

From the films of the 1930s to the later *Sound of Music* (1965)—which
resurrected the *Heimatfilm* for U.S. audiences by setting Salzburg outside
historical time and space—the influence of Austrian producers, directors,
and screenwriters was inestimable. Many were Jewish and were horrified by
the idealization of Austrian history and politics, yet they brought an Austrian
aesthetic in which ideals of purity, cultural refinement, and urban class dis-

tinctions persisted. This aesthetic gradually flowed into American cinematic imagery, in which white masculine transcendentals found expression in frontier-saga individualism, as opposed to the cosmopolitan Viennese nobles or even the impenetrable German Spartan. In the case of the white feminine transcendental, the desexualized maiden ideal, representing an oneiric Austro-Hungarian Empire, found itself resexualized and democratized in the United States. We see this American effect both in the tension in Greta Garbo's talky image between aloofness and vulnerability (cf. *Ninotchka* [1939], in which she eats a hotdog at a baseball game), and in Marilyn Monroe as directed by émigré Billy Wilder (cf. gender-bending and Marilyn's "I Wanna Be Loved by You" in *Some Like It Hot* [1959]). If the German transcendental was embodied in the white nurse, as Theweleit effectively shows (1987, 125–57), comparable feminine ideals were found in the Austrian *Heimatfilm*, and it is surprising to see how readily these images entered the American scene. Indeed, *The Sound of Music*, which revisited a distinctly Austrian genre two decades after the war, proved a smash U.S. hit four years running, amassing $50 million in box-office receipts over forty-three weeks. It was the false transcendental in this film—set in a de-Nazified Austria, featuring an ingénue from the convent, an impoverished aristocrat, and music like "Edelweiss"—that reconstructed Austrian political identities and fused love of country with love of family. Perhaps *The Sound of Music* provided American viewers with an escape from the turbulence of the 1960s, although their need for escape was relatively mild compared to the flight Viennese audiences sought in the mid-1930s (Vansant 1999, 180–81). In any case, the film clearly addressed powerful nostalgia for family and country.

The social and symbolic privileges, such as racial "coding," that such filmic images embodied relied on sedimented images whose power comes from their unconscious persistence (Shaheen 2001, 6–7). Tied to a range of affects, this persistence is awakened as "interpellation." The work of Althusser and others has shown that ideology is essential to a socially grounded subjectivity (Semmerling 2006, 4). If sedimented images and types form the glue and touchstones of myth, and if myth functions as an illusion of reality resting on an allusion to reality, then subjects define parts of themselves through recognition of mythic elements: "'That's right! That's true!' What . . . occurs is the formation, through a process of 'interpellation' [being hailed/called], of the individual's idealized self-image . . . an 'ideal ego' that constantly rediscovers itself in the application of ideologies" and their metanarratives (ibid.). It is uncontroversial that film exerted, almost from its inception, an interpellating influence on values and social stereotypes greater than that of most books.

"It is time to recognize that the true tutors of our children are not school-teachers or university professors but filmmakers," wrote Benjamin Barber in the *Nation* (quoted in Shaheen 2001, 5). This is the case even when the mythic oppositions set in place in the 1930s and '40s (civilized/savage, rational/frenetic, normal/pathological, pure/defiled, light/dark, etc.) are reworked and applied to new populations. As Jack Shaheen argues, Nazi propaganda "presented the lecherous Jew slinking in the shadows, scheming to snare the blond Aryan virgin [but] yesterday's Shylocks resemble today's hook-nosed sheiks, arising from fear of the 'other'" (6; cf. Leonardo 2007, 263). The images persist and attach to different populations conceived as "threatening" or repugnant.

Das Frauenparadies (1936): A Society Film, Musical Comedy, and *Heimatfilm*

To consider how fusion phenomena can be analyzed in the fascist rhetoric of types as depicted in filmic images of false transcendence, let us look at a rather conventional Austrian film. *Das Frauenparadies* was produced in 1936, the year the Rome-Berlin Axis was formed. This was the moment when "a politically polarized Austria . . . found itself at its most geopolitically disadvantaged [point] since the end of the Great War" (Dassanowsky 2008, 173). We hardly remember the films of that period, although German television has rebroadcast a number of them in the past decade. They responded to an urgent need for cinematic escapism, which was one of the few remaining avenues for "resolving social strife through the nostalgia and spirituality of Austro-fascist ideology" (ibid.). *Das Frauenparadies* combined the urbane society film (imperial Vienna) and the *Heimatfilm* (Austria as unsullied garden) with the "screwball" comedy that Hollywood also staged from the 1930s to the 1950s. Women's Paradise was the name of a fashion house that employed fifteen elegant saleswomen, all blond, all similarly dressed. It was run by two symbolic parents, an excitable matron and an ineffectual, old-empire Viennese. Using the remnants of his creative freedom to escapist ends, director Arthur Rabenalt (1905–1993) staged one Gary Field (played by Ivan Petrovich) as his leading man and as the Austrian version of a military engineer—only Gary sets up his experimental propellers in the offices of the fashion house itself, with the result that his aircraft scatters papers rather than bullets. The female lead is a platinum blonde from Sweden named Ingrid Holm. She arrives in Vienna to prepare her wedding with Gary, slated

to take place in Italy. Ingrid's role is to introduce light opera into the "society film," as she sings its three musical numbers. A minor star, Eva (Hortense Raky), belongs to the sales staff and is immediately smitten with Gary. She enhances the screwball element through her foibles, which turn into heroic sacrifice.

In close contact with Hollywood, the Viennese directors—those who expatriated as well as those who remained—developed innovative cinematic techniques, including camera traveling and lateral-aerial dual perspectives, framing songs with Busby Berkeley's geometric dance numbers, in which ballerinas formed kaleidoscopic shapes on revolving stages. In *Das Frauenparadies*, the central musical number unfolds in just this way: the star is dressed in white gossamer and is "worshipped" by the dancers around her. Yet the musical numbers stand apart from the film's plot, introducing mythic and nostalgic elements as Gary and Ingrid walk through an eighteenth-century garden, for example, where they are hailed as royalty by "peasants" in overalls and dirndls. The plot turns on the bankruptcy of Frauenparadies— a convent in the religion of fashion, unable to survive in contemporary Vienna—and the selfless sacrifice of Eva, who obtains money sufficient to pay off its debts by offering herself to Ingrid's German patron, Mühldorfer (Georg Alexander). Nobly, Mühldorfer requires no return, and Eva is able surreptitiously to add the funds to the contributions of the saleswomen. When Gary learns of her contribution, he suspects the worst of her, and their own budding romance is quashed. It is a suffering Gary who now joins Ingrid on the train as they depart for Venice, followed, unbeknownst to them, by Eva and Mühldorfer. Aboard the train, it becomes clear that Ingrid and Gary's liaison is doomed, and this has to do with the character of Ingrid herself. A "Nordic" woman who is neither mother nor maiden, Ingrid embodies the desexualized, white feminine transcendental that we find in both German and Austrian films of the period. Theweleit has shown how German films staged the de-eroticized "white goddess" to motivate the "man of steel" to brave his wars against "Others" (Theweleit 1987, 315; see also Linke 1999, 75–77). In Austrian cinematic logic, the feminine transcendental is closer to a Catholic Madonna.

Once settled in their sleeping cabins, Eva and Ingrid, and Gary and Mühldorfer, discover—not without hilarity—that they are sharing two bunk-bed compartments. Their talk of Vienna reveals cross-purposes in love and the sacrificial sexual purity of young Eva. The denouement anticipates the screwball train chase found in Billy Wilder's *Some Like It Hot*, yet is more consistent with 1930s mythic types. When Ingrid grasps that Eva's love for her

betrothed has taken the higher form of sacrifice (a German feminine ideal), and that her girlish naiveté has flowered into devoted faithfulness (Austrian purity), she encourages Eva to pursue Gary with inexplicable equanimity. Eva heeds Ingrid's urging to stop the train by yanking the emergency brake. When the locomotive comes to a jarring halt, Eva and Gary together leap from the train in their pajamas, crossing hill and dale, only to meet up with the Frauenparadies town car, packed with its proverbial "father," "mother," and staff of fashion nuns. Cutting back to the train, we see a ruffled Ingrid confronting Mühldorfer in an enigmatic exchange of complicity. Nothing of their fate is ever decided. In a higher sense, nothing *need* be decided, for that is not Ingrid's function in the myth.

The lightness of the comedy frames a false transcendence of liberation—into courtly elegance and privilege, escape out of time, and the merging of love and sacrifice. Yet this *légèreté* wields a normalizing force. The separability of Ingrid's musical numbers is deliberate. Her image as "Nordic," her blondness, and the angelic quality of her dress reiterate the Austrian white feminine transcendental. The thematic triviality of the songs belies the power of her presence in the film; beyond sex, beyond motherhood, she embodies the purity of the desexualized feminine myth.

Close-ups of the singer's face reveal the paradox, typical of German fascist art, of a desirable woman whose expressions betray no eroticism. The only other mythic pole available to a feminine transcendental was the maternal angel, also found in German ideals of the same period. As Theweleit puts it, "mothers and sisters seem here to have been revealed as the true love objects of these men [who march into war]. The words of the incest taboo have written 'the water is wide and they cannot get across.' We now also have a way of understanding why 'good' women have to be husbandless, why they have to be pale as death. . . . Why? Because the sons/brothers want it that way" (1987, 112). The sons and brothers embody the imperative of fascist masculinity: hegemony must be defended without distraction. In the aftermath of Weimar and Red Vienna, the myth rewrites history: "their father has failed them, and now [the sons] are stepping forward to do battle for his succession before Mother Germany. Patriarchy secures its dominance [in a paroxysm of privilege] under fascism in the form of a filiarchy. . . . Nothing but sons as far as the eye can see" (108).

Proceeding on desexualization, the feminine fascist transcendental arose out of the embourgeoisement and mass opening of the heritage of German aesthetics and natural philosophy. The Frauenparadies sales staff incarnate Lippe's observations on German mythmaking: "Water nymphs, nymphs

from that same fountain . . . the purest and most characteristic forces of a country represented as a garden with a fountain" (Lippe 1974, quoted in Theweleit 1987, 315). Nevertheless, the work of students of fascism like Theweleit and Jonathan Littell (2008) shows how the transcendentals, essential to the *process* unfolded in German language imagery, radicalized gender distinctions and roles. As indicated, the male transcendental was epitomized by Ernst Jünger as "a whole new race, energy incarnate. . . . These were the keenest assembly of bodies, intelligence, will, and sensation" (quoted in Theweleit 1989, 159).

Transcendence here fuses the microcosm of the soldier-genius-machine with the macro-organism of the race—of Aryan sons. This assembly required a protector—not simply in the armed divisions but transcendentally, in the form of a Pallas Athena (where the fathers had failed) beyond feminine domesticity. As Theweleit points out, "the newly constructed edifice of the bourgeois-absolutist state [was] founded upon the restructured sexuality of the 'high-born' woman, who is to become a model for all women. The flowing of the streams of desire is captured and held in a fountain; it bubbles up to please man . . . it is desensualized, 'white' water, perfect for irrigating the new ordered state" (1987, 316).

The opposite of such a race could only be aliens, projectively identified with formlessness, imbalance, rushing floods, animality, and a different sort of force—the very antipode of the "men of steel." The fascist male body stood resistant (through a perverse inversion of imperial aggression) as both exception and fragility: "Those hirsute giants, those large-eared Mongols with melon-shaped skulls, black stiff hair, flattened cheek bones . . . appeared as prehistoric monsters next to our young soldiers, with their fragile bodies" (Littell 2008, 53; cf. Linke 1999, 236).

Against this, "the sixteen- and seventeen-year-old boys were of . . . a crystalline idealism."[3] The ideal of the fascist body entailed uprightness, impenetrability, light, and dryness. In its "infancy," this ideal reinforced imaginary racial threats from Russians and Mongols, Slavs and Asians in the East, to Jews at home, to colonized people outlying. It consolidated its purity against a metaphysical enemy. For Theweleit, the Manichean logic structuring fascist values is exemplified by the literature of the Storm Division: dry force versus wet engulfment, the noontime sun versus fetid swamps, the visible gestalt versus the abyss of darkness. This is not so unlike worldviews justifying many Western imperial adventures. More remarkable is that fascism exploited every form of the culture industry. The message for culture was expressed in sexual-racial politics: the Aryan transcendental was a body of

discipline, able to contain the chaos of forces within. All that threatened to overflow the crystalline idealism had to be restrained or eliminated. The Aryan female ideal moved between the *bleiche Mutter* who could become the mother of the race and the Athena who neither could nor would marry or reproduce, because she served as a beacon. This is why singer Ingrid Holm relinquished her betrothed, the Austrian pastiche of the military aircraft designer, to the virginal Eva, who truly embodied the mythical ideal. That sums up the normative message of the film, its "happy ending."

The transcendental, constructed to bolster Aryan rhetoric and to motivate the fascist paramilitary, describes a "beyond" that never imagined opening a site that would be beyond race. That myth belongs to a different cultural context. Race "science" deployed a metanarrative for European hegemony in the twentieth century, and there has not been a time when the symbolic cluster abbreviated as "whiteness" was not the lodestar (and site of terror [cf. Eze 2001, 187]) in the Western imagination. When whiteness itself appears as "transcending race," but never as "raced"—when it concentrates "crystalline purity"—being "raced" becomes the problem of the "Other."

Blackface and the Spread of "Talkies"

The German and Austrian filmic mythologies differed in light of their histories and the ideological ends they intended. Yet they overlapped and entered the evolving U.S. cinema together. Antifascist, the immigrant film writers, producers, and directors initially embraced the new culture, but historian John Russell Taylor argues that German producers like Erich Pommer and directors like Fritz Lang "were roughly divided into two main clans. One, the *haute culture* . . . the other clan . . . [with] communistic leanings; each clan patronized the other" (1983, 54; see also 22). Munby argues that directors like Wilder, Preminger, and Edgar Ulmer, arriving in the United States, brought with them the understanding "of post-liberal society and the crisis of the individual" they had developed in anti-Semitic Austria (Munby 1999, 142). As unknowns, they gravitated to productions over which they exerted artistic control, some producing Yiddish-language films about the working classes, like *Yankl der Schmid*, directed by Ulmer in 1937, while others created socially critical works in collaboration with Ukrainian and African American communities, among others (ibid., 147).

The complexity of the exiles' experience cannot be exhaustively traced here. Yet, whether high culture (Preminger) or socialist (Wilder, Ulmer), the

shock of their encounter with American racism and its myths of freedom and self-making resulted in a number of noir films in the 1940s whose commentary on the host society was so powerful that the "major studios either suppressed or tried to divest themselves of [the] socially critical filmmakers" (Munby 1999, 149). It was the studios themselves that set up the two-tiered system of A and B productions, in which all A films were self-censoring in anticipation of world markets and the scrutiny of the Office of War Information (ibid.). It is impossible to review here the A productions of the 1930s, whose influence was clearly immense. Suffice it to say that the American studio moguls were conservative and anxious about social criticism and anti-Semitic backlash at least as early as 1934, when Louis B. Mayer gloated over the political defeat of the left-leaning writer Upton Sinclair in the California gubernatorial elections (Taylor 1983, 112–15). Taylor maintains that the Mayers and the Cohns (Columbia Pictures) were largely apolitical in their values, at least until the United States entered the war (114).

Immigrant artists from Vienna and Berlin confronted assimilation as a challenge and a problem. Wilder, for example, had grown up impassioned by American music and had published articles defending jazz as a genre (Munby 1999, 143). Yet, outside their incisive social commentaries, it is not wholly clear how the types and values they brought with them from Berlin and Vienna meshed with native images, flowing from what Michael Rogin has called the genetic triangle of American film production, as far as the meta-narrative about race is concerned: D. W. Griffith's 1915 silent *Birth of a Nation*, Jolson's *The Jazz Singer* (1927, the first "talkie" feature film), and David O. Selznick's 1939 *Gone with the Wind* (Rogin 1996, 14–15). These were costly A films, each introducing a crucial innovation. For Griffith, it was technique, investment, and the first mass-audience cinematic production. With *The Jazz Singer*, the talkie made its definitive entrance. *Gone with the Wind* secured the Technicolor future (15). In each case, the mythic reconstruction of the American past proceeded, violently in the case of *Birth of a Nation*, on the exaltation of white over black bodies. *The Jazz Singer* adapted the Scottish minstrelsy, transformed into blackface first by Irish and then by Jewish performers, which flourished in a host of Hollywood productions from the 1920s through the 1950s. Rogin points out that "American film was born in the industrial age out of the conjunction between southern defeat in the Civil War, black resubordination, and national integration; the rise of the multiethnic, industrial metropolis, and the emergence of mass entertainment, *expropriated from its black roots*, as the locus of Americanization" (15). For him, "blackface" is not just corking up as "appropriative identification"

and exclusion; it also refers to "African Americans who, whether or not literally under burnt cork, perform against themselves for white eyes" (18).

This formed the abject type on which the possibility of ethnic assimilation turned in the 1930s and '40s (cf. Winnubst 2004, 38–39; Seshadri-Crooks 2000, 158ff.). It was thus possible, even desirable, to "democratize" American white transcendentals, because they could be taken up by all those seeking to assimilate. Transcendentals could belong to "the people" so long as that people was en route to American whiteness. Whatever their origins, ethnic "white" actors washed the cork off at the end of the day. Indeed, the message of blackface was that Old World identities could be escaped (Rogin 1996, 79)—through maudlin identifications (e.g., Jolson singing "Mammy") and through the pseudomiscegenation and pretend access to African American "psychology" via the black masquerade. "As immigration and technological innovations were creating American mass culture [and mass sedimented images], the film . . . appropriated an imaginary blackness to Americanize the immigrant son" (80–81). This cultural institution of American racism, which persisted in animated cartoons into the 1970s, was doubtless one of the first "novelties" that the Austrian and German immigrants encountered. As the creation of an immovable abject type, it must have contributed to the disenchantment they experienced with American freedom and opportunity, as staged in 1940s film noir. The white transcendentals were thus positioned differently in the American metanarrative, whose symbolic poles were white over black rather than Aryan over Jew, Slav, and so on.

The racialization of violence in American cinema, overdetermined by a transcendental as democratized white ideals, thus proceeded along the color line and certainly in terms of "blood." One-drop conceptions resembled Aryan racism against Jews, Slavs, "Asians," and *mischlinge*, and this could not have been lost on the immigrant artists. German-language émigré cinema unwittingly contributed types that intertwined with emerging American images in the 1930s; the characters and plots moved in a different space in the binary polarities created by color-line racism and assimilation to whiteness through blackface. Yet, as *The Sound of Music* demonstrated, the romance of the escapist false transcendental endured, and we may wonder how much the white transcendentals have changed today, in a culture where "color blindness is really a misnomer in a color-obsessed nation," as Leonardo and others have shown (Leonardo 2007, 266; Palmer 1995; see also the chapter by Bonilla-Silva, Ray, and Seamster in this volume, citing Rodriguez 2009).

Aftermath

The brief comparison between Austrian, German, and American transcendentals was motivated by Adorno's claim that there is "no right behavior in the wrong world" (Adorno 2000, 164, 174). Nevertheless, by 1962, Adorno, the immigrant who returned to Germany, was urging his students to take moral responsibility for their values by abstaining from the culture industry's myths. Their power, he said, will "make us into what we are *supposed* to become" today (168). His point was that, through critique and dialogue, we can take responsibility for the myths *we believe we did not create.* Have I taken up that challenge?

Das Frauenparadies launched Ingrid Holm's film career. Having figured as the untouchable transcendental, she left Vienna in 1938 to work with Warner Brothers in England. In 1944, during the last German bombing of London, she was killed when a V1 struck her apartment building. Aino Bergo, alias Ingrid Holm, lost her life to a system of power in whose apotheosis she was consciously and unconsciously complicit. She was my aunt, the ideal of the family. I discovered *Das Frauenparadies* online in 2008, having grown up with her image, the ambiguity of which troubled me yet shaped my youthful values. I believe that we must start our demythification here, with our own families.

Notes

1. See Yancy's chapter in this volume (emphasis added).
2. "Approximately 240 Austrians worked as directors, actors, screenplay writers, composers, and choreographers in more than five thousand Hollywood films" between 1936 and 1965 (Vansant 1999, 170; figures from Steiner 1996).
3. "Memoirs of SS-Obersturmführer, Léon Degrelle, *Autoportrait d'un fasciste,*" quoted in Littell 2008, 53.

References

Adorno, Theodor. 1974. Culture industry reconsidered. *New German Critique* 6:12–19.
———. 2000. *Problems of moral philosophy.* Trans. Rodney Livingstone. Stanford: Stanford University Press.
Bergner, Gwen. 1995. Who is that masked woman? or, The role of gender in Fanon's *Black skin, white masks. Publications of the Modern Language Association* 110, no. 1: 75–88.
Brown, Michael K., Martin Carnoy, Elliott Currie, Troy Duster, David B. Oppenheimer, Marjorie M. Shultz, and David Wellman. 2003. *Whitewashing race: The myth of a color-blind society.* Berkeley: University of California Press.

Castoriadis, Cornelius. 1997. *World in fragments: Writings on politics, society, psychoanalysis, and the imagination*. Trans. David Curtis. Stanford: Stanford University Press.

Dassanowsky, Robert von. 2008. Screening transcendence: Austria's *Emigrantenfilm* and the construction of an Austrofascist identity in *Singende Jugend*. *Austrian History Yearbook* 39:157–75.

Douglas, Susan J. 1994. *Where the girls are: Growing up female with the mass media*. New York: Three Rivers Press.

Elam, Michele. 2011. *The souls of mixed folk: Race, politics, and aesthetics in the new millennium*. Stanford: Stanford University Press.

Eze, Emmanuel Chukwudi. 2001. *Achieving our humanity: The idea of a post-racial future*. London: Routledge.

Gilman, Sander. 1986. *Jewish self-hatred: Anti-Semitism and the hidden language of the Jews*. Baltimore: Johns Hopkins University Press.

———. 1991. *Inscribing the other*. Lincoln: University of Nebraska Press.

Good, David F., and Ruth Wodak, eds. 1999. *From world war to Waldheim: Culture and politics in Austria and the United States*. New York: Berghahn Books.

Husserl, Edmund. 1991. *On the phenomenology of the consciousness of internal time (1893–1917)*. Trans. John Barnett Brough. Dordrecht: Kluwer.

———. 2001. *Analyses concerning passive and active synthesis: Lectures on transcendental logic*. Trans. Anthony J. Steinbock. Dordrecht: Kluwer.

Ilyin, Natalia. 2000. *Blond like me: The roots of the blond myth in our culture*. New York: Touchstone.

Jünger, Ernst. 1926. *Der Kampf als inneres Erlebnis*. Berlin: Mittler und Sohn.

Klemperer, Klemens von. 1978. On Austrofascism. *Central European History* 11, no. 3: 313–17. http://www.jstor.org/stable/4545840.

Lacoue-Labarthe, Philippe, and Jean-Luc Nancy. 2005. *Le mythe nazi*. Paris: Éditions de poche.

Leonardo, Zeus. 2007. The war on schools: NCLB, nation creation, and the educational construction of whiteness. *Race, Ethnicity, and Education* 10, no. 3: 261–78. http://vocserve.berkeley.edu/faculty/ZLeonardo/NCLBandRace.pdf.

Linke, Uli. 1999. *Blood and nation: The European aesthetics of race*. Philadelphia: University of Pennsylvania Press.

Lippe, Rudolf zur. 1974. *Naturbeherrschung am Menschen*. Frankfurt am Main: Suhrkamp.

Littell, Jonathan. 2008. *Le sec et l'humide: Une brève incursion en territoire fasciste*. Paris: L'Arbalète/Gallimard.

Mann, Michael. 2004. *Fascists*. London: Cambridge University Press.

Mosse, George L. 1968. *Nazi culture: Intellectual, cultural, and social life in the Third Reich*. New York: Grosset and Dunlap.

———. 1975. *The nationalization of the masses: Political symbolism and mass movements in Germany from the Napoleonic Wars through the Third Reich*. New York: Howard Fertig.

Munby, Jonathan. 1999. *Heimat* Hollywood: Billy Wilder, Otto Preminger, Edgar Ulmer, and the criminal cinema of the Austrian-Jewish diaspora. In *From world war to Waldheim: Culture and politics in Austria and the United States*, ed. David F. Good and Ruth Wodak, 138–61. New York: Berghahn Books.

Palmer, Allen W. 1995. The Arab image in newspaper political cartoons. In *The U.S. media and the Middle East: Image and perception*, ed. Y. R. Kamalipour, 139–50. Westport, Conn.: Greenwood Press.

Rabenalt, Arthur Maria. 1978. *Film im Zwielicht: Über den unpolitischen Film des dritten Reiches und die Begrenzung des totalitären Anspruches.* New York: Olms Verlag.

Rodriguez, Dylan. 2009. *Suspended apocalypse: White supremacy, genocide, and the Filipino condition.* Minneapolis: University of Minnesota Press.

Rogin, Michael. 1996. *Blackface, white noise: Jewish immigrants in the Hollywood melting pot.* Berkeley: University of California Press.

Semmerling, Tim Jon. 2006. *Evil Arabs in American popular film: Orientalist fear.* Austin: University of Texas Press.

Seshadri-Crooks, Kalpana. 2000. *Desiring whiteness: A Lacanian analysis of race.* New York: Routledge.

Shaheen, Jack G. 2001. *Reel bad Arabs: How Hollywood vilifies a people.* New York: Olive Branch Press.

Steinberg, Shirley, and Joe Kincheloe. 2009. *Christotainment: Selling Jesus through popular culture.* Boulder, Colo.: Westview Press.

Steiner, Gertraud. 1996. Exile and Eldorado: Austrian filmmakers in Hollywood. Keynote address at Beyond the Sound of Music, a symposium held at the Center for Austrian Studies, University of Minnesota, 16–18 February.

Taylor, John Russell. 1983. *Strangers in paradise: The Hollywood émigrés, 1933–1950.* London: Faber and Faber.

Theweleit, Klaus. 1987. *Male fantasies I: Women, floods, bodies, history.* Trans. Chris Turner, Stephen Conway, and Erica Carter. Minneapolis: University of Minnesota Press.

———. 1989. *Male fantasies II: Male bodies; Psychoanalyzing the white terror.* Trans. Erica Carter and Chris Turner. Minneapolis: University of Minnesota Press.

Thorpe, Julie. 2010. Austro-fascism: Revisiting the "authoritarian state" 40 years on. *Journal of Contemporary History* 45:315–43. http://jch.sagepub.com/content/45/2/315.

Vansant, Jacqueline. 1999. Robert Wise's *The Sound of Music* and the "de-Nazification" of Austria in American cinema. In *From world war to Waldheim: Culture and politics in Austria and the United States,* ed. David F. Good and Ruth Wodak, 165–86. New York: Berghahn Books.

Winnubst, Shannon. 2004. Is the mirror racist? Interrogating the space of whiteness. *Philosophy and Social Criticism* 30, no. 1: 25–50.

5

Painting and Negotiating Colors

Lilia Moritz Schwarcz

Translated by Hermenegildo Galeana and Bettina Bergo

Comparatively speaking, Brazil has practiced a quite extensive and flexible use of "color" concepts. In other words, rather than use terms such as "race" or references such as ethnic origins, the most popular option is "to describe colors." Indeed, it is because of this that the country's self-definition also changes, depending on the context, the social situation, the region, or even on good (or bad) moods or states of mind. People change colors as they change clothes, as well as negotiate and seek out their situations.

My goal in this chapter is to use a series of examples drawn from Brazilian reality, which is also my own, to show how, in Brazil, this "social game" operates and, moreover, to show how, notably in the south, the aim is always "to whiten" color, since status typically rises and falls along a whiteness gradient. "Becoming whiter," "turning white," and "being white" are expressions that reveal aspirations to social ascent and privilege.

Case 1: Blacks Against Whites—A Game and Much More than a Game

In Brazil there is a proverb, as popular as it is uncanny: "At night, all cats are *pardo* [brown]." It is difficult to understand its precise meaning, because *pardo*, in rural areas, is almost a "noncolor." Never used as a self-definition, the term *pardo* appears only in official documents, when color is assigned by

an investigator. However, common sense links it to "black" or "mulatto." That is, we all know that a *pardo* is a "nonwhite." The logic of the proverb comes from its associative flexibility, and given the number of shared assumptions it embodies, it is important to feel the power of this phrase. In the darkness of night, will not all be equal? Yet being or becoming equal does not seem to be a positive value in this case. The proverb is used to express fear or the anticipation of some threat.

This proverb could be followed by another, however, which was presented at a conference by the writer Ferréz (Reginaldo Ferreira da Silva), who defines himself as "part of the periphery."[1] This proverb responds to the first one by adding, "[But] in the *favela* [slum] at night, even the Japanese are black,"[2] which shows a certain "extended" use of color in Brazil. In short, given Brazil's particular social conditions, actual origin is worth little; it is the context that prevails. Yet these variations, say, between black and *pardo*, presented as parallels with the night, do not seem innocent. Indeed, this "relationship between colors" appears constantly, and never in an accidental way. As Victor Turner has clearly shown in *The Forest of Symbols*, these are not constituent elements that we might remove from a reading of colors. Turner points out that among the principal symbols produced by human thought, the colors black, red, and white represent the products and materials of the human body, a claim demonstrated by their association with heightened emotions. To these symbols of bodily experiences corresponds a perception of power, or at least one system of classification within the domain of colors. Such colors would thus represent intensified physical experiences and, still more, experiences of relationality that distribute primordial classifications and procedures for naming reality. Colors would then amount to processes of synthesis and condensation (see Turner 1970).

To contextualize this discussion of Brazil, consider a sports ritual that occurs each year, toward the end of December, in the *favela* of Heliópolis, a neighborhood of São Paulo. This is a game of football that has the suggestive name *Pretos contra Brancos* (blacks against whites) and invariably takes place before Christmas. There is an obvious "dialogue" here between colors and names, and both play a central role in organizing the relationships and norms that prevail within the game as well as outside it. It provides a kind of laboratory for thinking about the correlation between nomination and color.

In his classic essay on the struggles around cockfights in Bali, the anthropologist Clifford Geertz has shown how games serve as an entryway to understanding a society and how a ritual condenses, amplifies, and often even creates elements that reveal the context in which it occurs (Geertz 1973).

Here, the game presents and reinforces conflicts, alliances, even ambiguities. Unlike the cockfights, Heliópolis football should be considered neither "national" nor illegal. Placing bets on the *Pretos contra Brancos* is not allowed. Yet the *pelada* (amateur soccer) should remind us of those famous "ritual games" whose result is determined in advance. In *The Savage Mind*, Claude Lévi-Strauss recalls these games—namely, the soccer played by the Gahuku-Gama of New Guinea, where two rival clans compete for the time necessary to reach a tie score.

I will not explore these examples further here. I would emphasize, however, their important analytic parallels. To the degree that competitive games are marked by a predetermined asymmetry, we find the opposite occurring in ritualized games: organizing events in accord with a preexisting level, these games *associate* groups that were initially asymmetrical and dissociated (*Pretos contra Brancos*). In *Culture and Practical Reason*, Marshall Sahlins discusses the ritualistic side of Western competitive games, adding that the results are no longer "regular" because they are no longer "structured." Indeed, he adds that in American football, for example, a tie score elicits disapproval comparable to infringements of the incest taboo: it would be like "kissing your sister" (Sahlins 1979, 65; for the English version, 1976, 76).

Likewise, in our ritual game of *Pretos contra Brancos*, no one knows in advance whether blacks or whites will win. What is known, however, is the *outcome*: over the year that follows, victory will be taken as evidence of the superiority of one group over the other, "naturalized" by the game itself. But let me return to Geertz's essay for additional parallels. In the Brazilian example, "to be mocked is to be accepted" (Geertz 1973, 282; Geertz [1977] 2000, 443–44), but a joke causes laughter only in a specific context. Outside that context, things can appear as a "signal of racism" (sinal de racismo).

Like the Balinese, our soccer fans spend significant time with their favorite players: they tout, praise, or disagree with the players selected to join the team in a given year. This part of the ritual also takes place in December, but its results (off the field) last the entire year. Initially, it involves mocking those named to the team, but as the game approaches, what matters is assembling the team and forgetting (or recalling) the previous year's game. To be sure, I am speaking of an essentially male ritual in which virility is played or staged with increasing intensity, as the matches follow one another in a season. Yet this fails to note the essential point, i.e., that there is no clear "cosmology," no overarching logic in these matches. As in cockfights, we are subjected to *internal* cosmologies that promote reflection on how these describe the Brazilian attitude "like colors, like names," but that also bind people to origins

or to biology. My objective is thus not to analyze soccer practices but rather to show how, through a *pelada*, played annually for the past thirty years, modes of naming and conceptualizing are created, updated, and modified for those who inhabit the peripheries of São Paulo. Described on the basis of their putative colors, they are also manipulated in this way.

The *pelada* gradually became something "traditional" for a nation that counts fingers on the hand of its five-hundred-year history. Over the course of three decades, this *pelada* was consolidated until it became "a classic," as the residents put it. And it was in the 1970s that the soccer fans, in more than twenty of the playing fields covering the region, began to engage in the *festa do Flor* (festival of flowers). Into the history of the game was woven the history of the *favela*, whose foundation dates to the same time. Thus it was in 1971 that the city of São Paulo (temporarily) transferred 150 families to a region between the Independence and Sacomão Rivers, in the Zona Sul of the city. In 1978, new housing was created, and sixty families were moved from the Vergueiro *favela*. At the same time, the activity of squatters led to the occupation of a large area, rather like an intense geographical lottery. In fact, this "improvisation" resulted in the largest *favela* in São Paulo (and the second-largest slum in Brazil and indeed in Latin America), which currently has one hundred thousand inhabitants, 49 percent of whom are children and adolescents. The Heliópolis/São João Clímaco complex now covers some one million square meters. Heliópolis, or Sun City, as it is called, has, moreover, serious structural problems. Forty percent of its households have no sewage, more than 60 percent of its streets are unpaved, and more than 250 families live in unhealthy, unsafe huts. In spite of its obvious deficiencies in infrastructure, however, the neighborhood is one of the best organized when it comes to fighting for better living conditions for its residents. In this sense, the game of *Pretos contra Brancos* represents one of many local activities.

Accompanying the growth of the *favela* was the formation of fans' collectives—dressed in black or white—true markers of color sets and other social indicators of difference. The practice is celebrated festively, with barbecue and beer, while awaiting the results of four games. The first game, called *Sucatão* (a reference to the advanced age of the players) is composed of group elders. Here, we find the game's founders, who can no longer run for very long; they endure barely five minutes of play and then rest "in the bathtub," near the opponents' goal. Next comes the *Veterano*'s turn—a group composed of middle-aged players. Here, the ball rolls more freely. Younger players are divided into two final delegations: the reserves, who participate in the first team, and, finally, the professionals or *Quadro Principal* (main scene).

This is the most important game of the day and to take part in it is, as the locals say, "to play a lot."

On the field, the "racial mockery" continues. As Senhor Ze Lauro Pereira— a man in his midsixties with thirty years' experience as a soccer player and the captain of the Flor de São João Clímaco team—puts it, "the boys will always make jokes." The captain (defined as white because of where he lives, outside the neighborhood) recounts, "they actually brought the box of bananas to throw at the blacks, but that's not a problem because, on the field and outside it, we're all friends." In fact, the entire ritual takes place as though there were a clear imaginary boundary between the public and private spheres: in the game there is no racism; outside it, there is nothing to discuss. Imaginary lines also define the territory of the *favela* and beyond. Finally, onto the regional boundaries is superimposed a hierarchy of colors: most residents of Heliópolis are *negro*, *preto*, mulatto, or *pardo*. Those who live outside Heliópolis are white, more by "right" than by color.

Another important personality on the field, the leader of the black team (the *pretos*), likewise says, "on the day of blacks against whites, people say things that, if it were a normal day, would cause problems." In fact, the event itself creates new meanings and organizes relations in that precise moment. We might also say that the game transforms everyday life into a kind of laboratory, repeating, modifying, and imprinting new meanings on the same scene. In the game, certain colors that do not appear, or are not mentioned, in everyday life are rigidly demarcated.

The important point is that actors and scenes are defined and redefined as the ball rolls freely in the field, but also throughout the entire year. In 2005, for example, there was no time to negotiate "who has color, and which color." The event has therefore become a vast debate in which not only the skills of the players but also their colors are discussed on the playing field. We see this in the pragmatic character of decisions that greatly affect the final color index of the players. Indeed, it is not merely the soccer game of "blacks against whites" that becomes a laboratory for the expanded uses that color has assumed in Brazil. Far from the biological definition of race and the model of the one-drop rule, Brazil lives with the description and nomination of colors. We practice, as Oracy Nogueira asserts, a bias of "brands" rather than of "origins," and our definitions evince more flexible degrees of color (Nogueira [1954] 1985, 19–94). That is, in contemporary social markers there operate criteria considerably more external—e.g., phenotypic traits— than so-called biological determinations. For this reason, the concept of race is often replaced in Brazil by the concept of color, and the words used to

describe color become quite slippery. It is no coincidence that in the *favela* of Heliópolis, when the players perform the classic ritual of "blacks against whites," they refashion the old model: formally, there are eleven black-skinned men against eleven white-skinned ones. In practice, however, things are not so clear-cut. The names are mixed together just as colors and definitions of color are blended. Each year, the players can redefine their team, or give themselves different names: green, molasses, coffee with milk, lamp-light, sunburned. The colors are defined, in turn, more in relative than in absolute terms. In the first place, the use of augmentative terms seems to have been acknowledged; the team of blacks, for example, has adopted the name *negão* as a form of self-elevation and esteem (auto elevação e estima). Moreover, in Heliópolis, definitions like coffee with milk, light or near mulatto, and green tea explain how colors, as much as the idea of being black, are negotiated and played out. Finally, the *morenos*, as color intermediaries, can afford the luxury of changing teams. Whites, by contrast, are whites, and have no need for a definition.

We might cite another, still more paradoxical datum: many Brazilians consider race a passing condition, almost a circumstance; and they point out that, in Brazil, in many cases people *are* not (não *se é*) something but *become* (se *está*) something temporarily. They see color as variable and, as such, they consider it as fluid as social relations and names. As in the Heliópolis *pelada*, with rare exceptions, anyone (except blonds) can change teams, because in Brazil the condition of being white or black is determined by the circumstances of the moment.

Yet the problem is not limited to names and colors. The most notable *given* is the contextual dependency of its application. The identification and choice of colors and names for colors are transformed in this way into a relational issue. Color varies from person to person, depending on location, time, and the observer, as well as his or her discernment. When the interviewer is lighter than the interviewee, the latter's answer may be "darker," and vice versa. When the interviewer was black and from his own *favela*, Marcelo, the captain of the white team, became whiter. When I, a "whiter" woman, was asking the question, Preguinho, the captain of the black team, called himself blacker, reflecting a certain "social use" of color. Now, these myriad terms point to a certain "Brazilian racial calculus." A remarkable thing is not only its multiplicity but the subjectivity and contextual dependency of its application (do Valle e Silva 1994, 70). The response depends on the people, the place (as we have seen), and still more on the context in which the interview takes place. In the bar (with "white" friends), Marcelo

called himself mulatto. In the game, he became black. With us, he was coffee with milk.

In this type of racial status, people of mixed race have advantages. The term *pardo*, by contrast, which our respondents never used, seems to be a kind of "overdetermination": it is not black or white, because in practice it approaches *negro* in popular representations. One person said that no one in Heliópolis was *pardo*.[3] Perhaps he was right; at night the cats are not *pardo* but mulatto or black.

It is time to try to "untie" this first "game." If there is no possible comparison between the representational quality of the "black versus white" game in Brazil and cockfighting in Bali, there nevertheless takes place here a *jogo absorvente* (an absorbing game), a deep game, where the rules follow nominational practices, all clearly relational and social. There is a clear correlation between the game and social status, between color and meaning, and above all there is a growing demarcation of opposite and circumstantial borders. *Pretos*, ultimately, are those who live in the *favela*; whites departed "a long time ago." There is a hierarchical migration patterned on color, clearly dramatized in the game.

We are working, nevertheless, with social constructions set in motion by these highly charged emotional experiences. The game, in this sense, does not seem to help relieve, but on the contrary exposes, almost didactically, the differences between the players. As Geertz said of cockfighting, this is "merely a game, but it is more than a game." It is not just a reflection but exacerbates racial sensibilities.

"And after all," Preguinho asks, "who is *preto* in Brazil?" The game is almost over, and we are not going to blow the final whistle. Nothing works as well as the local definitions: Preguinho spent some time every year playing for each side. Another player said, "someone turns around and shouts, 'Look over there, there is a white playing with the blacks!'" "Signals" can be names and, in our case, colors. But social colors do not respond to basic and biological stimulation; they respond to emotion, sensitivity, and thus can be intensified. With arbitrary limits, they vary in light of the response provided to a field of possibilities given in advance. Maybe the players are right; after all, only a judge has no color. Or does he?

The fact is that the colors are determined relationally and by turns. Therefore, we cannot think of whiteness, or "whitening," without understanding the role that this color plays in society as a whole. Social whiteness is so highly valued that it is naturalized (and looks like "no color"), and is some-

times invested with great social weight; it is the highest symbol of power and ascendancy in the social hierarchy. Who knows whether the judge has a color? If he does, by custom and history, it is white.

Case 2: Naming the Colors; In the Country of the Laboratory and the Racial Rainbow

The philosopher Kwame Appiah once said that "to insist on the notion of race is more disheartening for those who take culture and history seriously" (1997, 68). It is unfortunate, however, to note that this type of "disheartening" scenario remains strong and vigorous even today. Race is still—despite having been completely dismissed as a biological concept—a powerful concept. It persists as a historical and social construction, raw material for nationality discourses, and as a social marker that identifies and classifies people and situations. It is no coincidence that this concept would be used to think through the integration of other social groups such as Jews, Indians, gypsies, or even physically or mentally disabled persons. However, in the Brazilian case, this issue centered primarily on discussion about the native Indians, and then turned to the vast black population in the countryside and to the many examples of miscegenation. Or rather, in colonization projects, a necessary mixture of social groups was imposed (due to the lack of population in the metropolis), but the model favored, from the outset, a certain social whitening, or at least a hierarchy of values and models. This claim becomes all the more important when we recall that even before Brazil was Brazil, i.e., when there was still a Portuguese America, the theme of different colors and possibilities of "people" in Brazil was already part of the discourses, chronicles, images, and letters describing the country. Seventeenth-century travelers such as Thevet, Leiris, and Laet emphasized, on the one hand, an Edenic nature, and, on the other hand, a population given to customs considered "primitive" or "barbarian," in complete conformity with the classification of that age. The Portuguese chronicler Gandavo synthesized this kind of perception, albeit more negatively, asserting that Brazilians were a people without F, L, K: faith, law, and king.[4] The country's inhabitants, since the beginning of their foray into a long Western history, were already known as "other" and grasped under the sign of a lack: "lack of manners, but an excess of color." In this case, the difference was not *more* but *less*: lack of manners, less order, less responsibility. It is no accident that customs such as

cannibalism, polygamy, and nudity ignited the European imagination, which migrated from the East toward America, marveling at nature but distrustful of what would be a new humanity.

The ambiguity was such that it proved necessary, in 1534, for Pope Paul III to issue a papal bull confirming the "humanity" of the New World natives, and conferring upon them a "soul." But the mistrust continued, notably when eighteenth-century naturalists proceeded to observe nature and the American "naturals." In one case, George-Louis Leclerc, Comte de Buffon, published in 1749 the first three volumes of his *Histoire naturelle*, establishing that the natives were a people of children (notably because they had no body hair), thereby proving the youth of the continent. In another case, Buffon's colleague Cornelius de Pauw published in 1768 in Berlin *Recherches philosophiques sur les Américains, ou Mémoires intéressantes pour servir à l'histoire de l'espèce humaine* (*Philosophical Research on Americans, or Interesting Memoirs Toward the History of the Human Species*), which took the argument in a more strident direction, saying that these people were not children but decadent. Having already been children, they had passed through maturity, grown old, and thus become "degenerates."

The theme of degeneration entered deeply into the debate about America, and especially into that about Brazil, when, in the mid-nineteenth century, it was taken up again by local scientists well aware of the deterministic and racial theories in vogue at that time. In fact, in this context, the country was seen as a "racial laboratory" for the cross-breeding of races. The debate coincided with the campaign to end slavery in the country, and in this case it referred not so much to races as to isolated phenomena, above all to miscegenation. Indeed, against the argument of citizenship, a racialized model was counterpoised, denying the notion of equality among men. The assumption was not so much that the races (like ontological species) had different contributions, values, and qualities, but that the mixing of these races always gave rise to misfortune, imbalance, and degeneration. Employing this type of model, scientists from the Faculty of Law of Recife, like Silvio Romero and Tobias Barreto, or others from the Faculty of Medicine of Bahia and Rio de Janeiro, like Nina Rodrigues and Renato Kehl, advocated practices of social exclusion, measures against miscegenation, and the restriction of legal freedom—all in the name of the science of the time.[5] The idea was that such measures would "enliven" the validity of a white society and "discourage" the mixing, or the predominance, of a black population. Moreover, on the side of racial theories, the models of Italian criminal anthropology, whose most important exponent was Cesare Lombroso, were betting on the idea that crim-

inality was concentrated in mixed populations, also considered degenerate.[6] In this sense, incentives were offered to white European immigrants, and attempts were made to send former slaves back to Africa. The cornerstone of these policies was that civilization could only be the corollary of a white society of European origin. Whiteness continued as the strong value, justified by the models coming from biology, which tended to naturalize differences and forget history.

It is interesting to reflect that in the 1920s, Brazilians were one step away from social apartheid, and in 1930 we transformed ourselves into an "example of racial democracy." It is clear that the intellectual context was different, and that today the concept of race is being exchanged for the concept of culture, urging that it is not biology that explains societies but their stories, contingencies, and customs. In Brazil, the debate was led by a modernist generation, who—following the example of Mario de Andrade, Gilberto Freyre, Arthur Ramos, and many others—began to trace the black populations of Brazil and their contribution to the core of national thought, not as a lacuna, silence, or demerit but as a profound contribution. From poison to fortune, miscegenation was slowly turning into a "national brand," to the point that Brazil would serve, in 1947, 1951, and 1964, as a case study for UNESCO, as an example of idyllic and peaceful coexistence in a world marked by the hatred expressed in terms of race, origin, and culture. Examples of this are seen in terms such as *melting pot, racial democracy,* and *celeiro harmônico de raças* (harmonious nest of races), which pointed toward a cultural reversal and toward new representations of identity in Brazil. The evidence for a single pattern of race relations was called into question. It is no coincidence that, at the same moment, President Getúlio Vargas "nationalized" and decriminalized practices like *capoeira, samba,* and *candomblé.* He also transformed football into a mixed-race Brazilian sport. Also coming out of these winds of change was the transformation of *feijoada* into a national and mixed-race dish: the white of the rice, the brown of the *feijão* beans, the gold of the orange, the red of the pimento, and the green of our forests—all came to compose the new "aquarela do Brasil."[7] In this context, the prevailing view saw miscegenation as synonymous with inclusion in one form or another. But what this argument overlooked was precisely the ambivalence of the Brazilian model, which has always combined social inclusion with exclusion. Moreover, it overlooked the fact that a certain social hierarchy, one that virtually eternalized white predominance and privilege, was never dismantled. To be whiter, to act whiter, to marry whiter, to be born whiter always remained long-term aspirations.

Since then, everything has changed, yet remains similar. After the 1970s, with the resurgence of the black movement and the politics of affirmative action, with the results of the national census and new investigations in this domain, the question of race grows all the more pressing. It was hard to miss that, along with inclusion, there prevailed an uncomfortable social discrimination. It is enough to note that the official data show profound disadvantages for nonwhite people in access to employment, education, and housing, and in mortality rates and even in unequal marriages. Whites are better educated; they have a smaller likelihood of being fined or imprisoned, even when they commit the same crimes; they marry better; and they have better jobs and living conditions.

So it is not a recent development that race always gives us Brazilians something to talk about—for better or worse. On the one hand, there is no way to deny the evidence of what is, in fact, an exceptional coexistence. On the other hand, this same curious sociability endorses a one-time naturalized (and now *culturalized*) division that refers to "aptitudes" and customs. There is a sort of consensual compartmentalization of activities, which became explicit and then conventional, such that social inclusion may occur in music, in sports, and in the arts in general. But in other areas—in political practices, science, and social life—it is assumed that "everyone knows their place." Who knows whether the absence of discriminatory laws does not help, paradoxically, those who play on the silence and the prohibition of traditional practices of discrimination? After all, it is in the private sphere, the domestic one, and in commonsense practices that possibilities are closed off and obstacles of all kinds renaturalized. It is true that in Brazil there are no official racial discourses to legitimize the exclusion, discriminatory laws, and institutions, or even dichotomous schemes that impose strict limits on blacks and whites; however, segregation is still robust and mainly affects the poor, above all the black population, which is poorer than poor.

At the same time, there remains a fairly intact hierarchy resulting from many years of colonization and the exploitation of African slavery that spread throughout the country. This authoritarianism attached itself to the figure of the *Senhor Branco*, the white master (and if he is not white, he is certainly lighter), and to a notion of hierarchy present in politics, erudite culture, and in all higher positions, generally speaking. This is so much the case that *branco*, white or whiteness, turned into a social value, as shown in our census, or even in the PNAD, the national home survey, when Brazilians were questioned about their color. The result was a veritable "aquarela do Brasil."

Case 3: Sense and Nonsense, Census and Non-Census

In Brazil, the combination of definitions based on first-person descriptions of color and on economic and social situations generated a certain indeterminacy, which solidified in 1976 after the Instituto Brasileiro de Geografia e Estatística (IBGE) performed the National Household Sample Survey (PNAD in Portuguese). Unlike the census, in which color was determined by the researcher, in the PNAD, Brazilians attributed to themselves some 135 colors.

National Household Sample Survey (IBGE, 1976)

1. Brown-haired	29. Whitened	55. Rose-colored
2. Agalegada	30. A little whitened	56. Firm color
3. Alva	31. Bronze	57. Creole
4. Alva-dark	32. Bronzed	58. Waxed
5. Alvarenta	33. Dark little Indian	59. Sulphured
6. Alvarinte	34. Escaped ass or	60. Whitening
7. Alva-pink	donkey	61. Dark
8. Alvinho	35. Caboclo (white &	62. Semidark
9. Yellow	Indian)	63. Fogoio
10. Yellowed	36. Cape Verdean	64. Galega
11. Yellow-fire	37. Coffee	65. Kale
12. Light yellow	38. Coffee with milk	66. Jambo
13. Darkish	39. Cinnamon	67. Orange
14. Reddish	40. Brownish	68. Lilac
15. Blue	41. Thistle	69. Blond
16. Dark blue	42. Brown	70. Light blond
17. Bahian	43. Light brown	71. Fair-haired
18. Very white	44. Dark brown	72. Blondie
19. Very pale	45. Chocolate	73. Malay
20. Very brunette	46. Light	74. Seafaring
21. White	47. Little pale	75. Brown
22. Reddish-white	48. Copper	76. Half-yellow
23. White molasses	49. Colored	77. Half-white
24. White-brunette	50. Coffee-colored	78. Half-brunette
25. Pale white	51. Cinnamon-colored	79. Half-black
26. Burned white	52. Gourd-colored	80. Honeydew
27. Freckled white	53. Milk-colored	81. Mestizo
28. Dirty white	54. Gold-colored	82. Miscegenation

83. Mixed	101. Black	120. Retinta (cattle red)
84. Swarthy	102. Negrota	121. Rosa
85. Becoming swarthy	103. Pale	122. Roseyed
86. Brown-tan	104. Paraíba (state)	123. Rose-burned
87. Cinnamon-brownish	105. Parda	124. Purple
	106. Light parda	125. Redhead
88. Dark swarthy	107. Brown-parda	126. Russian
89. Clear swarthy	108. Black-parda	127. Coquette
90. Cinnamon swarthy	109. Polish	128. Heal
91. Dark rose apple	110. Near-clear	129. Saraúba
92. Morenada	111. Near-brown	(meringue)
93. Dark brown	112. Near-pale	130. Toasted
94. Dark, dark-closed	113. Little brown	131. Wheat
95. Morenão	114. Pushing white	132. Brunette
96. Dark brown	115. Near-black	133. Cloudy
97. Brown-purple	116. Burned	134. Green
98. Brunette	117. Beach burned	135. Red
99. Mulatto	118. Sunburned	
100. Little Mulatto	119. Regular	

While this is not the place to deal with all these definitions, we can at least attempt to think about some of them, especially in a chapter that aims to reflect on the importance of white privilege, of "being white and being defined as white," in Brazil, along with the relationships that developed from this claim. The IBGE survey generated a series of reactions, ranging from a direct, positive response, to more negative ones, and even to a certain irony with regard to "our color." Although census categories—white, black, indígena, yellow (amarela) and brown (pardo)—covered approximately 57 percent of the spontaneous responses, the collection of names proved more complex than the term *pardo*.

The survey results indicate the wealth of representations with regard to color and the degree to which its definition is problematical in Brazil. First, we see that most of the terms seek to describe color as accurately as possible. Yellow, green, blue and dark blue, very white and dirty white, and red are parameters that seek to reproduce coloring almost didactically, a clear demonstration that race in Brazil is also a matter of *brand*. There is little talk of *origin*: none of the terms refers to Africa, and even in the case of terms like "Polish" and "Bahian," actual descent is never mentioned. We should note

also the attention paid to diminutive and enhancing names. In this case, the divisions reveal the reproduction of stereotypes regarding blackness and female and male sexuality, with diminutives for women and enhancing terms for men.

Other terms show how certain racial and physiognomic attributes are held together. Some people gave their hair color, for example, as a means of self-definition, hair, of course, being joined to skin color. Having straight hair, blond hair, wavy hair, or hair that moves with the wind are all signs of distinction.

A new series of denominations—"miscegenic (miscigenação), tending-to-white (esbranquecimento), mixed"—all show the ascendance of Brazil's self-image as a mixed-race nation. More important, these terms attest to the large number of variations on the term "white," which shows how white is a social aspiration rather than a color. Definitions such as very white, white, reddish-white, white molasses, white-brunette, blond, pushing white (puxa-para-branca), pale white, light blond, freckled white, blondie, dirty white, whitened, regular, and a little whitened show how, out of the flexibility of concepts, one great projection is symbolically expressed. When one is not white, one may attempt to be. Interesting, too, is the term "regular," which, when considered in an alternative way and in a particular context, signifies white. That is, whiteness does not require definition. It is therefore normal, or "regular."

We should also not forget the names that use race as a transitional condition. "Beach burned, sunburned, toasted" all indicate that in Brazil it is not that people *are* (ser) something; they are *becoming* (está). This situation, in turn, always "pushes toward white" (puxa para o branco). That is, a person who answers "sunburned" tries to show that he or she is not black—or is black only in this particular context, and only temporarily. Nevertheless, the person sees and understands him- or herself as much whiter than an onlooker might perceive.

In addition, as we have seen, people very often negotiate color, depending on the context and on who asks the question. If the investigator is black, the answers will turn whiter, and if the investigator is white, the answers will turn blacker. Moreover, depending on where the survey is done, the research will yield similarly diverse results. In the northeastern region of Brazil, with its large black majority, to be lighter is to be white, an observation that we do not find present in the same way in the southern region of the country. Without claiming to have examined all the combinations that this list of colors could provide, we can note the descriptive character of this relationship,

which, rather than offering a solution to the plethora of colors oriented around whiteness, points to a fundamental ambiguity. These myriad terms reveal a "Brazilian racial calculus." In this calculus, the most notable datum is not the multiplicity of color names but the subjectivity and the contextual dependence of their application.

In fact, racial identification is a relational question in Brazil; varying from individual to individual, it depends on the location, the time, and the observer him- or herself. As the composer Caetano Veloso said, "Gil is dark enough a mulatto even to be called, in Bahia, a *preto* [black]. I am a mixed-race person light enough to be called *branco* [white] even in São Paulo" (Veloso 1997, 172). Furthermore, and for a long time, the application of census results in Brazil, and above all those of the color criterion, varied widely. As Lamartine Babo sang, "Your hair cannot deny, mulata. . . . But since color can't be grasped [a cor não pega], mulata, I want your love." That is, the hair does not lie about race, but color is not fixed. Hair functions as a rigid indicative datum, but the color can escape, disappear. This flexible datum in our social classifications, based more on color than on origin, allows race/color to be the object of extensive negotiation—at one moment it is the criterion that comes into view; at another it disappears from the official census.

One Brazilian model entails negating and camouflaging conflict even before it arises in an evident form, and the same thing goes for color. In a country that always claimed to be white—*se pretendeu branco*—and that defined itself during the period of empire as virtually European, the practice of camouflaging or hiding a part of the country's large black contingent was a constant. In 1900, for example, when the fact that Brazil was a black and mixed-race country could no longer be denied or hidden, officials simply removed the question of color from the demographic census. Thus, although the census has been conducted in Brazil in 1872, 1890, 1900, 1920, 1940, 1950, 1970, and 1980, on at least three occasions (1900, 1920, and 1970), the item "color" was not used at all.[8]

Negotiation about race and the "aspiration to be white" is evident as well in the story of the itinerant Saint Hilaire. According to this tale, Saint Hilaire saw a light mulatto with a troop of donkeys. The saint was surprised when he was informed that the mulatto was the owner of the animals. Immediately, he responded, "And so he is no longer a *mulato!*" (Arruda 1996, 288). Similarly, the Englishman Henry Koster, who was in Brazil in the time of Dom João (João VI was king of Portugal from 1767 to 1826), expressed his great surprise at encountering, around 1809, a black soldier in the Brazilian army

for the first time. Again, the answer Koster received in response to his questions about this man is revealing: in the opinion of witnesses, the soldier was not a black man but an officer (Koster [1816] 1942, 58). These examples, despite their historical remoteness, are echoed in many recent cases. A university professor was surprised when the interviewer in the 1980 census classified her as racially white. When she contested that classification, alleging that her color was *negro* or *pardo*, the interviewer replied, "but is the senhora not a professor at the Universidade de São Paulo?"

"Social race" is the expression that do Valle e Silva used to explain the mischievous use of color to suggest the "whitening effect" in Brazil (1994, 76). That is, discrepancies between attributed color and self-perceived color were related to individuals' own socioeconomic status. In this country of tones and fluid criteria, a color is almost a criterion for naming, varying according to place, time, and circumstances. It is also what, within certain limits, makes the "color line" in Brazil an attribute of intimacy, in which "official race" is distinguished from "social race." It is for this reason, moreover, that the racial statistics in the census are almost unreal, or at least difficult to interpret. Thus we can understand the campaign of the Instituto Brasileiro de Análise Econômica e Social, reported by the media in 1991, in light of the "white inflation" of the census; its slogan was "Don't let your color go blank [passar em branco]: respond with good sense [censo]."

Conclusion: "I Do Not Have That Problem"

It is not the case that only poor people manipulate color. Research done at the University of São Paulo found the same kind of fluidity in self-definition by color. To begin with, the local community reacted to the university's survey as though it were itself racist; even asking about skin color was seen as reprehensible. At the same time, those who answered the survey questions expressed the same aspiration to whiteness seen in the 1976 IBGE survey, and their answers likewise demonstrated a transitional comprehension of color. Given that the University of São Paulo is composed in the main of elite white-skinned people, it is astonishing how the local population explained whiteness—how, that is, they sought to describe a variety of tones and semitones in terms of whiteness. One group of students simply responded, "I do not have that problem." When pressed to explain what they meant by this statement, it became clear that to have "that problem"

meant to be black. Being white, in turn, is a condition: a certainty and an affirmation.

Of course, things are changing. Today, we frequently hear expressions of pride in the *raça negra* arising in parallel with government policies that have restored not only the history, memory, practices, and customs of the black race but also its self-esteem.

But the past no longer lives next door. In fact, white social and economic—but also symbolic—preeminence is part of the Brazilian reality. To perceive its force, it is enough to enter restaurants, clubs, public university halls (which, I might say, are the hardest to enter), cinemas, or large companies. It matters little that white privilege is the product of a social hierarchy established more by custom than by official policy: the point is that it still prevails, with few exceptions, the product of a national consensus.

This chapter began with a proverb, and it closes with another: "Those who are white understand each other."[9] Those who understand this saying tend to see the world as divided by colors. These colors in turn reflect and produce a set of privileges and distinctions manifested solely by external characteristics. Yet the proverb says more than this. It appears to refer to an agreement between whites, who share a ground of their own, and above all, a restricted one.

To adapt a haiku by the poet Pablo Leminski, "white clouds [do not] pass into clouds white" (nuvens brancas [não] passam em brancas nuvens).

Notes

1. Born in 1975, Ferréz is a Brazilian author, cultural critic, and activist from the Zona Sul (southern zone) *favela* of Capão Redondo in São Paulo. He helped found the literary collective Literatura Marginal (Marginal Literature) in the late 1990s.

2. "Na favela, de noite, até japonês é preto."

3. Edward Telles points out that while *preto* tends to mean black, the use of *negro* may be increasing because of the government's efforts to dichotomize racial classifications. See Telles 2004, 86. (Editors' note.)

4. See Schwarcz 2004, 90–117. (Editors' note.)

5. See Schwarcz 1999, 168–296. (Editors' note.)

6. See Lombroso [1876] 2006. (Editors' note.)

7. This is the title of a famous 1939 song by Ary Barroso. See Schwarcz 2003. (Editors' note.)

8. Racial data can also be drawn from the National Household Sample Surveys from 1976, 1984, and 1987.

9. Proverb quoted by the literary critic Arcádio Dias at Princeton University, April 2010.

References

Adorno, Sérgio. 1996. Violência e racismo: Discriminação no acesso à justiça penal. In *Raça e diveridade*, ed. Lilia Moritz Schwarcz and Renato da Silva Queiroz, 90–130. São Paulo: Edusp e Estação Ciência.

Andrews, George Reid. 1992. Desigualdade racial no Brasil e nos Estados Unidos. *Revista Afro-Asiática* 22:47–83.

Appiah, Kwame Anthony. 1997. *Na casa de meu pai: A África na filosofia da cultura*. Rio de Janeiro: Contraponto.

Arruda, Maria Arminda. 1996. Dilemas do Brasil moderno: A questão racial na obra de Florestan Fernandes. In *Raça, ciência e sociedade*, ed. Marcos Chor Maio and Ricardo Ventura Santos, 195–206. Rio de Janeiro: Editora Fiocruz/CCBB.

Azevedo, Thales. 1955. *As elites de cor, um estudo de ascensão social*. São Paulo: Companhia Editora Nacional.

———. 1966. *Classes e grupos de prestígio: Cultura e situação racial no Brasil*. Rio de Janeiro: Civilização Brasileira.

Banton, Michael. 1977. *The idea of race*. Boulder, Colo.: Westview Press.

Barcelos, Luiz Claudio. 1992. Educação um quadro das desigualdades raciais. *Estudos Afro-Asiáticos* 23:92–144.

Bastide, Roger, and Florestan Fernandes. 1955. *Relações raciais entre negros e brancos em São Paulo*. São Paulo: Unesco/Anhembi.

Bercovich, Alícia. 1987. Fecundidade da mulher negra: Constatações e questões. *Textos Nepo* 11:47–101.

Berquó, Elza. 1987. Nupcialidade da população negra. *Textos Nepo* 11:8–46.

Bhabha, Homi K. 1990. *Nation and narration*. New York: Routledge.

do Valle e Silva, Nelson. 1994. Uma nota sobre "Raça Social" no Brasil. *Estudos Afro-Asiáticos* 26:67–80.

Fernandes, Florestan. 1965. *A integração do negro na sociedade de classes*. 2 vols. São Paulo: Companhia Editora Nacional.

———. 1972. *O negro no mundo dos brancos*. São Paulo: Difusão Européia do Livro.

Freyre, Gilberto. 1933. *Casa-grande e senzala*. Rio de Janeiro: Maia e Schmidt/José Olympio.

Fry, Peter. 1982. Feijoada e soul food. In *Para Inglês Ver*, ed. Peter Fry, 65–86. Rio de Janeiro: Paz e Terra.

Geertz, Clifford. 1973. Notas sobre a briga de galos balinesa. In Geertz, *A interpretação das culturas*, 87–102. Rio de Janeiro: Zahar.

———. [1977] 2000. *The interpretation of cultures: Selected essays*. New York: Basic Books.

Guimarães, Antonio Sérgio Alfredo. 1997. Racismo e anti-racismo no Brasil. PhD diss., University of São Paulo.

Hall, Stuart. N.d. *A questão da identidade*. Campinas: IFCH/Unicamp.

Harris, Marvin. 1964. *Patterns of race in the Americas*. New York: Walker.

Hasenbalg, Carlos A. 1979. *Discriminação e desigualdades raciais no Brasil*. Rio de Janeiro: Biblioteca de Ciências Sociais.

Hasenbalg, Carlos A., Nelson do Valle e Silva, and L. C. Barcelos. 1989. Notas sobre miscigenação racial no Brasil. *Estudos Afro-Asiáticos* 16:188–97.

Koster, Henry. [1816] 1942. *Viagem ao nordeste do Brasil*. São Paulo: Companhia Editora Nacional.

Lombroso, Cesare. [1876] 2006. *Criminal man.* Trans. Mary Gibson and Nicole Hahn Rafter. Durham: Duke University Press.

Marx, Anthony W. 1996. A construção da raça e o Estado-Nação. *Estudos Afro-Asiáticos* 29:32–53.

Nogueira, Oracy. [1954] 1985. *Tanto preto quanto branco: Estudos de relações raciais.* São Paulo: Queiroz.

Pierson, Donald. 1971. *Brancos e pretos na Bahia: Estudo de contacto racial.* São Paulo: Companhia Editora Nacional.

Posada, J. E. M. N.d. Cor segundo os censos demográficos. Manuscript.

Ramos, Jair de Souza. 1996. Dos males que vêm com o sangue: As representações raciais e a categoria do imigrante indesejável nas concepções sobre imigração da década de 20. In *Raça, ciência e sociedade,* ed. Marcos Chor Maio and Ricardo Ventura Santos, 65–92. Rio de Janeiro: Editora Fiocruz/CCBB.

Rodrigues, Raimondo Nina. [1894] 1957. *As raças humanas e a responsabilidade penal no Brasil.* Bahia: Progresso.

Romero, Silvio. [1888] 1953. *História da literatura brasileira.* Rio de Janeiro: Imprensa Nacional.

Rosenberg, Fulvia. 1990. Segregação espacial na escola paulista. *Estudos Afro-Asiáticos* 19:65–83.

Sahlins, Marshall. 1976. *Culture and practical reason.* Chicago: University of Chicago Press.

———. 1979. *Cultura e razão prática.* Rio de Janeiro: Zahar.

Sansone, Lívio. 1992. Cor, classe e modernidade em duas áreas da Bahia: Algumas primeiras impressões. *Estudos Afro-Asiáticos* 22:143–74.

———. 1996. Nem somente preto ou negro: O sistema de classificação racial no Brasil que muda. *Afro-Ásia* 18:165–87.

Schwarcz, Lilia Moritz. 1993. *O espetáculo das raças: Cientistas, instituições e questão racial no Brasil, 1870–1930.* São Paulo: Companhia das Letras.

———. 1996. Questão racial no Brasil. In *Negras imagens,* ed. Lilia Moritz Schwarcz and Letícia V. S. Reis, 120–54. São Paulo: Edusp.

———. 1998. Nem preto, nem branco: Muito pelo contrário. In *História da vida privada IV,* ed. Lilia Moritz Schwarcz, 210–43. São Paulo: Companhia das Letras.

———. 1999. *The spectacle of the races: Scientists, institutions, and the race question in Brazil, 1870–1930.* Trans. Leland Guyer. New York: Hill and Wang.

———. 2003. Not black, not white, just the opposite: Culture, race, and national identity in Brazil. Center for Brazilian Studies Working Paper CBS-47–03. Oxford: Oxford University Press.

———. 2004. *The emperor's beard: Dom Pedro II and the tropical monarchy in Brazil.* Trans. John Gledson. New York: Farrar, Straus and Giroux.

———. 2007. Pretos contra brancos ou dando e mudando nomes. In *Nomes: Género, etnicidade e família,* ed. João de Pina-Cabral and Susana de Matos Viegas, 219–44. Lisbon: Almedina.

Skidmore, Thomas E. 1976. *Preto no branco: Raça e nacionalidade no pensamento brasileiro.* Rio de Janeiro: Paz e Terra.

Souza, Juliana Beatriz Almeida de. 1996. Mãe negra de um povo mestiço. *Estudos Afro-Asiáticos* 29:85–102.

Sowell, Thomas. 1995. *Race and culture: A world view.* New York: Basic Books.

Tamburo, Estela Maria Garcia. 1987. Mortalidade infantil da população negra brasileira. *Textos Nepo* 11:23–57.

Telles, Edward. 2004. *Race in another America: The significance of skin color in Brazil.* Princeton: Princeton University Press.

Turner, Victor W. 1970. *The forest of symbols: Aspects of Ndembu ritual.* Ithaca: Cornell University Press.

Turra, Cleusa, and Gustavo Venturi. 1995. *Racismo cordial.* São Paulo: Ática.

Twine, France Winddance. 1978. Black-white income differentials: Brazil, 1960. PhD diss., University of Michigan.

———. 1993. Aspectos demográficos dos grupos raciais. *Estudos Afro-Asiáticos* 23:16–24.

———. 1994. Uma nota sobre raça social no Brasil. *Estudos Afro-Asiáticos* 26:54–78.

———. 1997. *Racism in a racial democracy: The maintenance of white supremacy in Brazil.* New Brunswick: Rutgers University Press.

Veloso, Caetano. 1997. *Verdade tropical.* São Paulo: Companhia das Letras.

Wood, Charles H. 1991. Categorias censitárias e classificação subjetiva da população negra brasileira. In *Desigualdade racial no Brasil contemporâneo*, ed. Peggy A. Lovell and Alícia M. Bercovich, 87–134. Belo Horizonte: Cedeplar/UFMG.

6

I Was an Honorary White Man:
Reflections on Space, Place, and Origin

Mark McMorris

1

The land is visible. Whenever I think of my history, I picture a large tract of land planted out in green crops destined for the boiler house and the commodity markets. Situated at the edge of recall, the men are no more than dark forms. They are anonymous and generic, replaceable by other dark forms without any loss of labor power. The image gives me an idea, that I am the same as them. And why not? Among the scattered bodies, there is at least one that concerns me in particular. Whenever I think of my history, I picture a mountain redoubt littered with the muskets of British soldiers. I am not concerned with the dead. The fighters are anonymous but obviously unmanageable. I have to do with one of these men in particular. Dark forms in forests, in trackless mountains: I am the same as them.

2

My friend, an American, one day amazed me by saying that I was regarded by our co-workers as an honorary white man. This was not an insult—not a compliment either. Both of us, from a distance, prior to any speech, are persons of African descent. Tilted toward certain likelihoods that it is our task to frustrate or to confirm. But I was not seen as black, my co-worker said. In

some measure, my origin in the anglophone West Indies exempted me from the logic of color—the delirium of race—specific to the United States.

What was not being said, I am fairly sure, was that I should henceforth strive to be regarded as a black man. I was not being accused of trying to pass, or of acting white, because the image in the mirror was not something I deliberately sought to influence. Creature of twin histories planted elsewhere, I wasn't sufficiently on the inside to be doing anything. It was an American drama. Therefore, I had to be of American origins to act—to be seen as a protagonist instead of as a dupe, or as an incidental chance. The closest I can come is to say that I wasn't from either side of the tracks, but in some respects I was obviously from the other side, and in still other respects, the same side, as whoever cared to pin down my location. If this seems an obscure way of putting it, the fault is not mine. The whole subject is a deep hole filled with fog.

I won't bore you with the obvious, that color is only an initial index of identity and can be trumped by spoken dialect, or social status, or place of birth. The opposite is true—that exterior signs can mask a so-called black essence. Staring at the moon's bright disc above the swamps, a black man haunted by the famous one-drop rule might with a clear conscience allow his white appearance to speak for him. A poet writes:

> The last hill burned,
> the sea crinkled like foil,
> a moon ballooned up from the Wireless Station. O
> mirror, where a generation yearned
> for whiteness, for candour, unreturned.
> (Walcott 1986, 46)

The mirror can't make you white, whatever it shows of the luminous skin. Yearning is not proof. To decide on a man's race, as in the story of Faulkner's Joe Christmas, you have to inspect the blood itself. Only then can one be certain, because only in the visible blood is the truth of race indelible. All of this is well known. What my friend was talking about, in saying that I was regarded as an honorary white man, had the logic of the blood at the bottom of it. The logic of the blood says that blackness begins at conception, gestates in the womb, and exists at birth. Let us say that I had been born in Louisiana to black American parents but fostered out to Jamaicans at three months and adopted by them. From that point on, my life unfolded exactly as it has. Do you see what I am getting at? It would not be all the same whether or not I

let it generally be known that I had been born in Louisiana. Or one might say that it is a silly hypothesis, since I have set the blood's influence at naught, and that is precisely what the quarrel has been about. Ah, you were born in Louisiana. Something changes, structures of interaction tilt forward or sideways, the density of space fluctuates. But you probably have to be American to say what, how, and why.

3

What you carry on your back is invisible except through the mirror of encountered people, in the place you enter, on the other side of a line that you cross. The line is not always in the same place. It is a magic line, a moveable border like a river that changes course when the earth moves. The land bordered by this line is called the nation, or the memory of myth and origins. Expanded into a surface, the infinitesimal abstract object of geometry, the widthless waist of an hourglass—the line soon appears below your feet as topography, with forests, mountains, and cities. I do not perceive the inward scar of the line, though there are other scars and other errors.

Born in Clayton, a rural town in North Carolina, my friend moved through institutions that replicated, for her, the social structure of the plantation.

At one time, the land about Clayton held an army on the march that made a road where there was none. People gathered because of this road. The farmland was good, and labor was very cheap. When it appeared, the railroad multiplied the chances of prosperity and the track served to define a border. The track, which joined two points in the direction of the train's motion, separated the neighbors by place. One spoke then of the other side of the tracks. To cross spectral parallel lines at right angles beneath the moon—to cross from the other side—was both a trivial and an impossible step.

Sustaining and sustained by the railroad, the town-land entered a golden age of agriculture and industry. We see that the place now holds lumber plants, a brick kiln, a cotton gin, a gristmill, a sawmill, tobacco warehouses, cotton mills, and a turpentine distillery. Blackened by coal dust, a man stands between the coal car and the furnace. The dust on his skin is an heirloom handed to sons and daughters. Prices rise and fall, techniques change faster than some can adapt, war breaks out, and the line temporarily falters. But this line is not so frail. Harder than steel tracks, it goes inward and infects every thought: a scar. Perceptible and cryptic, known and invisible, a shadow

whose real body has disappeared, the scar lies wholly on the surface of the man's skin. But this surface is infinitely deep—a bottomless *signans*. To be sure, born of the dust, the scar may be replaced by empty space—a mathematical idea that has no physical counterpart. The scar is a hypothesis, like a theory of epicycles, durable and precise, able to explain many phenomena. Therefore, the man's body is also a hypothesis. But that is no consolation.

4

An honorary white man must be distinguished from a Native and a Negro. A Native is the creature of conquest and colonization—the occupation of foreign lands by a Western power. A Negro is the creature of the plantation. The status of honorary white man is intelligible as the manipulation of signs derived from plantation society: on the one hand *master*, on the other hand *slave*. The Manichean structure joining the two has a physical reality: the slaves live over there, the masters live here, the fields of death lie between them. Every meeting between the two sides restates the division of power: on shipboard, at the auction, in the United States Constitution. The slave learns his position as the master learns his. The structure survives the plantation. Or the plantation survives as mental model: a conceptual metaphor.

An honorary white man has been granted a kind of blessing—the grace to be free from the dynamic structure that defines social life as a contest between slaves and masters. This is because he began life as a Native. The Native is open to seeing things our way—how else to justify conquest, except as a school? But the Negro—can anything be done? The black blood aside, we have wounded him too deeply to hope now for a change. But a Native, like a barbarian, can be civilized, and may come to love us as his benefactors. "As soon as the barbarians were reconciled to obedience, their minds were opened to any new impressions of knowledge and politeness" (Gibbon [1776] 1996, 33). The mind of a barbarian is like a palimpsest: it can be erased so as to produce a clean surface for new writing. That's how I think about the status of honorary white man. As a Native, as a barbarian, I have never been locked into place as the master's opposite in the dynamic of American racial power. The contest does not define the initial condition of my social self. But what I have learned is that it is possible to experience the Negro's position regardless.

5

One evening I set out from Washington, D.C., to drive to North Carolina. A friend of mine had moved to the state twenty-five years ago, and had been living in the city of Raleigh, about fourteen miles from Clayton. Jamaicans are liable to show up anyplace. They are like the Chinese. Another fellow about my age had gone from Accra to Kingston to Charleston, a coastal city of South Carolina, other friends to the exurbs of Atlanta, and one even to Vancouver, British Columbia, a place so remote from Kingston that I thought of him as a castaway, trapped by the perpetual ice. Some lands are so much a part of legend that they cannot be visited. Having been written about, in novels and memoirs and scripture, they seem only to exist as writing, fabulous places lifted out of the realm of desire, the province of others exclusively. It's unthinkable to find oneself in those places, just as it's unthinkable to find oneself in a fable, re-created as an illusion. The places in the Old and New Testaments are like that. Though people must once have lived in Bethlehem, or Jericho, one does not ever expect to be in those cities, since their being is of a different order. They do exist, but in a way inseparable from childhood stories, even if maps place them on a level with less fabulous lands. A host of circumstances causes a shift of place to the domain of fabulous pictures, set within the floating signs of the imaginary. The southern United States lies in such a domain for me.

In between D.C. and Richmond are exits perilous to stray into at night, if you are black. South and west of Richmond, on Interstate 85, the country is wooded, with an asphalt strip carved and laid down in the midst, so that drivers at night travel through a corridor of shadowy trees, an isolated tunnel, cut across by rain and filled at a distance with fog. The road wet with headlamps, the opposite lanes are hidden. The interior hallway goes on for how many miles, and what lies on the roads off the infrequent exits, within the trees, in the taverns and clubhouses, what if the car has a flat tire on this slick road, who will stop and with what purpose, what motels are safe to approach, where is this, for it feels like I have gone to a foreign country.

In my own eyes, I am a member of a class of persons defined by their race. The fate of the race in the archives of the world's knowledge concerns me because it is my own fate too. Prey to mystical thinking, I believe that a book describing the deeds of dark-skinned Africans prior to the rise of the Athenian empire will affect, for better or worse, my own self-perception. (The rain does not fall on everyone, and some lands are barren.)

There is in many instances a remarkable coincidence between certain classical observations on sub-Egyptian Ethiopia and the facts as reconstructed by Africanists. As early as Herodotus Meroë was described as a great city, reported to be the capital of all Ethiopia. The Greeks had received accounts of the Twenty-Fifth Ethiopian Dynasty [which ruled Egypt]. . . . The statement—attributed by Strabo to Megasthenes—that Tearco the Ethiopian advanced as far as Europe perhaps echoes reports of the power of an Ethiopian people who conquered Egypt. (Snowden 1970, 119)

Meroë, capital of the empire of Kush, is only one of several powerful centers of civilization founded by black Africans on the continent. It does not occur to me to think that a white man's own self-perception is anchored in history, reflected in the *res gestae* of the race he calls his own.

My urgent desire was to complete the journey intact. I pulled off the interstate and sent an e-mail to a friend, mainly to curb foolish thoughts. The convenience store was brightly lit, the floor spacious. No one cared when I stepped inside, bought a bottle of water, and went to stand on the pavement out of the rain. Think of it like this. I don't know what it feels like to be white. I don't yearn for the mirror. The moon's whiteness is not my ideal self. I don't know if whiteness has a feeling associated with it in the bodies and minds of white people. I feel black, use that name for the cause of the sensation, whenever I become aware that I have been marked by race. The awareness comes and goes a hundred times in an ordinary day. On the road to North Carolina, the sensation of being black grew until it brought on something like an existential vertigo, a hollowing out, a confidence of physical risk, founded on knowledge and ignorance. Once I got lost on a very narrow road in New Hampshire, on a very dark night, in a rainstorm. Around every corner was more of the black night, more bush, trees, rain. The road was interminable. For whatever reason, I did not feel blackness as peril. I did not feel that race would determine my future on that night.

The sensation of being black is related to the fear of being mistaken for someone else. I am a West Indian.

    3. PLEBIAN Your name, sir, truly.
        CINNA Truly, my name is Cinna.
    1. PLEBIAN Tear him to pieces! He's a conspirator.
        CINNA I am Cinna the poet. I am Cinna the poet!

4. PLEBIAN Tear him for his bad verses! Tear him for
his bad verses!
CINNA I am not Cinna the conspirator.
4. PLEBIAN It is no matter; his name's Cinna! Pluck but
his name out of his heart, and turn him going.
3. PLEBIAN Tear him, tear him! *[They kill him.]*
(Shakespeare, *Julius Caesar*, 3.3.26–35)

He is Cinna, but more might be said: that which he is not. Cinna the poet is
not the conspirator. The plebians confuse the name with the person; they
assume that the name dwells within and so marks the body, like the blood.
Imagine a situation in which you will be killed anyway because you have the
same color as a target. I am not the Cinna you want—makes no difference
to the mob. Do you then say, I am Cinna the poet, and I am Cinna the conspirator, since our fates are the same? When you deny that you are Cinna,
you wish to correct an error. But in the act of denial is a pointing elsewhere,
over to other bearers of the name. In trying to save yourself, you recognize
that others equally innocent are not saved.

6

Being from Kingston, I am used to the idea of garrison communities at war
with one another. I am familiar with places like Belfast, for instance. A place
is a historical artifact. Its opposite is space. (A similar space-place distinction
has been made by Stuart Hall.) Space is the absence of artifice, a pure geometry unmarred by the will to power. Space is the illusion of absolute freedom
to come and to go, a domain unconditioned by the distribution of social and
economic prohibitions: unified, continuous, permeable in every direction,
and theoretically limitless. The subject entering such a space experiences no
psychic ordeal. The gravity of power ignores the body and consents but to
maintain its own impalpability and invisibility. The iron partitions I once saw
in Belfast are the visible memorials of a conflict transposed onto the streets
of the city, so that space itself seemed wounded, still the platform of a violent
contretemps. Different again is the clustering of people by ethnicity, whether
by their own choice or by the prejudice of influential realtors, as one finds in
a city like New York. People seek out their own, or are forced to. They go to
their own place and stay there.

For all of its manifest scars, I experienced the city of Belfast as a space that was theoretically permeable to me. A blunt artifact of other people's history, the wall loomed over the houses, declaring the hostility of the two sides it stood between, but in no way was it meant for me. The plot made visible by the wall was not my plot. In that narrative, black lay on the outside—had no mass—and so I was free to treat the fragmented, discontinuous, impermeable spaces of the city as the relic of a benign episode, unrelated to the color of my skin. The menace gathered about the Shankill Road was entirely unrelated to my appearance.

At the origin, one acquires knowledge. At the origin, one says, I see. If you put two different origins side by side, you can retrieve information on the difference between two people. When I went to Clayton, I expected to find some news of the past. There are no signs of what must have happened here once, I said. Along Main Street the buildings are like boxes made out of brick, one or two stories high. I parked in an empty lot, down the street from Jones Lunch, a popular diner. In that direction lies the bank, in this direction lies the auto-service garage. Beyond the buildings lie the railroad tracks, which I am told separate the town into two zones.

Thinking again of what I saw in Clayton of distinguishing marks, I could name other business places: Glen's Barber, Clayton Steak House, Kirby's Precision Cuts, Shelton's Furniture (gone out of business). I could say that a visitor's perception can touch only the surface of things, and that these were generic, like coins you can exchange with anyone from anywhere. Tranquil describes the morning. The place was divided by a secret ordinance. Everyone knew everyone else. A black family sat in one of the booths over against the wall to the left. Small tables held the rest of the floor, and a counter held the right, pushed back and in, away from the tables a little. My assignment was to talk to the people inside the restaurant in order to learn about the origin. But maybe the purpose of talking was to experience the normalcy of the folks, not so much to learn anything of the town's people, or its history, or its present troubles, and so on, but to see that it was possible to talk to them. I was supposed to take the town out of the realm of fable. That was all. Well, I said, I don't need to talk to these people in order to believe that they lead ordinary lives. I need to leave.

The sun was shining. I was looking around, feeling disappointed, the inertia of a tourist with no more sights to see. No doubt but that anyone who saw me sitting on this bench would assume I'd crossed from the other side, or that I was a visitor, and would soon depart, and return to my own town

with its own opaque social logic. Perhaps another way of describing the sensation of being black is to say that space has degrees of force, or that the skin has a variable mass. What the mass of the skin attracts and is gripped by is the space around it in the restaurant, or on the sidewalk, like a planet in the vicinity of the sun. According to this metaphor, the sensation of being an honorary white man is more or less imperceptible: the mass of the skin falls away to zero, and one is no longer aware of it. The artifact of history—the place—has no hold on your autonomy as a subject.

7

The imaginary of the West once labored under the conclusion that History had bypassed Africa. A tropology cultivated this fact. Lord Lugard, 1922: "in Africa to-day we are . . . bringing to the dark places of the earth, the abode of barbarism and cruelty, the torch of culture and progress" (Lugard [1922] 1965, 618). Some metaphors last forever. This image of a continent unlit by the torch of progress we absorbed in the West Indies. I grew up with the idea that people from places in West Africa—Ghana, Benin, Senegal, Mali, other lands of the colonial imaginary—were savages in loincloths brandishing spears. This belief was a problem, since we were from those places ourselves once. Black, we were orphans of the West, without a respectable past over there. West Indians had evolved beyond their origin in Tarzan's jungle, we said, tutored and grown on other soil.

In fact, the lessons of our masters had been absorbed so well that we were able to retrieve an alternative truth about our local history. Educated, we exchanged the dumb slave for the strategy-conscious Maroon, the whipped dog for the rebel. Across the interior landscape, the songs were lit of the great houses blazing, the charred fields abandoned, servitude redeemed by violence. The culture exploded. Elsewhere, scholars such as Frank Snowden, Basil Davidson, and Cheikh Anta Diop vivified the concept of civilizations indigenous to Africa. "The Kushites now began writing in their own language in an alphabetic script which has yet to be understood," Davidson says. "Meroe became very much a civilization in its own right; and this civilization was one of considerable depth and range of culture" (Davidson 1995, 40). The tale of the dark origin was false. The illusion of barbarous Africa had been created by wicked men, and we had been deceived. Presumably, when a white person looks at the Elgin Marbles he feels a kinship with the radiant

whiteness of the heroes, as if looking into a mirror and seeing a nobler self looking back. But the mirror can show other faces, other designs.

8

One generation's experience of race is not that of the descendants. Born into a time and place of riddles, my parents escaped into the Civil Service. In the United States of America, written into the law and embodied in the Sheriff, Jim Crow segregated the place.

Maybe more deeply in the United States than in the West Indies, the old order still prevailed of masters and slaves when I was young. There was distressing poverty in the city, penal-style labor and illiteracy in the countryside, but there were no night riders: a simple note of difference between the two countries.

Not far from where my friend grew up in North Carolina, a roadside placard welcomed travelers to Smithfield. Printed on the sign was the name Ku Klux Klan. The warning remained in place until the 1980s.

References

Davidson, Basil. 1995. *Africa in history: Themes and outlines.* Rev. and exp. ed. New York: Simon and Schuster.

Gibbon, Edward. [1776] 1996. *The decline and fall of the Roman Empire.* Vol. 1. New York: Modern Library.

Lugard, Frederick D. [1922] 1965. *The dual mandate in British tropical Africa.* 5th ed. Hamden, Conn.: Archon Books.

Shakespeare, William. 1986. *William Shakespeare: The complete works.* Ed. Alfred Harbage. New York: Viking Press.

Snowden, Frank M., Jr. 1970. *Blacks in antiquity: Ethiopians in the Greco-Roman experience.* Cambridge: Belknap Press of Harvard University Press.

Walcott, Derek. 1986. *Collected poems, 1948–1984.* New York: Farrar, Straus and Giroux.

3

Troubling Privilege

7

Whiteness as Insidious: On the Embedded and Opaque White Racist Self

George Yancy

The white complicity claim maintains that all whites, by virtue of systemic white privilege that is inseparable from white ways of being, are implicated in the production and reproduction of systemic racial injustice.

—Applebaum 2010, 179

I argue that I cannot escape whiteness, nor can I discount the ways I am reproducing whiteness. I argue that I cannot claim to be nonracist, to rest in the ideal of a positive racial identity.

—Warren 2001, 465

Avoiding White Racist Exposure

"I see an angry black professor!"[1] That was the response of one white male professor who had listened to a talk that I had given on the theme of racial embodiment and the phenomenological dimensions of what it feels like to be an "essence" vis-à-vis the white gaze. I had engaged in a critical discussion about the ways in which black bodies are profiled, stereotyped, and dehumanized within the context of antiblack racism. I theorized the ways in which the white gaze functions to foreclose the black body from the realm of personhood, how the white gaze renders the black body ontologically truncated,

fixed like an essence. My aim was to bring attention to the racial and racist dynamics of quotidian social encounters, to defamiliarize everyday social encounters in order to expose the *lived* reality of white racism and its impact on the everyday experiences of black people. I wanted to create a receptive space within which whites in attendance would be willing to make an effort to suspend (to the extent to which this is possible) their own assumptions about the operations of white racism and allow themselves to be affected by black *Erlebnis* (lived experience), to glimpse what it means to encounter white gazes. For the one white male professor, however, I was simply angry, my judgment was clouded, and therefore my philosophical observations were nugatory.

While I certainly spoke with passion, there was no physical display of anger. All that he could see, though, was my "anger," my "hostility." On further reflection, I asked myself: what if I had been angry? When did anger and the simultaneous disclosure of pain and suffering become incompatible? After his dismissal, I asked the women in the audience if they were angry about the ways in which pornography can function as an act of violence and violation, as a form of bodily fragmentation, "visual mutilation," and reduction. Most of them agreed, though in barely audible voices. My use of this example was designed to communicate the point that anger can function as a place of passion, as a place of urgency. Quoting Toni Morrison, I said, "Anger is better. There is a sense of being in anger. A reality and presence. An awareness of worth" (1970, 50). My sense is that my "anger" functioned as the fulcrum around which the white professor's entire narrative of my talk revolved. In "seeing" only my "anger," he not only failed to hear me, but in the process he was able to shore up his whiteness. In other words, "I see an angry black professor!" can be described as the deployment (whether consciously or unconsciously) of a white "distancing strategy" that enables whites to "avoid being positioned as racist or implicated in systemic oppression" (Applebaum 2010, 42).

During the talk, part of my objective was to put whiteness on display, to mark it, to perform a countergaze from the perspective of a critical black male subjectivity. Marking whiteness in the presence of whites can be a profoundly disquieting experience for them, especially when the agent doing the marking is a person of color—in this case, a *black male*. As raced and engendered, I am a black professor, and yet I am also the "hypersexual beast," the "raper of white women," the shadow lurking in the dark. The context can become downright volatile. "I see an angry black professor!" functioned to

erase my critical subjectivity. I became the quintessential angry black man, a powerful racist trope that signified that I was out of control and possibly in need of some form of discipline. Perhaps for the white professor, I was the epitome of the raging black male on the precipice of violence, the academic Willie Horton. Toward the end of my talk, another white male professor, an older gentleman, felt that I had failed members of the audience. He said with a note of irritation in his voice, "You leave us with *no* hope." I responded, "Why do you want hope? My objective here is not to bring white people hope, to make them walk away feeling good about themselves." He responded with a faulty inference: "Then you must be angry!"

Hope has always played an essential existential role in the lives of black people living in white America. Black people have long rebelled against the absurdity of white racism through a blues sensibility that continues to emphasize the power of transcendence through hope. Hence, it wasn't that I was unfamiliar or unconcerned with the power of hope, that incredible capacity to look absurdity in the face and yet to affirm life. Rather, I was curious about the function of this white man's desire that I should have left white people with hope. Indeed, for me, "I see an angry black professor!" and "You leave us with *no* hope" functioned as two sites of white obfuscation. In the former case, as already argued, I was reduced to the mythical angry black male, rendering all that I had to say about whiteness and white racism of little or no value. The latter case functioned to elide the gravitas of the immediacy of black pain and suffering and the virulent ways in which white racism continues to function with such frequency in our contemporary moment. On my analysis, both men failed to *tarry* with the reality of racism and the profound ways in which people of color must endure such racism.

This refusal to tarry with the reality of racism and black pain and suffering was not new. In many invited talks, I have explored what I have come to call the "elevator effect." I describe how, within the context of an elevator, white racism is performed through the activity of a white woman clutching her purse and what this means in terms of the interpellation of the black body as criminal. I have noticed that many whites, after I present the elevator effect, will immediately ask questions that challenge the epistemic status of black people and their capacity *to know* when an act is racist. For example, I have been asked:

- What if the purse strap broke, and instead of holding it for fear of being robbed, the white woman is attempting to fix it?

- What if the white woman is claustrophobic, and therefore she is simply anxious about being in an enclosed space, as opposed to being in an enclosed space with a black man?
- What if the white woman on the elevator is really a cardboard image of a white woman, one that the black man only assumes to be real?
- What if the white woman is exhibiting behavior that resembles racist behavior, but such behavior is really the result of obsessing about not wanting to appear racist? In short, what if the white woman ends up emulating racist behavior for fear of appearing racist?

It is the sheer *alacrity* with which these questions are posed that makes me skeptical. Rare are the times when whites will actually attempt to understand what the experience is like for the black male in the elevator. The failure or refusal to tarry might very well indicate the power of white narcissism. The last question, for example, may result from feelings of guilt, of having been in precisely similar circumstances/physical spaces where the racist fear of black bodies erupted. It is as if the white woman who posed the question has glimpsed her own guilt and begins to obsess about her "innocence" in the form of declaring herself not racist but only mistaken as such. In short, the hypothetical objection is the vehicle through which she relives, at the level of fantasy, her experience of having been in the presence of a black body, only this time she gets to live that moment as racially innocent. The declaration "I am not being racist, only exhibiting behavior that mimics racism because I am really anxious about appearing to be racist to you" functions as a performance of a false moment of transcendence beyond racism. Sara Ahmed writes, "This white subject might even be anxious about its own tendency to worry about the proximity of others" (2004, par. 7), but in doing so there is a gesture toward white purity.

The questions given above are taken very seriously by whites who raise them. I don't deny this. Yet they are often communicated in a tone that says, "See! I got you. You were so wrong about me." Indeed, the "what if" structure of their questions has the effect of calling into question black people as epistemic subjects and installing whites as all-knowing epistemic subjects, especially regarding their own lack of racism. So many whites whom I have encountered are so quick to deploy the hypothetical scenario that they not only fail to tarry with the pain and suffering of black people, but they also fail *to hear* the complexity and reality of the racist situation that has been described. "You leave us with *no* hope" functions in precisely this way. The actual desire for hope, which is the subtext of the accusation, looks toward

the future and can function to point beyond the racist mess that whites *currently* continue to perpetuate. The process of hoping for the end of white racism, or hoping for a panacea for the problem of white racism, can function as a way of distinguishing oneself from those "really racist whites for whom there is no hope." As a "good white," one is already positioned beyond the muck and mire of contemporary forms of white racism; one has already come to terms with one's racist *past*. I firmly believe that whites ought to possess hope, for "without hope, the future would be decided, and there would be nothing left to do," but I am critical of forms of hope that "rush to 'inhabit' a 'beyond' to the work of exposing racism, as that which structures the present" (Ahmed 2004, par. 59). I encourage whites to dwell within spaces that make them deeply uncomfortable, to stay with the multiple forms of agony that black people endure from them, especially those whites who deny the ways in which they are complicit in the operations of white racism. I want them to *delay* the hypothetical questions, to *postpone* their reach beyond the present. Reaching too quickly for hope can elide the importance of exposure. Ahmed writes, "To hear the work of exposure requires that white subjects inhabit the critique, *with its lengthy duration,* and to recognise the world that is re-described by the critique as one in which they live. The desire to act in a non-racist or anti-racist way when one hears about racism, in my view, can function as a defense against hearing how that racism implicates which subjects, in the sense that it shapes the spaces inhabited by white subjects in the unfinished present" (par. 57).

The unfinished present is where I want whites to tarry, to recognize the complexity and weight of the current existence of white racism, to attempt to understand the ways in which they perpetuate racism, and to begin to think about the incredible difficulty involved when it comes to undoing white racism. Ahmed *locates* this tendency to flee the unfinished business of white racism vis-à-vis whites who ask, "But what can we do?" She argues, "But the question . . . can work to *block* hearing; in moving on from the present towards the future, it can also move away from the object of critique, or place the white subject 'outside' that critique in the present of the hearing. In other words, the desire to act, to move, or even to move on, can stop the message 'getting through'" (par. 56). So, while I would not argue that *all* cases of offering hypothetical scenarios or critiques of incidents that black people point to as racist are really modes of obfuscation or flight on the part of whites who deny (consciously or not) their own racism, I, like Ahmed, want to interrogate how that type of white response moves "too quickly past the exposure of racism and hence 'risks' such concealment" (par. 57) of their own white

racism. My sense is that "I see an angry black professor!" and "You leave us with *no* hope" both functioned to relocate the two white males "outside" the framework of my analysis of the pervasive, complex, and insidious nature of white racism. As such, they were able to retreat from exposure and find shelter from acknowledging the unfinished present of white racism.

The metaphor of "finding shelter" in the face of the reality of white racism is powerful in terms of identifying the ways in which white people obfuscate the reality of their whiteness and insidiously reinscribe and reinforce white power and privilege. During a class where we had been discussing bell hooks's understanding of whiteness as a site of terror, I asked the students in what ways they thought whiteness, in our contemporary moment, constitutes a site of terror. I wanted to get a sense of how white students related to hooks's understanding of whiteness as a site of "traumatic pain and anguish that remains a consequence of white racist domination, a psychic state that informs and shapes the way black folks 'see' whiteness" (1992, 169). My hope was that they might get a sense of whiteness from the perspective of black people. I also wanted them to begin to interrogate whiteness as a site and signifier of "goodness" and "purity" and as something benign. One white student said that she did not understand how her whiteness could possibly be a site of terror as she did not own any black people as slaves and was not violent toward black people. She was able to rush past the aim of the question by dissociating *herself* from a certain period in American history and thus relegating white terror to the remote past. It was then that a black student shared how she had attended an all-white school and how she was referred to as "the black girl." She specifically explained how she felt denuded of her subjectivity, her complexity. She made sure to specify how psychologically damaging it felt *to be treated* as "the black girl," not simply to be nominated as such. Another white student interjected, "I know exactly what she means! I lived in a black neighborhood and they referred to me as 'the white girl.'"

Without belittling my white student's experience, this was an important pedagogical and philosophical opportunity to point out how the failure of exposure operates insidiously. It is not enough, though, to point to the fact *that* whiteness is insidious; one must show *how* whiteness is insidious. In this classroom situation, there was a rush to identify with the black student's experience. The white student placed under erasure the specific reality and gravitas of the black student's experience of whiteness as terror by shifting the discussion away from the black student's experiences to that of *her own* (white) situation of being an object of insult within the context of a black

neighborhood. "I am just like you" also suggested that there is nothing specifically special about being white (or black for that matter) in America, despite the fact that America is a country predicated upon white privilege and white power. The fact is that there is a morally atrocious and enduring history of black people being the objects of white insults, which is not to deny that whites have also experienced the sting of black insults. Black people, however, have not only been the targets of white vitriolic speech and a long history of racial stereotyping, but they have also been the targets of state-sanctioned racial violence that was inextricably linked to such vitriolic speech. In short, whites have had the historical collective ideological and material power to enforce such hate speech and degrading racist stereotypes. Through the process of conflating or flattening important differential experiences, the white student sought shelter; she avoided the exposure of how she, *as white*, undergoes processes of racial interpellation that are different from the ways in which black people undergo processes of specific *white racist* interpellation.[2] She was not attentive to the unfinished present of whiteness and how it positions her differently. She did not tarry with or allow herself to be addressed by the experiences of the black student. As such, she did not hear what was being communicated. Her feelings of white fragility became valorized at the expense of the black student's feelings. Moreover, the discussion of whiteness as terror was replaced by a discussion of whiteness as innocence through both of the white students' responses. In both cases, the white student was able to disarticulate herself (or certainly imagine herself to have done so) from the history of whiteness and the ways in which whiteness continues to assert its power and privilege. Both white students reasserted their whiteness qua privilege precisely through the presumption of themselves as simply individuals, autonomous and nondescript, that is, interchangeable with anyone else.

Within the contexts of talks and in the classroom, I have witnessed many whites who attempt to position themselves beyond the fray of white privilege and power. I would argue that they imagine themselves as *completely* autonomous agents, free from the power of white racist effective history. Yet whiteness is precisely the *historical* metanarrative that affects their sense of themselves as atomic individuals, and as sites of exclusive transcendence (Birt 2004). Whites see themselves, even if unconsciously, as raceless, as abstract minds, as constituting the transcendental norm. This conception of the white self has complex historical links with European modernity and imperialism. This view presupposes a problematic philosophical anthropology that comes with a misanthropic dialectic, that is, black people vis-à-vis

whites are ontologically collapsed into pure facticity, constituting the very quintessence of racial assignment and racial degeneracy/inferiority. This view of the white subject obfuscates its status as *raced*, elevating it to the status of the human qua human. As a result, white subjects come to see the problem of race as an issue for people of color.

The Embedded White Racist Self

When introducing undergraduate and graduate students to questions of white privilege, I deploy Peggy McIntosh's seminal article, originally published in 1988, which explores white and male privilege, a staple reading within the area of critical white studies. In that article, McIntosh gives forty-six examples of white privilege. The majority of her examples powerfully identify ways in which white privilege continues to exist. For example, she writes, "I can go shopping alone most of the time, pretty well assured that I will not be followed or harassed" ([1988] 1997, 293–94). A significant part of what makes McIntosh's article so powerful is the way in which she conceptualizes the white self as complicit in the systemic operational power of white privilege. I have had white students object to the example above only later to recant, realizing, for example, that they were probably stopped by security as they entered a store because of their age, choice in attire, or multiple tattoos and piercings. I have never had a white student say that she was stopped *because she is white*. My objective in using McIntosh's work is to get white students to think about the deeper ways in which their whiteness functions to sustain white racism, even as they are, understandably, resistant to the appellation "racist." It is important to note that McIntosh actually clears a conceptual space for understanding her own white identity as racist. She writes, "In my class and place, I did not see myself as racist because I was taught to recognize racism only in individual acts of meanness by members of my own group, never in invisible systems conferring unsought racial dominance on my group from birth" (298). Thinking about racism in terms of what is systemically conferred or bestowed, McIntosh includes as racist herself *and* those from her group (other whites) who are recipients of the conferral or bestowal of racial dominance from birth.

One of my white students argued that if he and a black guy walked into a store together and the black guy was followed by the white security guard, this in no way makes him (my white student) racist. Rather, it is the white security guard, the one who carries out the "individual act of meanness," who

fits the racist stereotype. The student, however, overlooked the way in which *he* is still the recipient and perpetrator of racial dominance. As white, he gets to walk into stores without anyone doubting the integrity of his character and intentions. As Zeus Leonardo notes, "[White] privilege is granted even without a subject's cognition that life is made a bit easier for her" (2009, 75). This white student nevertheless gets to walk into the store on the basis of presumptive innocence that is dialectically linked to the black guy's presumptive guilt. As Applebaum notes, "Privilege also consists in the presumption of white moral integrity that is, in the larger picture, contingent upon the co-construction of the black as morally suspect" (2010, 29). There is, in short, a parasitic relationship, one governed by a racial Manichean divide where whites position themselves as the positive term of the divide. Indeed, within the context of white racist domination, this hierarchical binary assumes the form of a "metaphysical" structure (Martinot 2010, 24).

The difficult challenge is to get white students to understand the profound ways in which they are implicated in a complex network of racist power relationships, the ways in which racism constitutes a heteronomous web of white practices to which they, as whites, are linked as both beneficiaries of such a web and as co-contributors to the web's continual function. White racial oppression, power, and privilege can be conceptualized as uneventful acts of being white, like walking into a store and not being followed. In this way, white racial oppression, power, and privilege are "connected to one's very being constituted as white" (Applebaum 2010, 30). As Stephanie M. Wildman and Adrienne D. Davis argue, "Because part of racism is systemic, I benefit from the privilege that I am struggling to see. . . . All whites are racist in this sense of the term, because we benefit from systemic white privilege. Generally whites think of racism as voluntary, intentional conduct, done by horrible others. Whites spend a lot of time trying to convince ourselves and each other that we are not racist. A big step would be for whites to admit that we are racist" (2008, 114–15).

Many of my white students have difficulty accepting what I call the "embedded conception of the white racist." This embedded conception of the white racist self helps them to appreciate the ways in which they have missed the social ontologically robust ways in which they are *not* self-identical substances moving through space and time, fully self-present and fully autonomous, etymologically, a "law" unto themselves. Theorized as embedded within a preexisting social matrix of white power,[3] one that is fundamentally constitutive, though not deterministic, my students are encouraged to think critically about ways in which they are *not* sites of complete self-

possession, but sites of dispossession.[4] Part of the meaning of the process of dispossession is that one is not *the* ego-logical sovereign that governs its own meaning, definition, and constitution. The white embodied self is "transitive" (etymologically, "passing over"); its being presupposes others, signifying a relational constitution that takes place within the context of material history and situational facticity. The white embodied self is constituted through its connectivity to discursive and material practices that are fundamentally racist and in terms of which the white self is already consigned a meaning; it is an embodied white self that has already been given over to embedded and embodied white others. My white students, then, have already undergone processes of racist interpellation by the time white racism even becomes an issue for them, something to be critically and seriously reckoned with. Some of my white students have even gestured toward the desire to "abandon" their whiteness. However, as Tamara K. Nopper argues, whites remain "structurally white" (her term), despite the fact that they "go around saying dumb things such as, 'I am not white! I am a human being!' or, 'I left whiteness and joined the human race,' or my favorite, 'I hate white people! They're stupid'" (2003). Another way of stating this is that "privilege is also granted despite a subject's attempt to dis-identify with the white race" (Leonardo 2009, 75). The embedded and embodied white self is already the product of an anterior multitude of white epistemic assumptions, privileges or immunities, perceptual practices, and forms of white bonding that are experienced as unextraordinary. Judith Butler writes, "The body has its invariably public dimension. Constituted as a social phenomenon in the public sphere, my body is and is not mine. Given over from the start to the world of others, it bears their imprint, is formed within the crucible of social life" (2004, 26). While Butler is not theorizing whiteness within the context of that statement, what she says is relevant to my understanding of white constitution.

I try to get my white students to understand the ways in which they are materially linked to the public and private worlds of white others, and how the simple act of walking into a store with (white) racial impunity/immunity constitutes the site of a body that "bears the imprint" of white silent assumptions, moral integrity, and greater freedom of bodily mobility/comportment. Here, too, they fail to tarry with the reality of their embeddedness. Again, inflecting the work of Butler, they attempt to elide their racist constitution and, by extension, their vulnerability. Constitution-cum-vulnerability is the process in which their emergence in the world as white is put into play *ab initio*. However, there is no preexisting, stable, vulnerable *white self* that is exposed to white racism. Moreover, there is no ahistorical material "white"

vulnerable body that is the starting point of the white self. John Warren argues, "The color of one's skin cannot be separated from the practices that have historically constructed it—pigment is a product of a stylized repetition of acts" (2001, 462). I would argue that vulnerability and racial constitution/subjection are coextensive. My white students attempt to "build a notion of 'autonomy'" (Butler 2004, 26) upon the rejection of this deeper sense of their white historical constitution and precariousness. As such, then, they reject their existential fragility and white racist sociohistorical conditionedness in the name of an untenable conception of autonomy (ibid.). Hence, no matter how much my white students attempt to "fix" themselves or attempt to make themselves invulnerable, they are "already given over" (ibid., 28), beyond themselves. They are already dispossessed by social forces that fundamentally belie the assumption that the white self is a site of autogenesis or self-creation beyond social structures that have positioned them in particular ways. I encourage my white students to think about their white embedded and embodied selves as products of *the "law" of the other*, that is, ways of having undergone interpellation, citation, and sociostructural positioning beyond their intentions, especially "good intentions," beyond their sense of themselves as "self-lawed" or as the site of exclusive transcendence. The larger aim is to get them not to rush past the question of accountability.

Some of my white students think that the mere act of acknowledging their complicity is sufficient or that their newfound resolve to fight against white racism places them squarely outside the social matrix of whiteness. As Applebaum notes, however, "No white person can stand outside the system" of white power (2010, 46). And while it is true that not all whites are affected by whiteness in the same way, "all whites," according to Barbara Trepagnier, "are infected" by whiteness (2010, 15). It is here that my students begin to discover that the rabbit hole of whiteness is deeper than they had initially imagined. I explore with my white students what it means to say that they do not "stand outside" the system of whiteness. I also explain to them that they are also *infected* in profound ways at the site of their white psyches, a point that they often are reluctant to acknowledge.

The Opaque White Racist Self

My white students also resist what I refer to as the "opaque conception of the white racist." Most of them rely on the assumption that they can ascertain

their own racism through a sincere act of introspection. They assume that if they "look" deep enough they will be able to ascertain the limits of their racism. On this view, my white students presume that when it comes to ascertaining the complexity and depth of their own racism, they possess the capacity for absolute epistemic clarity and the self is transparent. Given contemporary whites' moral investment in the rhetoric of a colorblind United States, despite their embeddedness within systemic white racist practices, and the social stigma against being called a racist, I would argue that "introspection as ordinarily understood is more often an imaginative *construction* than a retrieval process" (Berlak 2008, 55) or an effective process for ascertaining the "truth" about the internal depth of one's white racism.

As one embarks upon the process of giving an account of one's "racist limits," the white racist self has already "gotten done" by white racism in fundamentally and profoundly constitutive ways. The white self that attempts to "ascertain such limits" has already arrived too late (Butler 2005, 79) to determine the complex and insidious ways in which white racism has become embedded within her white embodied self. It is not that there is no transparency at all; rather, the reality of the sheer depth of white racialization is far too opaque.

In *Black Bodies, White Gazes*, I argued that whiteness is a profound site of concealment, that whiteness is embedded within responses, reactions, good intentions, postural gestures, and denials. I argued that whiteness is a form of ambush. I argued that the moment a white person claims to have "arrived," that is, to have achieved "complete" antiracist mastery, she often undergoes a surprise attack that belies any sense of arrival. Within the context of *Black Bodies, White Gazes*, however, I did not connect the process of ambush to what I now see as indicative of a deeper opaque white self, one that is alien to itself, one that is a site of dispossession.

Indeed, it seems to me that the condition for ambush is linked to a white self that has undergone a process of *arrival*. Arrival, in this sense, signifies that one has undergone anterior processes of white subject formation. For example, the antiracist activist Tim Wise shares a story that demonstrates the insidious nature of whiteness and the opacity of the white racist self. In 2003, he boarded a 737 headed to St. Louis. "I glanced into the cockpit," he writes, "and there I saw something I had never seen before in all the years I had been flying: not one but two black pilots at the controls of the plane." Despite all of the antiracist work that he had done and the antiracist training

that he provides, Wise admits that he thought, "Oh my God, can these guys fly this plane?" (2005, 133). What is powerful about this disclosure is that Wise also points out that what *he knew to be true* was of little help. The domain of justified true beliefs was of little help. Despite the fact that he knew that black pilots are more than capable of flying planes, his racism triumphed. Wise's experience demonstrates how white racism is embedded within one's embodied habitual perceptual engagement with the social world and how white racism is woven into, etched into, the white psyche, forming an opaque white racist self.

So just as the white subject undergoes white racist interpellation within the context of white racist systemic structures and institutional practices, the white self undergoes processes of interpellation vis-à-vis the psychic opacity of the white racist self. One responds, as it were, to the hail of one's "immanent other"—the opaque white racist self. If Wise had been asked before he boarded the plane to share his thoughts about black pilots, he probably would have given an account that identified how important it is to see more "racial" diversity and how this challenges the white monochromatic field of commercial piloting. Yet Wise was *not* asked to provide such an account, an account that would have involved a narrative of racially blinkered, even if sincere, introspection. His response, in short, would have not revealed anything racist. But Wise was besieged by what he would otherwise have disavowed, had he been asked. The ambush is intelligible against the background of a white racist prehistory that "has never stopped happening" (Butler 2005, 78). I would argue that these moments of ambush, moments of unknowing, are profound moments of dispossession, which implicate forms of white racist relationality that install white racist sensibilities and iterative white racist norms. While Butler theorizes dispossession/foreignness as an important basis of ethical connection with others, I theorize dispossession/foreignness as a source of insight for understanding the phenomenon of ambush. Thus Wise's dispossession/foreignness to himself within the context of white racism takes the form, "I *don't* know myself as I thought I did," or "I am other to myself despite my assumptions to the contrary." Given my theorization of white self-formation as involving one's "immanent other," my sense is that this opacity places a limit on self-knowledge regarding one's own white racism. The experience of ambush interrupts and undermines a form of white epistemic arrogance to give a full account of the complex dimensions of one's white racist self. My white students gain solace from the belief that they possess the capacity to give a

transparent and full account of their "nonexistent" racism, which has the impact of securing the illusion of self-control and a conception of themselves as postrace or as postracist whites. Given the density of internalized white racism, however, their accounts of themselves *will* fail. They will undergo the upsurge of an ambush experience, its sting, and perhaps they will experience the feeling of vertigo that discloses profound uncertainty regarding the white racist self, that is, an experience of aspects of the white self as outside their control.

Conclusion

It is important that whites linger under the weight of this analysis. The process of lingering is not meant to encourage whites to engage in an abstract flirtation with some species of philosophical nihilism, perhaps eventually throwing up their hands in a theatrical gesture of ultimate failure, or to engage in some form of disinterested cynicism. Part of the objective is to get whites to linger with the question: *How does it feel to be a white problem?* The objective, though, is not to "guilt" white people. Lingering with this analysis is not meant to paralyze action and critique but to instigate action and critique, though always with the understanding that white antiracist action and critique take place within a systemic white racist context of white power and privilege and within a context where white psychic life is formed through sociality, resulting in an opaque (and dispossessed) white self that is prior to a conscious and deliberate act of taking up the issue of one's own white racism. The reality of *"having been given over from the start"* (Butler 2005, 77) signifies a white racist social embeddedness and a racist psychic opacity that operate insidiously. As whites resist white racism, it is within this complex social and psychic arena that the battle takes place. Unlike Nopper, I don't think that being a white antiracist as such is an oxymoron, though I do hold that white antiracists are indeed *racists*. There is nothing contradictory in that statement. Being a white antiracist and yet being racist aren't mutually exclusive. Rather, being a white antiracist racist signifies tremendous tension and paradox, but not logical or existential futility. In fact, and in conclusion, it is from this site of paradox, tension, and deep frustration that white antiracist racism must begin to critique itself and to give an account of itself, even as these processes are bound to encounter limitations and failures.

Notes

1. An earlier version of this chapter appeared in Yancy 2012, chapter 6.
2. This does not mean that the ways in which black people undergo white racist interpellation are exactly the same or are experienced in exactly the same way.
3. Of course, people of color are also embedded within this matrix, but the results of their embedded reality are experienced differently from whites. We must also caution against conflating the ways in which different groups of people of color experience their embedded reality within this matrix. This also applies to the ways in which people of color are differentially positioned along multiple axes vis-à-vis whites.
4. I use this term in the philosophical spirit of Judith Butler, particularly in terms of its poststructural implications, though I restrict its use here in reference to white subject formation.

References

Ahmed, Sara. 2004. Declarations of whiteness: The non-performativity of anti-racism. *borderlands e-journal* 3, no. 2. http://www.borderlands.net.au/vol3no2_2004/ahmed_declarations.htm.

Applebaum, Barbara. 2010. *Being white, being good: White complicity, white moral responsibility, and social justice pedagogy.* Lanham, Md.: Lexington Books.

Berlak, Ann. 2008. Challenging the hegemony of whiteness by addressing the adaptive unconscious. In *Undoing whiteness in the classroom: Critical educultural teaching approaches for social justice activism,* ed. Virginia Lea and Erma Jean Sims, 47–78. New York: Peter Lang.

Birt, Robert. 2004. The bad faith of whiteness. In *What white looks like: African-American philosophers on the whiteness question,* ed. George Yancy, 55–64. New York: Routledge.

Butler, Judith. 2004. *Precarious life: The powers of mourning and violence.* New York: Verso.

———. 2005. *Giving an account of oneself.* New York: Fordham University Press.

hooks, bell. 1992. *Black looks: Race and representation.* Boston: South End Press.

Leonardo, Zeus. 2009. *Race, whiteness, and education.* New York: Routledge.

Martinot, Steve. 2010. *The machinery of whiteness: Studies in the structure of racialization.* Philadelphia: Temple University Press.

McIntosh, Peggy. 1988. White privilege and male privilege: A personal account of coming to see correspondences through work in women's studies. Working Paper #189, Wellesley Centers for Women, Wellesley College, Massachusetts.

Morrison, Toni. 1970. *The bluest eye.* New York: Knopf.

Nopper, Tamara K. 2003. The white anti-racist is an oxymoron: An open letter to "white anti-racists." In *Race traitor* (Autumn). http://racetraitor.org/nopper.html.

Trepagnier, Barbara. 2010. *Silent racism: How well-meaning white people perpetuate the racial divide.* Boulder, Colo.: Paradigm.

Warren, John T. 2001. Performing whiteness differently: Rethinking the abolitionist project. *Educational Theory* 51, no. 4: 451–66.

Wildman, Stephanie M., and Adrienne D. Davis. 2008. Making systems of privilege visible. In *White privilege: Essential readings on the other side of racism*, ed. Paula S. Rothenberg, 109–15. New York: Worth Publishers.

Wise, Tim. 2005. *White like me: Reflections on race from a privileged son*. New York: Soft Skull Press.

Yancy, George. 2012. Looking at whiteness: Tarrying with the embedded and opaque white racist self. In Yancy, *Look, a white! Philosophical essays on whiteness*, 152–75. Philadelphia: Temple University Press.

8

White Privilege: The Luxury of Undivided Attention

Heidi A. Zetzer

Peggy McIntosh (1989) refers to white privilege as "unearned assets," a trea-
sure trove of gifts that are invisible to white folks and a source of annoyance,
envy, and dismay to people of color. In the field of counseling and psychotherapy, privilege is a concept that is closely tied to other hard-to-see phenomena: color blindness (Neville, Worthington, and Spanierman 2001),
aversive racism (Dovidio and Gaertner 2000), microaggressions (Sue et al.
2007), white racial identity development (Helms 1995), and white racial consciousness (Rowe, Bennett, and Atkinson 1994).

The standards of the profession require that clinicians develop cultural
competence (American Psychological Association 2003). European-American
psychologists in training are called upon to become aware of their privilege,
examine their prejudices and biases, learn about other cultures, and blend
their developing awareness and knowledge with culturally adapted counseling skills. The multicultural counseling dyad, with its explicit mission of one
person wholly understanding another, is excellent terrain for the exploration
of white privilege.

Here, white counselors actively aim to witness their racism and privilege
with the purpose of promoting the development of trusting, helping relationships with clients of color. The white counselor's journey from sleepy uncon-
sciousness, through the dissonance of discrepant views of oneself compared
to those of people of color, toward an integrated self, with full humility and
awareness, requires changes in the deep structure of ego and identity. White
privilege stands directly in the way of necessary and dramatic losses and gains

of this sort. It is the superglue of white supremacy, an invisible adhesive that binds even the most well-meaning white people (Wolf 1995) to the status quo. Its invisibility is the chief problem, and the mechanisms that maintain it are deeply psychological (Thompson and Neville 1999; Utsey and Gernat 2002).

Witnessing one's own racism and letting go of privilege requires that white trainees and their elders acknowledge past and present injuries to people of color. This type of change is unpleasant and distressing. The dissonance between one's perception of oneself as a nonracist person and evidence to the contrary is usually alleviated by pursuing one of two options: (a) increased entrenchment or (b) gradual attitude or behavior change (McConnell and Brown 2010). Constructive dissonant experiences lead to a surrender of white privilege and movement toward a positive white identity (Helms 1995; Spanierman and Soble 2010). There are intra- and interpersonal struggles all along the way for white psychologists and their students. White privilege is rich with entitlements, which are difficult to relinquish because white socialization labels them as *deserved*. Even the most virtuous individuals may find it difficult to give up the comfort and status of white privilege. While it is difficult to find a suitable metaphor for racism and white privilege, one does come to mind.

I am a well-meaning white person. I have worked on my issues for some time, and I have been invited to tea at the home of a colleague who is a person of color. I appear wearing my favorite boots, but unbeknownst to me, they are caked with mud. I don't see the mud, and I don't notice my colleague's look of dismay as I tramp from room to room, complimenting her décor and dirtying the residence. The crud on my soles is racism, and it has been accumulating over the course of my life. White privilege is my lack of awareness that it's there, my inability to notice the context in which I am bumbling around, and my failure to recognize the gracious hospitality of my colleague, who is reacting to my violation by struggling to find a way to stop me from damaging her home without eliciting defensiveness. If I were paying attention, I would be able to see this struggle. If I could witness the insensitivity of my own actions, I could acknowledge her predicament. She is in a double bind (Mahmoud 1998), and together we are in what Sue and his colleagues call a "psychological dilemma" (Sue et al. 2007, 275).

On one side of the dilemma is my colleague, who would like me to stop. However, if she confronts me, she is at risk of greater insult because I might get defensive. Such a response will suggest that not only am I *completely unaware of what I am doing, but I am intent on remaining oblivious of my impact*

on her. On my side, perhaps I sense that something is awry. I feel anxious. My autonomic nervous system prepares itself. My psychological defenses are at the ready. I may not be aware of this, but I have been guarding against accusations of racism my entire life. My colleague and I are trapped in a dilemma with no easy resolution for her. If I persist in my ignorance, I will be okay. She is the one who will get to "hold" the negativity of this event.

While many acts of racism far exceed the insult and injury associated with defiling someone's home in this way, this is a vivid dramatization of how white privilege allows me to prioritize my comfort over that of another person, prevents me from acknowledging the impact of my actions on people, keeps me from apologizing, and stops me from offering to repair the damage to the home *and* to my relationship with my colleague. Ordinarily, I would engage in whatever reparative efforts might be needed, but this confrontation would imply racism on my part, and it is simply too difficult for me to accept.

I have never made such an egregious error in someone's home. But I have inadvertently trampled on feelings, used noninclusive language, uttered or alluded to stereotypes, taken charge, perpetuated monoculturalism, and then hoped for a "free pass" from friends and colleagues of color, who at any moment might care enough about me to say, "Heidi . . . can I talk to you about something?" Once this happens, I can choose to listen or I can leap to my own defense.

The purpose of this chapter is to examine the role that white privilege plays in preventing change in multicultural relationships and, by extension, systems and institutions by reinforcing the status quo, blocking growth in white racial consciousness, and placing the burden of psychological dilemmas on people of color. I use lessons from social psychology and multicultural counseling and psychotherapy to illuminate barriers to multicultural development, and I use psychodynamic psychotherapy theory to craft recommendations for developing a positive white identity that is characterized by a capacity for empathy, openness to experience, and respectful engagement, all of which are likely to lead to the emergence of healthy work environments characterized by nondefensive personnel and a capacity for continued multicultural growth.

New Racism and White Privilege

My grandparents referred to their "cleaning lady" as "the colored gal." Her obstreperous irreverence and lack of appreciation were a constant source of

irritation to them. Both of my elders are deceased, and their old-fashioned racism has died with them, but the notion of white superiority and patronizing benevolence is still present in my generation. The overt racism of my grandparents has been replaced by a modern version that Bonilla-Silva (2003, 272) describes as the "new racism." It is characterized by hard-to-name racist undertones, covert discriminatory practices, politically correct language (which includes ardent claims of reverse racism), the identification of "safe" minorities that masks fears of the "unsafe" ones, and the continuation of a "racialized social system" that is damaging to everyone involved. Other authors have described this phenomenon as "modern racism" (McConahay 1983) and "aversive racism" (Dovidio and Gaertner 2000). The whole psychological contraption is held together by white privilege.

White Privilege

Frances Kendall writes eloquently about white privilege, which she defines as "an institutional, rather than personal, set of benefits granted to those of us who, by race, resemble people who hold the positions of power in our institutions. . . . White privilege has nothing to do with whether or not we are 'good' people. . . . Privileges are bestowed on us *solely because of our race* by the institutions with whom we interact, not because we deserve them as individuals" (2006, 63–64).

We can see this privilege in the latitude taken by Bill O'Reilly as he interviewed President Obama on Super Bowl Sunday in 2011 (Fox News 2011). What institutional benefit did Mr. O'Reilly possess as he interviewed the president? He had the authority to define the public discourse. Some might assert that this benefit was *earned*, but how does one go about *earning* the right to interrupt and ask repeated, irrelevant, and intrusive questions to the president of the United States? Based on what accomplishment is someone entitled to ask the leader of the free world, "Does it disturb you that so many people hate you?" In response, Obama smiled, laughed, and looked down. Obama replied, "The truth is that the people, and I'm sure previous presidents would say the same thing, whether it was Bush, or Clinton, or Reagan, or anybody, the people who dislike you don't know you." O'Reilly persisted, "But they *hate* you!"

O'Reilly introduced this question by saying that he had asked it of President Bush, but the two sociopolitical contexts are not equivalent. President Obama was in a racial double bind (Mahmoud 1998). He could express condemnation and fulfill a racial stereotype, or he could sidestep the accusations and appear evasive. Privilege allows white folks like Bill O'Reilly and me to

ignore history, to disregard our own racial identities, and to stake an entitled claim to inquire into others' thoughts and feelings but avoid delving into our own. In most circumstances, we can leave it up to the person of color to manage his or her response in a way that protects our self-image. We get to tramp around in interracial relationships without paying attention to our own behavior.

Some might argue that it is O'Reilly's unique personality and his designated role as an interviewer that afforded him the freedom to disrespect the president and the office, but the broader context cannot be ignored. The interview was peppered with microaggressions, which the president managed graciously and nondefensively, but was he equally free to be bossy, argumentative, and controlling of the discourse? How does race, our own and the other person's, influence our interactions? And to white folks in particular, how do we manifest white privilege in our interpersonal exchanges?

The Nexus of New Racism and White Privilege: Racial Microaggressions
Microaggressions are manifestations of the new racism. They are "brief, everyday exchanges that send denigrating messages to certain individuals because of their group membership" (Sue 2010, 24). Racial microaggressions are "subtle insults (verbal, nonverbal, and/or visual) directed toward people of color, often automatically or unconsciously" (Solórzano, Ceja, and Yosso 2010, 60). According to Sue (2011), microaggressions are characterized by four psychological dilemmas: (1) a clash of racial realities, in which the person of color doubts her own perceptions and white folks deny the incident and/or their intent; (2) invisible expressions of unintended bias, in which the white participant might be sincerely complimentary, but offensive; (3) minimization of harm by the white participant; and (4) racial double binds in which the person of color is harmed by staying silent and harmed by expressing hurt, anger, or indignation. The white participant perceives harm only when challenged.

O'Reilly's flurry of questions and observations of the president was intrusive and wearying. For example, O'Reilly asked, "What's the *absolute worst part* of being president of the United States?" To which President Obama answered humorously, "First of all, I've got a jacket on on Super Bowl Sunday. If I wasn't president, that would not be happening." O'Reilly, noticing the president's open collar, replied, "Yeah, I have a tie. You don't have a tie." At the close of the interview, O'Reilly asked, "But are you actually going to *watch* the game? You're going to sit down and you're going to watch it? You know football? You know, like, *blitzes* and *coverage* and all that?" The president asserted,

"Oh, I know football, man." "You do?" O'Reilly asked. "'Cause I know you're a *basketball* guy!"

The difficulties in this exchange lie in the subtext. O'Reilly emphasized only the negative aspects of the president's job, the perceived deficits of the president, and doubts about the president's knowledge of football. Granted, this might have been pure politics, and no claims may be made about O'Reilly's intentions, but it is impossible to ignore the fact that this exchange took place between a white broadcaster and a black president.

The Psychodynamics of White Identity Development/White Racial Consciousness

Models of white racial identity development and white racial consciousness have been developed for white people in general (Helms 1995; Spanierman and Soble 2010) and applied to counselors in training (Sabnani, Ponterotto, and Borodovsky 1991). Though each model has its own nuances, the journey starts with a white person's "lack of awareness as a racial being" (stage 1). "Interactions with other cultures" (stage 2) lead to the cognitive dissonance of discovering that one holds erroneous beliefs about self and race (stage 3), and then to antiracist positions and a "pro-minority stance" (stage 4). This is followed by disillusionment and a temporary return to a pro-white stance (stage 5), and finally culminates in a fully integrated positive view of oneself and others as racial beings (stage 6) (Sabnani, Ponterotto, and Borodovsky 1991, 82). Change is driven by cognitive dissonance, and growth can be halted or furthered depending on how the dissonance is resolved. Development varies across domains. For example, a white person might be "pro-minority" in the workplace but oppose miscegenation.

A common feature across models is the appearance of *negative affect* in stages 2 and 3. *White guilt and anger* appear in stage 2, and *anxiety or distress* associated with cognitive dissonance occurs in stage 3. Both stages include threats to a white individual's view of himself as a "good" (i.e., nonracist) person (Dovidio and Gaertner 2000). The emotions elicited in stages 2 and 3 provoke psychological responses that work to eliminate these negative feelings by either (a) defending against them (Utsey and Gernat 2002), or (b) working through them. Just as in other life domains, human responses to perceived threats may be *adaptive* or *maladaptive*. For example, guilt may be associated with genuine feelings of remorse and may motivate new behaviors (adaptive), or it may provoke self-hatred and hostile actions toward others

(maladaptive) (McCullough et al. 2003, 24). Similarly, a person's feelings can have an *activating* or *inhibiting* effect. For example, shame tends to be inhibitory, while anger is often activating. An individual's ability to acknowledge and manage the internal conflict influences her behavioral response. McCullough et al. (13) refer to this inner (psychodynamic) conflict over feelings, and the very human effort to avoid the conflict, as "affect phobia": a fear of feelings!

In the context of the new racism, a chief barrier to racial understanding and harmony lies in white folks' effort to avoid painful feelings. A lack of awareness about the choices that are being made to cope with negative emotions impedes individual and organizational multicultural development. The intergenerational transmission of racism and privilege among white folks includes teaching future generations how to manage their affect phobia and guard against threats to the individual and collective view of white people in general as *good and kind*.

When threats to one's self-concept occur, a person's propensity for adaptive or maladaptive thoughts, feelings, and behaviors is guided by his or her learning history (McCullough et al. 2003, 25). White folks first learn how to cope with these feelings in their families. In my childhood family, raising doubts about one another's race-related attitudes and behaviors elicited condemnation and rejection from the other members. Family distress was used to prevent members from questioning one another's views. I learned to cope with the negative feelings related to our racism in the same way that children in alcoholic families learn to cope with destructive drinking, by following the family rules: "Don't talk. Don't trust. Don't feel" (Black 2002, 33–54). I had to turn to colleagues and friends of color to learn about white racism and my role in its perpetuation (Zetzer 2011).

Information-Processing Strategies as Psychological Defenses

Helms's model of white racial identity development (WRID) (1995, 2005) offers useful propositions about how white folks perceive, process, and avoid negative feelings associated with critical incidents in our lives as racial beings (Spanierman et al. 2008; Utsey and Gernat 2002). Helms refers to each step as a "status," which consists of a specific set of information-processing strategies that drive the expression of psychological defenses.

Helms's model is a "progressive" rather than a "defensive" scheme for the emergence of a positive white identity that is grounded in principles of

equality rather than white supremacy (Croll 2007). Racial statuses are at first consonant with a benign inattention to race and racial differences (e.g., race doesn't matter), then dissonant with those expectations (e.g., uh-oh, race matters), then wrought with inner turmoil (e.g., race matters *too* much for me!) that is eventually resolved (e.g., I can manage racial matters). *How* white folks move from one status to the next has not been well defined. Psychotherapeutic principles of change, specifically those that relate to affect phobia and its treatment (McCullough et al. 2003), may be used to illuminate and facilitate the WRID process, for which each burst of growth requires an adaptive response to negative feelings.

White folks face a constant struggle with negative feelings. This is no surprise. This type of change is difficult! It happens "on the inside" and is rarely shared. Each generation of white families fails the next by first avoiding and then denying the impact of race and racism in our society. White privilege protects against realizing the painful effects of affect-phobic responses on white people and people of color. Self-reflection is not required when one resides in a system that is designed to guard against insight. Another one of my elders used to say, "Don't fix it if it ain't broke," and as long as white folks agree that "it ain't broke," there is little incentive to change.

The Role of (In)Attention in Psychological Dilemmas

A common theme in Sue's (2011) varied descriptions of microaggressions caused by psychological dilemmas is the lack of awareness on the part of the white initiator. In the context of a racial microaggression, the offender is frequently oblivious to the transgression, just like my happily and unknowingly soiling the carpets of my gracious colleague.

In a seminal article, still considered to be the state of the field, Posner and Petersen (1990, 26) describe three types of attention that are anatomically separate but part of a "unified system for the control of mental processing": (1) involuntary orienting to sensory events, (2) detecting signals for focal (conscious) processing of visual and semantic events (more recently known as executive attention), and (3) maintaining a vigilant or alert state for high-priority targets.

Most of the research on attention has studied visual and auditory processing of simple tasks, not anything as complicated as a psychological dilemma triggered by a microaggression. However, it is useful to understand that attention is a complex neurological phenomenon that moderates human perfor-

mance even in interracial interactions (Richeson and Trawalter 2005). For example, basic research has shown that the general scanning of one's visual field produces the same amount of interference as the monitoring of a single location. As soon as a viewer detects a target, however, the orienting function of attention is activated and begins to consume cognitive resources, which interferes with most other cognitive operations (Posner and Petersen 1990, 33).

Extrapolating from this literature, the occurrence of a microaggression in an interracial exchange orients the observer to the affront (the target or threat) and instantly detracts from other types of cognitive processing. In the case of a racial microaggression with a white initiator and a person of color as the recipient, privilege allows the initiator to assume that her worldview is normative while the other person's view is skewed. Thus the disruption will affect the initiator only if she also detects a "target" (threat) (e.g., she is actually confronted by the recipient or recognizes the offense herself). Once this occurs, the initiator is equally compromised. So an unintended microaggression has the potential to trigger shifts in attention that compromise the smooth operation of human interaction for both parties. Both people may become cognitively depleted while they struggle with managing the complexities of the interaction.

Fluctuations in attention have been proposed as one of the mechanisms that affect performance in wide range of studies on *stereotype threat* (Schmader, Johns, and Forbes 2008, 336). Stereotype threat is a "predicament in which members of a social group (e.g., African Americans) 'must deal with the possibility of being judged or treated stereotypically, or of doing something that would confirm the stereotype'" (Steele and Aronson 1995, 401, quoted in Nguyen and Ryan 2008, 1314). The effect is seen when there is "a significant threat to self-integrity, the sense of oneself as a coherent and valued entity that is adaptable to the environment" (Schmader, Johns, and Forbes 2008, 337).

Negative stereotypes have detrimental effects on performance. For example, Latino and African American research participants who are informed that a test measures intelligence (threat condition) perform more poorly than Latino and African American research participants who are told that the same test measures problem-solving abilities (no threat condition) (Steele and Aronson 1995; Steele 1997). Latino and African American participants in the threat condition also perform more poorly than white participants in the threat condition (Gonzales, Blanton, and Williams 2002). Stereotype threat has been shown to impair the performance of women on math tests (Spencer, Steele, and Quinn 1999) and to erode the math scores of white

males when they are informed that they will be compared to Asian men (Aronson et al. 1999). Similarly, white participant performance on the Implicit Associations Test (IAT) (Greenwald, McGhee, and Schwartz 1998) is negatively affected by the threat of being perceived as racist (Frantz et al. 2004). In one study, white participants, who were highly motivated to control expressions of prejudice, showed stronger pro-white scores than those in the neutral or masked condition. The threat of appearing racist actually lengthened their response times in a way that made them look *more* prejudiced, not less.

Schmader, Johns, and Forbes proposed an integrated process model of stereotype threat. The threat elicits an internal state of cognitive imbalance that activates a physiological stress response, monitoring processes, negative thought processes, and an effort to suppress the experience of the threat that in turn has a negative impact on working memory and ultimately on performance on both sensory motor (automatic processing) and cognitive and social tasks (controlled processing). The exact influence of each of these components is unknown, but working memory seems to be the "core cognitive faculty that is implicated in cognitive and social stereotype threat effects" (2008, 337).

The Role of Attention, Emotion, and Working Memory in WRID

Our social and cognitive processes are neurologically interconnected and rely heavily on working memory (Schmader, Johns, and Forbes 2008, 337). The emotional and behavioral flexibility of the human condition allows us to survive and even thrive despite threats in our environment (Greenwald 1980). The strategies we use vary based on our learning histories and represent our best effort at consciously or unconsciously navigating interpersonal terrain. Models of WRID and resistance to change have centered primarily on beliefs and behaviors (D'Andrea 2003; Helms 1995; Thompson and Neville 1999). The role of attention and emotion in helping or hindering WRID is not well understood. A psychodynamic approach to WRID suggests that white folks have the capacity to unlearn maladaptive emotive routines, but this type of change requires therapeutic conditions that extend beyond the call to "get over it" (Zetzer 2011, 14).

Overcoming defenses and helping people live authentically by learning "how to respond to themselves and others in affectively open, honest, and appropriate ways" (McCullough et al. 2003, 32) is an explicit goal of human-

istic and psychodynamic psychotherapies (Rogers 1961; Shedler 2010). If we assume that white folks' defenses are driven by *learned responses to negative emotions*, then multicultural educators, including those who train counselors and clinicians, might enhance the effectiveness of their programs by designing interventions that "treat" affect phobia. In psychotherapy the focus is on (a) systematically (with gradation) exposing and encouraging participants to tolerate the activating affect (e.g., guilt), (b) encouraging participants to avoid defensive responses that suppress unwanted emotions, and (c) using anxiety-regulation strategies to reduce or modify anxiety, guilt, shame, or pain linked to the activating event (McCullough et al. 2003, 29).

The successful resolution of each status of WRID requires potent ingredients. Many of these ingredients are already present in graduate psychology training programs that promote interracial, multicultural (Betita et al. 2001), and difficult dialogues (Sue et al. 2009; Sue 2011). Dialogue is an effective tool, but what is needed to witness and "grow out of the problem" (Conoley 2011) of the new racism is a greater focus on helping white folks in general, and white trainees in particular, tolerate and appropriately express the feelings that inevitably arise when examining whiteness as a system of racial privilege (Andersen 2003, 25). Feelings of guilt, shame, regret, loss, anger, and dismay are difficult to embrace. Expressing these emotions in the context of a supportive relationship may be the key to developing a positive white identity that is characterized by openness to experience, authentic engagement with others, and a willingness to participate in social reform.

Overcoming Affect-Phobic Responses in Multicultural Education with Psychotherapeutic Principles and Techniques

According to the principles of short-term dynamic therapy for affect phobia, "the more the patient is able to experience affect verbally, physiologically, and in the imagined action of fantasy, the more thorough the desensitization of conflict will be" (McCullough et al. 2003, 177). Exposure to unwanted feelings will elicit anxiety and trigger psychological defenses, which may be restructured by (a) teaching students to identify defenses and evaluate the maladaptive and adaptive qualities of their feelings (122–23), (b) pointing out the strengths that exist alongside the defenses, and (c) empathizing with the defenses, which reduces the shame that is associated with recognizing them.

Structured learning experiences that systematically invite and then maintain the experience of affective arousal will help white students learn to tolerate

and transform their fully identified feelings into adaptive responses. This is accomplished through systematic and sustained exposure paired with proper levels of compassion. Compassion is given short shrift in U.S. culture. Public shaming is typical of our collective response to racist remarks. Shaming is silencing and produces an immediate outcome that terminates the public discourse. It attributes "the problem" to one person, not the collective. Curiously, shaming leaves the role of privilege unexamined. In a sense, it helps sustain the status quo. What if shaming were replaced with empathetic expressions of dismay and explicit requests for accountability, an apology, and restitution? Public discourse of this type would provide a language for naming feelings of embarrassment or guilt and promote opportunities for construction of a "positive self-image and adaptive connections to others" (McCullough et al. 2003, 235).

Finally, multicultural educators can help white folks and white trainees "grow out of the problem" of racism and white privilege by replacing goals driven by "avoidance motivation" (I want to avoid being seen as racist) with goals guided by "approach motivation" (I want easy, authentic interracial relationships) (Conoley and Conoley 2009, 12–13). Approach goals are associated with greater optimism than avoidance goals, and with stronger persistence (Elliot, McGregor, and Gable 1999) and higher productivity in generating creative solutions (Friedman and Förster 2001). Positive psychology (Conoley and Conoley 2009) and solution-focused therapy (De Jong and Berg 2008) may offer multicultural educators other helpful strategies for transcending shame and sustaining hope. The "miracle question" is a good place to start: "Now, I want to ask you a strange question. *Suppose* that while you are sleeping tonight and the entire house is quiet, a *miracle* happens. The miracle is that the problem that brought you here is solved. However, because you are sleeping, you don't know that *the miracle has happened.* So when you wake up tomorrow morning, *what will be different* that will tell you that a miracle has happened and the problem which brought you here is solved?" (de Shazer 1988, 5).

The Miracle Question in the Muddy-Boot Metaphor

I would know that a miracle occurred because my colleague and I would have an easygoing interracial relationship in which we could offer each other feedback on the ways in which we appear prejudiced, biased, insensitive, or racist, and these exchanges would result in rich and meaningful dialogue that is filled with gratitude for each other's authentic expressions.

Here's how the muddy boot incident would go: After I've tracked dirt into the hallway, my colleague politely and firmly points out my offense. Neither one of us is distracted by stereotype threat. We tolerate our feelings of anger and dismay or embarrassment and shame and stay in the present moment (no activation of psychological defenses). We have positive and compassionate perceptions of ourselves (we are both "good" people who make mistakes) and adaptive perceptions of each other. She tells me that she has had to deal with this many times before and that she is weary. I empathize. I apologize. I offer to pay for the cleanup. I offer to clean up the mess myself. I feel bad, but I am not ashamed. I recognize that I am imperfect. We leave the interaction satisfied that we understood each other's perspective and we continue to feel committed to each other's mutual growth. We drink tea and laugh at ourselves.

References

American Psychological Association. 2003. Guidelines on multicultural education, training, research, practice, and organizational change for psychologists. *American Psychologist* 58:377–402.

Andersen, Margaret L. 2003. Whitewashing race: A critical perspective on whiteness. In *White out: The continuing significance of race*, ed. Ashley W. Doane and Eduardo Bonilla-Silva, 21–34. New York: Routledge.

Aronson, Joshua, Michael J. Lustina, Catherine Good, Kelli Keough, Claude M. Steele, and Joseph Brown. 1999. When white men can't do math: Necessary and sufficient factors in stereotype threat. *Journal of Experimental Social Psychology* 35:29–46.

Betita, Juliet, Keith Mar, Muriel Shockley, and Heidi Zetzer. 2001. Challenging racism, privilege, and oppression: Building bridges through multicultural dialogue. Workshop presented at the Multicultural Center, University of California, Santa Barbara, November.

Black, Claudia A. 2002. *It will never happen to me: Growing up with addiction as youngsters, adolescents, adults.* Center City, Minn.: Hazelden Publications.

Bonilla-Silva, Eduardo. 2003. New racism, color-blind racism, and the future of whiteness in America. In *White out: The continuing significance of race*, ed. Ashley W. Doane and Eduardo Bonilla-Silva, 271–84. New York: Routledge.

Conoley, Collie W. 2011. What positive psychology has to offer psychotherapy. Presentation at Cottage Hospital Psychiatric Grand Rounds, Santa Barbara, Calif., 23 February.

Conoley, Collie W., and Jane C. Conoley. 2009. *Positive psychology and family therapy: Creative techniques and practical tools for guiding change and enhancing growth.* New York: Wiley.

Croll, Paul. 2007. Modeling determinants of white racial identity: Results from a new national survey. *Social Forces* 86:613–42.

D'Andrea, Michael. 2003. Expanding our understanding of white racism and resistance to change in the fields of counseling and psychology. In *Culturally diverse*

mental health: The challenges of research and resistance, ed. Jeffery S. Mio and Gayle Y. Iwamasa, 17–37. New York: Brunner-Routledge.

De Jong, Peter, and Insoo Kim Berg. 2008. *Interviewing for solutions*. Belmont, Calif.: Brooks/Cole.

de Shazer, Steve. 1988. *Clues: Investigating solutions in brief therapy*. New York: W. W. Norton.

Dovidio, John F., and Samuel L. Gaertner. 2000. Aversive racism and selective decisions: 1989–1999. *Psychological Science* 11:315–19.

Elliot, Andrew J., Holly A. McGregor, and Shelly Gable. 1999. Achievement goals, study strategies, and exam performance: A mediational analysis. *Journal of Educational Psychology* 91:549–63.

Fox News. 2011. Bill O'Reilly interviews President Obama. 6 February. http://video .foxnews.com/v/4526781/bill-oreilly-interviews-president-obama/#sp=show-clips.

Frantz, Cynthia M., Amy J. C. Cuddy, Molly Burnett, Heidi Ray, and Allen Hart. 2004. A threat in the computer: The race implicit association test as a stereotype threat experience. *Personality and Social Psychology Bulletin* 30:1611–24.

Friedman, Ronald S., and Jens Förster. 2001. The effect of promotion and prevention cures on creativity. *Journal of Personality and Social Psychology* 81:1001–13.

Gonzales, Patricia M., Hart Blanton, and Kevin J. Williams. 2002. The effects of stereotype threat and double-minority status on test performance of Latino women. *Personality and Social Psychology Bulletin* 28:659–70.

Greenwald, Anthony G. 1980. The totalitarian ego: Fabrication and revision of personal history. *American Psychologist* 35:603–18.

Greenwald, Anthony G., Debbie E. McGhee, and Jordan L. K. Schwartz. 1998. Measuring individual differences in implicit cognition: The implicit association test. *Journal of Personality and Social Psychology* 74:1464–80.

Helms, Janet E. 1995. An update on Helms' white and people of color racial identity models. In *Handbook of multicultural counseling*, ed. Joseph G. Ponterotto, Jesus M. Casas, Lisa A. Suzuki, and Charlene M. Alexander, 181–98. Thousand Oaks, Calif.: Sage Publications.

———. 2005. Challenging some of the misuses of reliability as reflected in the evaluations of white racial identity attitudes scale (WRIAS). In *Handbook of racial-cultural psychology and counseling: Theory and research I*, ed. Robert T. Carter, 360–90. New York: Wiley.

Kendall, Frances E. 2006. *Understanding white privilege: Creating pathways to authentic relationships across race*. New York: Routledge.

Mahmoud, Vanessa M. 1998. The double binds of racism. In *Re-visioning family therapy: Race, culture, and gender in clinical practice*, ed. Monica McGoldrick, 255–67. New York: Guilford Press.

McConahay, John B. 1983. Modern racism and modern discrimination: The effects of race, racial attitudes, and context on simulated hiring decisions. *Personality and Social Psychology Bulletin* 9:551–58.

McConnell, Allen R., and Christina M. Brown. 2010. Dissonance averted: Self-concept organization moderates the effect of hypocrisy on attitude change. *Journal of Experimental Social Psychology* 46:361–66.

McCullough, Leigh, Nat Kuhn, Stuart Andrews, Amelia Kaplan, Jonathan Wolf, and Cara L. Hurley. 2003. *Treating affect phobia: A short-term dynamic psychotherapy*. New York: Guilford Press.

McIntosh, Peggy. 1989. White privilege: Unpacking the invisible knapsack. *Peace and Freedom*, July–August, 10–12.

Neville, Helen A., Roger L. Worthington, and Lisa B. Spanierman. 2001. Race, power, and multicultural counseling psychology: Understanding white privilege and color-blind racial attitudes. In *Handbook of multicultural counseling*, 2nd ed., ed. Joseph G. Ponterotto, Jesus M. Casas, Lisa A. Suzuki, and Charlene M. Alexander, 257–88. Thousand Oaks, Calif.: Sage Publications.

Nguyen, Hannah-Hahn D., and Ann Marie Ryan. 2008. Does stereotype threat affect test performance of minorities and women? A meta-analysis of experimental evidence. *Journal of Applied Psychology* 93:1314–34.

Posner, Michael I., and Steven E. Petersen. 1990. The attention system of the human brain. *Annual Review of Neuroscience* 13:25–42.

Richeson, Jennifer A., and Sophie Trawalter. 2005. Why do interracial interactions impair executive function? A resource depletion account. *Journal of Personality and Social Psychology* 88:934–47.

Rogers, Carl R. 1961. *On becoming a person*. Boston: Houghton Mifflin.

Rowe, Wayne, Sandra Bennett, and Donald R. Atkinson. 1994. White racial identity models: A critique and alternative proposal. *Counseling Psychologist* 22:120–46.

Sabnani, Haresh B., Joseph G. Ponterotto, and Lisa G. Borodovsky. 1991. White racial identity development and cross-cultural counselor training: A stage model. *Counseling Psychologist* 19:76–102.

Schmader, Toni, Michael Johns, and Chad Forbes. 2008. An integrated process model of stereotype threat effects on performance. *Psychological Review* 115:336–56.

Shedler, Jonathan. 2010. The efficacy of psychodynamic psychotherapy. *American Psychologist* 65:98–109.

Solórzano, Daniel, Miguel Ceja, and Tara Yosso. 2000. Critical race theory, racial microaggressions, and campus racial climate: The experience of African American college students. *Journal of Negro Education* 69, nos. 1–2: 60–73.

Spanierman, Lisa B., Euna Oh, V. Paul Poteat, Anita R. Hund, Vetisha L. McClair, Amanda M. Beer, and Alexis M. Clarke. 2008. White university students' responses to societal racism: A qualitative investigation. *Counseling Psychologist* 36:839–70.

Spanierman, Lisa B., and Jason Soble. 2010. Understanding whiteness: Previous approaches and possible directions in the study of white racial attitudes and identity. In *Handbook of multicultural counseling*, 3rd ed., ed. Joseph G. Ponterotto, Jesus M. Casas, Lisa A. Suzuki, and Charlene M. Alexander, 283–299. Thousand Oaks, Calif.: Sage Publications.

Spencer, Steven J., Claude M. Steele, and Diane M. Quinn. 1999. Stereotype threat and women's math performance. *Journal of Experimental Social Psychology* 35:4–28.

Steele, Claude M. 1997. A threat in the air: How stereotypes shape intellectual identity and performance. *American Psychologist* 52:613–29.

Steele, Claude M., and Joshua Aronson. 1995. Stereotype threat and the intellectual test performance of African Americans. *Journal of Personality and Social Psychology* 69:797–811.

Sue, Derald Wing. 2010. *Microaggressions in everyday life: Race, gender, and sexual orientation*. New York: Wiley.

———. 2011. Microaggressions in everyday life: Race, gender, and sexual orientation. Workshop presented at the National Multicultural Conference and Summit, Seattle, Washington, 26 January.

Sue, Derald Wing, Christina M. Capodilupo, Gina C. Torino, Jennifer M. Bucceri, Aisha M. B. Holder, Kevin L. Nadal, and Marta Esquilin. 2007. Racial microaggressions in everyday life. *American Psychologist* 62:271–86.

Sue, Derald Wing, Gina C. Torino, Christina M. Capodilupo, David P. Rivera, and Annie I. Lin. 2009. How white faculty perceive and react to difficult dialogues on race: Implications for education and training. *Counseling Psychologist* 37:1090–115.

Thompson, Chalmer E., and Helen A. Neville. 1999. Racism, mental health, and mental health practice. *Counseling Psychologist* 27:155–223.

Utsey, Shawn O., and Carol A. Gernat. 2002. White racial identity attitudes and the ego defense mechanisms used by white counselor trainees in racially provocative counseling situations. *Journal of Counseling and Development* 80:475–83.

Wolf, Naomi. 1995. The racism of well-meaning white people. In *Skin deep: Black and white women write about race*, ed. Marita Golden and Susan R. Shreve, 37–46. New York: Doubleday.

Zetzer, Heidi A. 2011. White out: Privilege and its problems. In *Explorations in diversity: Examining privilege and oppression in a multicultural society*, 2nd ed., ed. Sharon K. Anderson and Valerie A. Middleton, 11–24. Belmont, Calif.: Brooks/Cole.

9

The Costs of Privilege and Dividends of Privilege Awareness: The Social Psychology of Confronting Inequality

Tracie L. Stewart and Nyla R. Branscombe

A crucial aspect of privilege for many white Americans is blindness to the institutionalized racial biases that benefit them on a daily basis. As white Americans ourselves, we, the authors of this chapter, well remember our first experiences with confronting our group-based privileges and the subsequent, often painful, ever enlightening process of realizing our group's role in perpetuating inequality and our own responsibility to work toward reducing this inequality. One purpose of many diversity-training exercises is to remove privilege "blinders" such as these and to ensure that white Americans become aware of racial inequality (Dovidio et al. 2004; Stewart et al. 2003; Tatum 1997). Historical inequality in the distribution of resources across members of different racial groups means that disparities in education (Vaught 2009), health care (Orsi, Margellos-Anast, and Whitman 2010), and the legal system (Pewewardy and Severson 2003) will continue in the future even if "equal opportunity" policies and practices are fully enacted in the present. As we, the authors, came to realize through our own racial identity development, ignoring this history means that its legacy continues. Therefore, making people aware of such historical inequality may be critical for eliciting support for social change and reducing prejudice in the present.

We contend that if heightened awareness of white privilege is to be effective in improving intergroup attitudes and actions, whites must feel collective guilt—remorse following the recognition that one's group has illegitimately

harmed another group and has not repaired the damage (Branscombe, Doosje, and McGarty 2002; Halley, Eshleman, and Vijaya 2011). In recent years, considerable research has been directed toward understanding the antecedents and consequences of experiencing "white guilt," a term representing race-based collective guilt (Swim and Miller 1999). Although the term "white guilt" is sometimes used disparagingly, some see collective guilt stemming from one's group's historical racial injustices and the ways in which whites continue to benefit from illegitimate race-based advantages as an appropriate and useful emotional response.

However, as we ourselves have experienced, multiple barriers exist both to whites' acknowledgment of white privilege and to their acceptance of feelings of collective guilt about their illegitimate advantages. But when these barriers are overcome, there is mounting evidence that introducing whites to the costs of their privilege may pay substantial dividends in reducing prejudice and increasing antidiscrimination action (Branscombe 2004). In this chapter, we consider psychological research on factors that impede whites' acknowledgment of white privilege and their associated feelings of collective guilt. We then highlight recent research that has shown that if these barriers are overcome, substantial improvements in intergroup attitudes and actions are possible.

Barriers to the Awareness of White Privilege

White Americans, including the present authors, are conditioned well not to see the systems that confer illegitimate advantages on them. Instead, as whites, we are raised to believe that our society allows anyone to accomplish whatever he or she wants, if the person just works hard enough. Consequently, whites are often unaware of the many ways in which our social institutions privilege some groups while illegitimately disadvantaging others. Of course, we are reminded from time to time to help others who are less privileged. But that reminder tends to place the focus on the ways in which some individuals and groups in our society have been underprivileged, rather than on the ways in which whites are overprivileged. This is a crucial difference. Considering how to help others who have not capitalized on the promise of our "great society," and on our generosity in helping them, can easily lead us to question why *they* are disadvantaged, rather than to the goal of how to correct the biased systems that illegitimately perpetuate the status quo in favor of the privileged. Accounting for inequality in terms of "our privilege" puts us,

as white Americans, in the equation, whereas accounting for inequality in terms of "their disadvantage" undercuts any perceived role of the privileged in the perpetuation of inequality (see Powell, Branscombe, and Schmitt 2005).

In her classic paper, Peggy McIntosh (1988) outlines a few of the invisible advantages that whites experience on the basis of their skin color. In an attempt to make the invisible visible, she directs our attention to the advantages held by whites, such as being able to give a presentation to a powerful group without putting one's race on trial, being relatively confident that one will not be treated with suspicion when shopping, and easily finding dolls and picture books for their children that feature people of their own racial group. These advantages generally go unseen by whites. Whites assume that their experiences are normative. Similarly, we as whites tend to see ourselves as simply being "normal," rather than as having any particular racial identity (Helms 1992; Tatum 1997).

If one challenge to white privilege awareness is the invisible nature of many white privileges, can the problem be solved simply by making these privileges more visible? It turns out that this is easier said than done. To varying degrees, we, as whites, are motivated to maintain a positive sense of ourselves and our group, and acknowledging the existence of white privilege threatens that goal (Branscombe, Schmitt, and Schiffhauer 2007; Unzueta and Lowery 2008). Sharp resistance may arise to attempts to get white Americans to face and accept the reality of their privileges. Accepting that reality means that whites can no longer see themselves as normative or the social standard, which is an unsettling and distressing feeling to many of us. And whites tend not to feel terribly comfortable with being told that they are experiencing privileges based on their group membership, that their accomplishments may not be due exclusively to their own merit, and that other groups face disadvantages as a result of the privileges whites carry around with them. White Americans with a strong racial identification may be particularly resistant to such awareness of the privileges associated with their race (Branscombe, Schmitt, and Schiffhauer 2007). If we have a strong identification with being white, we have more to lose by acknowledging that the accomplishments of whites are the result of group privileges rather than simply of individual efforts. Thus the acknowledgment of white privilege is particularly threatening to individuals high in white identification, and their resistance is likely to be greater.

For those teachers and diversity trainers who nonetheless take on the challenge of helping whites become aware of their social privileges, research has

found that the response of white participants tends to be one not of gratitude but of defensiveness, resentment, and other negative emotions (Case 2007). For junior professors, this negative response is not inconsequential, given that student evaluations may play an important role in the assessment of their work. It is thus reasonable to ask whether the outcome is worth the effort and the costs of teaching white students to be aware of their privilege. As we discuss below, the answer seems to be that the benefits of such training can be considerable. But the key to transforming whites' awareness of in-group privileges into more positive intergroup attitudes and engagement in concrete antiracism actions lies in ensuring that we, as whites, take on a feeling of collective guilt for our group privileges. However, people have plenty of defenses against collective guilt, so this project is inherently challenging.

Barriers to Collective Guilt

Recent research suggests that collective guilt is a critical ingredient in the effectiveness of white privilege awareness in reducing intergroup biases (Powell, Branscombe, and Schmitt 2005; Stewart et al. 2010). But there are barriers to eliciting collective guilt in paradigms aimed at introducing whites to their illegitimate advantages. For one thing, whether through diversity training or other life experiences, white Americans who become aware of racial inequalities often find this awareness quite distressing (Helms 1990; Tatum 1997). Thus, for whites, defensive mechanisms aimed at protecting our positive sense of our group may automatically kick in when we are confronted with our group privileges. One important strategy for defending against feelings of collective guilt is to minimize the perceived harm that white people have done to nonwhites (Miron, Branscombe, and Biernat 2010), which is especially likely among highly identified white Americans. Other defensive reactions are likely among whites for whom identification with their racial group is a strong component of their identity (Branscombe, Schmitt, and Schiffhauer 2007).

Such persons may attempt to distance themselves from the actions of the larger group. By emphasizing their individuality and lack of personal responsibility, they are able to experience less culpability for the harm done. Distancing oneself and one's immediate family—for example, by proclaiming that one's family has no known history of perpetuating slavery (Ansell and Statman 1999)—can minimize collective guilt. Either of these related responses

can serve the function of protecting self-esteem; reminders that one (and one's family) had no hand in creating the biased and unequal system can absolve one of responsibility for correcting it. Denying our role in the perpetuation of racial inequality allows whites to sidestep feelings of collective guilt (Branscombe, Slugoski, and Kappen 2004; Mallett and Swim 2007).

Another self-protective response to being made aware of white privilege is our attempt, as whites, to legitimize existing inequality. Whites may acknowledge that, yes, race-based inequality exists, but then rationalize that whites are not actually responsible for it. The myth of American meritocracy allows us to argue that our group may not be responsible for the privileges that benefit us and disadvantage others. Explicitly or implicitly, we may construct a legitimizing argument that if members of other groups would simply work harder, or be more responsible, or otherwise embody the Protestant work ethic, then this inequality would not exist. To the extent that inequality can be seen as legitimate, collective guilt can again be averted (Miron, Branscombe, and Schmitt 2006). Indeed, research has found that in order to experience collective guilt, members of the dominant group must recognize their group's privileges, feel somewhat responsible for this inequality, and perceive the inequality as unjustifiable (Branscombe 2004; Mallet and Swim 2007). For example, a high-ranking white male executive would need to acknowledge that his success stems in part from career networks to which he has access through his membership in social clubs that have historically been exclusive to whites and that continue to be majority-white and to be uncomfortable affiliations for members of other racial groups.

In addition, institutional authorities may discourage individuals in dominant groups from feeling collective guilt. Consider President Ronald Reagan's urging that Americans move beyond guilt concerning issues of race and return to the "good old days" of the 1930s, when, in Reagan's view, there was greater racial harmony (Jones 1997, 103). Similarly, consider former Australian Prime Minister John Howard's instruction to Australian citizens that white guilt is an unhelpful and unnecessary emotion (Augoustinos and LeCouteur 2004). Such dismissals of collective guilt make it easier for citizens to deny collective guilt, and put obstacles in the way of reparations aimed at remediating continuing inequality. The position of authorities like Reagan and Howard is understandable given that institutions naturally attempt to protect themselves, to maintain the status quo. And such feel-good messages are likely to be well received. When given the choice to feel good or bad about one's group, most people opt for the positive social identity. But recent research suggests that feel-good messages are not likely to

facilitate improved intergroup attitudes or to encourage support or action for alleviating racial inequality (Stewart et al. 2010; Stewart et al. 2012). Another impediment to eliciting collective guilt through heightening white people's awareness of white privilege is the feeling that working to reduce racial inequality will require a tremendous amount of effort, and even then may fail. Brehm's (1999) theory of emotional intensity holds that factors that impede the function or goal of an emotion can act as deterrents to feeling that emotion, as well as to engaging in actions consistent with the goals of that emotion. In other words, if it is difficult or impossible for me to reduce racial inequality, then I'm not going to feel guilty, because there's nothing I can do about it.

Consistent with this theory is the finding of Schmitt et al. (2008) that white American men who believed that their actions could reduce gender inequality, but that the necessary efforts to do so were particularly burdensome, did not feel significant levels of collective guilt. In this case, the perception that the actions necessary to reduce inequality were inordinately taxing acted as a deterrent to the feeling of collective guilt (i.e., "you're asking too much of me, so I'm not going to feel bad about gender inequality"). Another recent study examined the effects of the belief that one's efforts, however great, would fail to alleviate racial inequality (Stewart et al. 2010). Consistent with Brehm's theory, the researchers found that this belief acted as a deterrent to feeling collective guilt. It seems fair to conclude that privileged individuals will feel collective guilt about their unearned advantages only if they believe that they can reduce this guilt through actions that do not seem overly daunting and are perceived as likely to be effective. The absence of either of these conditions can undermine feelings of guilt.

Dividends of Privilege Awareness and Associated Collective Guilt

In an evaluation of a popular diversity-training exercise, members of the majority group made to experience the ways in which their group is privileged through participation in a prejudice simulation reported heightened negative self-directed affect concerning their group's advantages (Stewart et al. 2003). Given the numerous diversity-training approaches involving positive messages that are available, is a prejudice-reduction approach aimed at confronting whites about their illegitimate privileges in our society, and inducing guilt about these privileges, really a useful strategy? With so many "feel-good" approaches out there, do we really need this focus on the negative?

A decade of social psychological research suggests that the answer to this question quite clearly is "yes." Confronting white Americans with their illegitimate advantages and inducing collective guilt about these advantages is a powerful means of achieving both reduced prejudice and increased antidiscrimination actions by members of the majority group on behalf of disadvantaged out-groups. As noted above, one privilege held by many white Americans is blindness to the institutionalized racial biases that confer benefits on a daily basis. Interventions aimed at removing the blinders have been quite effective in reducing racial prejudice by eliciting feelings of collective guilt. For example, in two studies by Powell, Branscombe, and Schmitt (2005), participants were presented with statements about racial inequality framed as either white privileges or black disadvantages. The authors found that heightening awareness of in-group advantages, as opposed to out-group disadvantages, facilitated lower prejudice toward disadvantaged out-group members. And this prejudice reduction was mediated by greater collective guilt in participants who focused on white privileges.

In addition, a growing body of research has demonstrated the importance of pairing heightened awareness of white privilege with perceived efficacy in reducing inequality in order to improve both interracial attitudes and antidiscrimination activism (Stewart et al. 2010; Stewart et al. 2012). We (Stewart et al. 2010) examined the effects of increasing white American college students' awareness of their illegitimate advantages, relative to their African American peers, on their attitudes toward African Americans and their willingness to engage in actions aimed at reducing racial discrimination. We presented them with facts about the underrepresentation of African American faculty at their university and the social and educational impact on African American students of this lack of African American role models and mentors. In order to communicate that this underrepresentation (common at many American universities) was unjust, we added a fictional statement adducing evidence that this underrepresentation was a result of discrimination. One group of white students was told that their efforts to increase the representation of African American faculty on campus were highly likely to succeed; another group was told that their efforts were highly unlikely to succeed.

White students in the first group later reported more positive attitudes toward African Americans and engaged in more antidiscrimination actions than white students in the second group. Specifically, they took a greater number of flyers to post on campus lobbying for the hiring of more African American faculty. There was thus a direct positive effect of efficacy on participants'

intergroup attitudes and actions. However, the effects of efficacy on these outcomes were also mediated in part by greater collective guilt in the first group of students. Consistent with Brehm's (1999) model, participants who felt that their actions were unlikely to be effective in reducing inequality rejected feelings of collective guilt, given their belief that this guilt could not readily be alleviated by reforming the biased system. In other studies, we (Stewart et al. 2012) examined whether higher efficacy beliefs were essential to obtaining effects of white privilege awareness on racial attitudes. Our findings suggested that the effects of white privilege awareness and subjects' belief in the efficacy of their efforts to reduce inequality were cumulative. In other words, we obtained stronger positive effects when the independent effects of efficacy and privilege awareness were combined. Notably, we found that the effects of efficacy beliefs on prejudice reduction were not limited to participants lower in white identification. Heightened awareness of white privilege, paired with a belief in efficacy in reducing inequality, reduced prejudice equally for participants, regardless of how strongly they identified themselves as whites.

Thus a number of studies show positive benefits of heightened white privilege awareness on prejudice reduction and increased antidiscrimination action. Furthermore, research has found that beliefs concerning efficacy in reducing inequality can bolster these effects. Consequently, there is evidence that diversity-training exercises can produce positive change in participants. When we make people aware of the inequality from which they benefit, but also help them understand that they can do something to reduce this inequality, they are more likely to take part in efforts for change. It is also notable, however, and perhaps somewhat ironic, that making people feel *better* about what they can accomplish makes them feel *worse*—greater collective guilt— about existing inequality. But this unpleasant feeling of guilt turns out to be a good thing for bias reduction and collective action on behalf of disadvantaged groups.

Conclusion

Does the elicitation of collective guilt in white Americans about our illegitimate advantages have a place in the design of effective diversity-training initiatives? Certainly, there are less potentially aversive approaches to diversity training that do not involve confronting white Americans with our race-based privileges and the associated disadvantages faced by members of other racial groups. Although feel-good approaches to racial reconciliation have

intuitive appeal, a growing number of social psychology studies suggest that diversity training that skirts the uncomfortable issue (for whites) of white privilege is missing out on a powerful tool for social change.

The social costs of continuing white privilege are considerable. Disparities persist in areas ranging from health care, to education, to housing and beyond, disparities that mean that many U.S. citizens never have the opportunity to realize potential social contributions. However, it is becoming increasingly clear that heightened awareness of this privilege creates subversive possibilities for change in both intergroup attitudes and social action (Powell, Branscombe, and Schmitt 2005; Stewart et al. 2010; Stewart et al. 2012; Tatum 1997). Educating white Americans about their illegitimate race-based privileges and pointing toward constructive strategies to reduce racial inequality often prompt feelings of collective guilt. And this negative affective state leads to quite positive outcomes, including improved attitudes toward members of other racial groups and greater engagement in antidiscrimination action. For the goal of reducing white Americans' racial prejudice and combatting racial inequality, a growing body of research suggests, simply and clearly, that guilt is good.

References

Ansell, Amy, and James Statman. 1999. I never owned slaves. In *The global color line: Racial and ethnic inequality and struggle from a global perspective*, ed. Pinar Batur-Vanderlippe and Joe Feagin, 151–73. New York: Emerald Group.

Augoustinos, Martha, and Amanda LeCouteur. 2004. On whether to apologize to indigenous Australians: The denial of white guilt. In *Collective guilt: International perspectives*, ed. Nyla R. Branscombe and Bertjan Doosje, 236–61. New York: Cambridge University Press.

Bandura, Albert. 1997. *Self-efficacy: The exercise of control*. New York: Cambridge University Press.

———. 2006. Toward a psychology of human agency. *Perspectives on Psychological Science* 1:164–80.

Branscombe, Nyla R. 2004. A social psychological process perspective on collective guilt. In *Collective guilt: International perspectives*, ed. Nyla R. Branscombe and Bertjan Doosje, 320–34. New York: Cambridge University Press.

Branscombe, Nyla R., Bertjan Doosje, and Craig McGarty. 2002. Antecedents and consequences of collective guilt. In *From prejudice to intergroup emotions: Differentiated reactions to social groups*, ed. Diane M. Mackie and Eliot R. Smith, 49–66. Philadelphia: Psychology Press.

Branscombe, Nyla R., Michael T. Schmitt, and Kristin Schiffhauer. 2007. Racial attitudes in response to thoughts of white privilege. *European Journal of Social Psychology* 37:203–15.

Branscombe, Nyla R., Ben Slugoski, and Diane M. Kappen. 2004. The measurement of collective guilt: What it is and what it is not. In *Collective guilt: International perspectives*, ed. Nyla R. Branscombe and Bertjan Doosje, 16–34. New York: Cambridge University Press.

Brehm, Jack W. 1999. The intensity of emotion. *Personality and Social Psychology Review* 3:2–22.

Case, Kim A. 2007. Raising white privilege awareness and reducing racial prejudice: Assessing diversity course effectiveness. *Teaching of Psychology* 34:231–35.

Dovidio, John F., Samuel L. Gaertner, Tracie L. Stewart, Victoria M. Esses, Marleen ten Vergert, and Gordon Hodson. 2004. From intervention to outcome: Processes in the reduction of bias. In *Education programs for improving intergroup relations: Theory, research, and practice*, ed. Walter G. Stephan and W. Paul Vogt, 243–65. New York: Teachers College Press.

Halley, Jean, Amy Eshleman, and Ramya M. Vijaya. 2011. *Seeing white: An introduction to white privilege and race*. Lanham, Md.: Rowman and Littlefield.

Helms, Janet E. 1990. *Black and white racial identity: Theory, research, and practice*. New York: Greenwood Press.

———. 1992. *A race is a nice thing to have: A guide to being a white person or understanding the white persons in your life*. Topeka, Kans.: Content Communications.

Jones, James M. 1997. *Prejudice and racism*. New York: McGraw-Hill.

Mallett, Robyn K., and Janet K. Swim. 2007. The influence of inequality, responsibility, and justifiability on reports of group-based guilt for ingroup privilege. *Group Processes and Intergroup Relations* 10:57–69.

McIntosh, Peggy. 1988. White privilege and male privilege: A personal account of coming to see correspondences through work in women's studies. Working Paper no. 189. Wellesley College, Wellesley Centers for Women.

Miron, Anca M., Nyla R. Branscombe, and Monica Biernat. 2010. Motivated shifting of justice standards. *Personality and Social Psychology Bulletin* 36:768–79.

Miron, Anca M., Nyla R. Branscombe, and Michael T. Schmitt. 2006. Collective guilt as distress over illegitimate intergroup inequality. *Group Processes and Intergroup Relations* 9:163–80.

Orsi, Jennifer M., Helen Margellos-Anast, and Steven Whitman. 2010. Black-white health disparities in the United States and Chicago: A 15-year progress analysis. *American Journal of Public Health* 100:349–56.

Peters, William. 1987. *A class divided: Then and now*. New Haven: Yale University Press.

Pewewardy, Nocona, and Margaret Severson. 2003. A threat to liberty: White privilege and disproportionate minority incarceration. *Journal of Progressive Human Services* 14, no. 2: 53–74.

Powell, Adam A., Nyla R. Branscombe, and Michael T. Schmitt. 2005. Inequality as ingroup privilege or outgroup disadvantage: The impact of group focus on collective guilt and interracial attitudes. *Personality and Social Psychology Bulletin* 31:508–21.

Schmitt, Michael T., Daniel A. Miller, Nyla R. Branscombe, and Jack W. Brehm. 2008. The difficulty of making reparations affects the intensity of collective guilt. *Group Processes and Intergroup Relations* 11:267–79.

Stewart, Tracie L., Jacqueline R. La Duke, Charlotte Bracht, Brooke A. M. Sweet, and Kristine E. Gamarel. 2003. Do the "eyes" have it? A program evaluation of Jane Elliott's "blue eyes/brown eyes" diversity training exercise. *Journal of Applied Social Psychology* 33:1898–921.

Stewart, Tracie L., Ioana M. Latu, Nyla R. Branscombe, and H. Ted Denney. 2010. Yes we can! Prejudice reduction through seeing (inequality) and believing (in social change). *Psychological Science* 21:1557–62.

Stewart, Tracie L., Ioana M. Latu, Nyla R. Branscombe, Nia L. Phillips, and H. Ted Denney. 2012. White privilege awareness and efficacy to reduce racial inequality improve white Americans' attitudes toward African Americans. *Journal of Social Issues* 68, no. 1: 11–27.

Swim, Janet K., and Deborah L. Miller. 1999. White guilt: Its antecedents and consequences for attitudes toward affirmative action. *Personality and Social Psychology Bulletin* 25:500–514.

Tatum, Beverly D. 1997. *Why are all the black kids sitting together in the cafeteria? And other conversations about race.* New York: Basic Books.

Unzueta, Miguel M., and Brian S. Lowery. 2008. Defining racism safely: The role of self-image maintenance on white Americans' conceptions of racism. *Journal of Experimental Social Psychology* 44:1491–97.

Vaught, Sabina. 2009. The color of money: School funding and the commodification of black children. *Urban Education* 44:545–70.

10

Unpacking the Imperialist Knapsack:
White Privilege and Imperialism in Obama's America

Eduardo Bonilla-Silva, Louise Seamster, and Victor Ray

"But what on earth is whiteness that one should so desire it?" Then always . . . silently but clearly, I am given to understand that whiteness is the ownership of the earth forever and ever, Amen!
—Du Bois 1920, 29

For many commentators and far too many Americans, the election of a black man as the forty-fourth president of the United States of America is prima facie evidence that racism is over.[1] Accordingly, too many people believe that notions such as racial domination, white supremacy, and white privilege have lost their analytical purchase. Banner headlines heralded Obama's election as breaking a final symbolic barrier (Nagourney 2008). This symbolism has real effects, and in the looking-glass world of white racial politics, whites now see themselves as an oppressed minority despite empirical evidence to the contrary (Norton and Sommers 2011). We argue that the collective hallucination surrounding the meaning of Obama's election for racial politics in the United States should end. Obama's election represents neither a sea change in the racial order nor a break with historical patterns of U.S. imperialism. In many ways, Obama's blackness is "the best possible shell" for the smooth operation of the American political regime.[2]

From its inception, the United States of America has been an "empire state" whose "racial formation" (Omi and Winant 1994) was welded to expansionist practices—first across the continent through manifest destiny, and

then through extraterritorial colonization (Jung 2011). Historically, the spoils of the American empire have been distributed along racial lines. The United States' enslavement and subjugation of blacks, its genocidal policies toward Native Americans (Smith 2005), its seizure of Mexican lands (Montejano 1987), the Japanese internment during World War II, and the continued curtailing of options and opportunities for Americans of color have all fed white coffers (Feagin 2000; Oliver and Shapiro 2006; Marable [1983] 2000). Racialized concerns have been central to U.S. foreign policy in keeping our guns trained on the "wretched of the earth" (Fanon 1968), as imperialist projects serving U.S. interests extract resources from nonwhite countries. Although scholars of whiteness studies have amply demonstrated the benefits accruing to whites in the domestic sphere (Roediger 1991; Brodkin 1996), left unexplained are the ways in which America's foreign agenda—as a global racialized practice—is shaped and justified through racialized concerns (Lutz 2006).

Obama's election—cathartic as it may have seemed—has not transcended this globally racialized system. Obama's rise is the culmination of nearly forty years of racial restructuring, wherein both political parties have promoted nonwhites to work in the trenches of empire (Bonilla-Silva 2013; Bonilla-Silva and Seamster 2011). We will show how this partial success—a push for inclusion in the system, rather than the transformation of that system—has created a situation where some people of color, according to Angela Davis, have become incorporated into the "machinery of oppression" (Davis 2005, 29). We argue that Obama represents the pinnacle of this incorporation.

By analyzing Obama's imperial presidency as a manifestation of white supremacy, we also seek to enlarge the concept of white privilege. In McIntosh's (1989) important early formulation, the concept of white privilege was tied to a number of personal advantages. However, by focusing on individual advantages, even antiracist whites aware of their privilege may miss the historical and current imperial projects tied to white supremacy. For many, acknowledgment of privilege has become its own rationale, detached from goals of social justice (Golash-Boza 2013a). Andrea Smith recently noted that "as the rituals of confessing privilege have evolved in academic and activist circles, they have shifted our focus from building social movements for global transformation to individual self-improvement" (Smith 2012, 278). This is still true of the field of whiteness studies today: Andersen (2003) notes astutely that some scholars of whiteness, while claiming to be writing about privilege, tend to elide institutional power from the discussion, so that "all of the mechanisms and sites of racial domination and subordination disappear

from view." In order to maintain its explanatory power, we must bring the idea of white privilege into a cogent analysis of our racialized social system (Bonilla-Silva 1997), reconceptualizing white privilege to encompass the themes of war, globalization, neoliberalism, immigration—some of the pressing racial issues of our day.

As Marx famously noted, history tends to repeat itself, "the first time as tragedy, the second time as farce" (Marx [1852] 1978, 594). The tragedy, as W. E. B. Du Bois pointed out in his early treatise on white privilege, "The Souls of White Folk," was the colossal damage wrought by European and American imperialism. The farce is the present enactment of neoimperialism partially carried out by nonwhite leaders, still in the ultimate service of white supremacy. And as in the first iteration, where the damage was done in the name of benefiting the world's nonwhite peoples, our own invasions, governmental interventions, and structural adjustment strategies are conducted in the name of helping what Du Bois called the "Darker Peoples." The difference, of course, is that white privilege can now be advanced through a "black mask" (Fanon 1967). To show this, we first outline how the structural transition from Jim Crow to the "new racism" created the conditions of possibility for the election of a black president while simultaneously curtailing the progressive thrust of any candidate. Second, we briefly review some of Obama's foreign and domestic policies to show how they continue to disproportionately target nonwhites for the benefit of white people. We end with an analysis of the implications of this farce for the continuity of white privilege, as well as resistance against it.

Hoping for Incorporation: The Historical Construction of Postracial Politics

The Obama phenomenon is the product of the fundamental racial transformation that transpired in America in the 1960s and 1970s. Unlike Jim Crow, the new racial order that emerged—the "new racism"—reproduces racial domination mostly through subtle and covert discriminatory practices that are often institutionalized, defended with coded language ("*those* urban people" or "*those* people on welfare"), and bonded by the racial ideology of color-blind racism (for a full discussion of the "new racism," see Bonilla-Silva 2013, chap. 4; cf. Smith 1995). Compared to Jim Crow, this new system seems genteel, but it is extremely effective in preserving systemic advantages for whites and keeping people of color at bay. The new regime is, in the immor-

tal lyrics of Roberta Flack's song, of the "killing-me-softly" variety. This new regime came about as the result of various social forces and events that converged in the post–World War II era, particularly as people of color led the twentieth century's battles against racism and its twin, economic inequality (Winant 2001). The most visible positive consequences of this process are well known: the slow and incomplete school desegregation that followed the 1954 Supreme Court decision in *Brown v. Board of Education*; the enactment of the Civil Rights Act of 1964, the Voting Rights Act of 1965, and the Housing Rights Act of 1968; and the haphazard political process that brought affirmative action into life. Perhaps most strikingly, however, the victories of people of color in the United States have in some cases incorporated nonwhites into the machinery of racial oppression. In fact, as Charles Payne (2007) points out, once movement radicals have pushed to change a racial system, the system is likely to make accommodations by extending opportunities to people less likely to rock the boat. This is exactly what has happened with the current generation of crossover black politicians.

Obama's rise is perhaps one of the best examples of this historic shift, but the structural shift is apparent in the racial politics of both U.S. political parties. In the post–civil rights era, as a number of scholars have pointed out (Bonilla-Silva 2013; Bobo, Kluegel, and Smith 1997; Dovidio 2001), overt racism has been largely discredited. The delegitimization of openly racist practices, however, has not stopped either party from adjusting to the new racial order. For the past forty years, the Right's so-called southern strategy has actively courted whites who feel that their privileges are being eclipsed by people of color. This ideological shift in tactics is perhaps best captured in the words of Reagan advisor Lee Atwater, who claimed that the Republicans "start[ed] out in 1954 by saying, 'Nigger, nigger, nigger,' [but] by 1968, you can't say 'nigger'—that hurts you. . . . So you say stuff like forced busing, states' rights, and all that stuff . . . blacks get hurt worse than whites" (Herbert 2007).

Instead, the Right actively cultivated a "color-blind" rhetoric that in practice was clearly meant to undermine and reverse racial progress. The creation of the Tea Party and manufactured furor over the Affordable Care Act show this policy in practice. And despite the protests of academics who subscribe to the oxymoronic myth of "principled conservatism," strong evidence links racial animus to opposition to progressive policy (Tesler and Sears 2010; DeSante 2011). The color-blind backlash also benefited from what Adolph Reed calls "anti-affirmative action, affirmative action appointments" (2001, 121) such as Supreme Court Justice Clarence Thomas. Obama himself

questioned the continued importance of affirmative action and touts so-called universal policies, avoiding engagement with policies that disproportionately affect blacks (Kuhn 2008). This policy shift on race issues created a situation where the Bush cabinet was among the most diverse in U.S. history—all the while pursuing a brutal foreign and domestic agenda.

The Left also adopted a color-blind approach to campaigning and governance. Today's electorally oriented minority politician (1) is not the product of social movements, (2) usually joins the party of choice while in college, (3) moves up quickly through the party ranks, and, most significantly, (4) is not a race rebel. The new breed of minority politicians, unlike their predecessors, are not radicals talking about "the revolution" and "uprooting systemic racism." Obama's 2008 campaign and his postelection strategy fell clearly within the lines of the current dominant racial ideology. Obama's first campaign did not directly address race until the manufactured furor over the comments of Reverend Wright forced his hand. Even then, Obama's "race speech" refused to address black grievances directly and equivocated about the historical and current magnitude of racial inequality (for a full discussion of Obama's strategic postracial appeals, see Bonilla-Silva 2013). Since then, Obama has been mostly reticent on issues of race, addressing racial issues only when forced.

Post–civil rights minority politicians like Obama are not truly about deep change but about compromise. If they were truly about fundamental change and frontal challenges to the American social order, they would not be the darlings of the two mainstream parties. Although some post–civil rights minority politicians may, from time to time, "talk the talk," their talk is rather abstract, almost to the point of being meaningless, and they seldom if ever "walk the walk." For instance, Obama talked during the campaign about corporate lobbyists but said nothing about *corporate power*; complained about "big money" in politics yet raised more money than *any* politician in American history; subscribed to the Republican lie about a crisis in Social Security and is likely to follow through with policies to "save" a program that is actually solvent;[3] and talked about alternative energy sources and clean energy yet was in bed with folks in the "clean coal" and "safe nuclear energy" camp (see Street 2009, chap. 1).

Despite the fact that Obama's presidency has not heralded a postracial society, contemporary (white) common-sense thinking dismisses an analysis grounded in racial inequality and calling for racial redress as outdated. America has a black president, goes the argument, and we are closer than ever to achieving our nation's promise of equality. How can the United States

still be enacting the logic of white supremacy if our leader is not white? But several facts militate against the reasoning that Obama's election means that we have overcome. First, the empirical evidence since 2008 refutes the idea that Obama's election represents a sea change in white racial opinion (Hutchings 2009; Pettigrew 2009; Tesler and Sears 2010; Parks and Hughey 2011; Ross and Agiesta 2012; Richomme 2012). In fact, some anti-egalitarian whites may have voted for Obama simply to *demonstrate* that racism is over (Knowles, Lowery, and Schaumberg 2009). And despite the claims of some that Obama's campaign was a larger movement for progressive goals, protest movements against the imperial wars in Iraq and Afghanistan collapsed after the election (Heaney and Rojas 2011), implying that Democratic imperialism is acceptable.

Second, shortly after the 2008 election, Dylan Rodríguez astutely connected Obama's rise to the emergence of a "multicultural white supremacy" (2009). Beginning with Hall's (1980) assertion that racism needs to be analyzed in its historically specific articulations, Rodríguez argues that Obama represents the symbolic incorporation of nonwhites into a multiracial regime in which white power remains at the core. Significantly, as Rodríguez notes, this has occurred because traditional white supremacy is no longer viable in today's society. We now recognize the first iteration of Western imperialism as a "tragedy," in the Marxist sense, so a blatant recuperation of these politics would be actively resisted. Instead, Rodríguez writes,

> The signature of the "post-civil rights" period is precisely marked by such changes—compulsory and voluntary—in the comportment, culture, and workforce of white supremacist institutions: selective elements of police and military forces, global corporations, and major research universities are diversely colored, while their marching orders continue to mobilize the familiar labors of death-making (arrest and justifiable homicide, fatal peacekeeping, overfunded weapons research, etc.). While the phenotype of white supremacy changes—and change it must, if it is to remain viable under changed historical conditions— its internal coherence as a socialized logic of violence and dominance is sustained and redeemed. (Rodríguez 2008)

This incorporation is not simply tied to domestic policies but is part of the larger historical pattern of racialized imperialism (Mills 1997). For the first time in history, through their collective silence, people of color have become incorporated into the empire. This is unfortunate, as blacks and other people

of color led anti-imperialist efforts in the past (Carmichael 2005). Indeed, as we demonstrate in the next section, Obama's policies represent a historical continuation with the American imperialist tradition.

The Audacity of War Crimes: Foreign Policy Since 2008

So far, we have established that, far from dismantling racism, Obama's election served to prop up white supremacy in the post–civil rights era. But we also wish to emphasize the ways in which Obama's actions have maintained white supremacy through imperialist interventions abroad and racial repression at home. In short, his presidency represents continuity not only with the previous administration but with decades of interventionist, imperialist American presidencies that have always served to promote white power.[4] As Tariq Ali noted in 2010, the Left's mistake was to assume that George W. Bush's foreign policy was aberrant, while Obama represented America's "true face—purposeful but peaceful, firm but generous, humane, respectful, multi-cultural" (Ali 2010, 99). But Obama is an imperialist statesman. Before his election, drunk on his "hope liquor" (Bonilla-Silva 2013), many relied on his vote against the Iraq War as a badge of anti-imperialism rather than focusing on his promise to escalate the war in Afghanistan. After five years of his presidency, the predator drones and bombs have destroyed Obama's antiwar street cred. As Ali wrote, "There was no fundamental break in foreign policy, as opposed to diplomatic mood music, between the Bush 1, Clinton, and Bush 2 Administrations; there has been none between the Bush and Obama regimes. The strategic goals and imperatives of the US imperium remain the same, as do its principal theatres and means of operation" (ibid.). This is only clearer several years further into Obama's presidency.

Despite the Nobel Peace Prize and campaign promises, Obama has left many of Bush's worst policies in place and has openly defended a large number of them. For instance, Obama has continued the euphemistically named "extraordinary rendition" program, which consists of kidnapping third-country nationals and flying them to countries that are known to engage in torture (Mayer 2009; Alterman 2011). He has also been reluctant to prosecute known torturers within the CIA, putting him at odds with Eric Holder (Johnston 2009).

Obama has also reversed course on shutting down the United States' local torture camp at Guantánamo Bay. Despite a campaign promise to close this abscess on the U.S. body politic, Obama reopened military tribunals for Guan-

tánamo detainees in 2011; the camp is still open in 2014 and Obama has reversed course, saying that the notorious prison will remain open and military tribunals can continue (Shane and Lander 2011). This is despite the history of torture there and the many innocents who continue to be wrongly held (Mayer 2009). As if Orwell and Kafka got together to design the prison and its rationalization, the very contravention of international law and the nebulous legal status afforded the prisoners when they were captured now serve to justify their indefinite detention. At the end of 2013, the military quietly cut back information flows from Guantánamo, including statistics on the dire state of hunger strikers (Rosenberg 2014). Meanwhile, Americans are still holding (and, according to detainee and Afghan official testimony, torturing) at least sixty prisoners under indefinite detention in Afghanistan's Bagram prison, with no plans to close down after December 2014 (Hanly 2013). This treatment contrasts sharply with the treatment of white so-called homegrown terrorists, despite the fact that the Department of Homeland Security (2009) recognizes the threat from the white Right.

The war in Afghanistan is a disaster. Obama's embrace of Afghanistan as the "good war" has done nothing to stem the corruption of the Afghan government or U.S. contractors (Reuters 2010). The list of problems in Afghanistan is as troubling as it is long (Mitchell 2011). The military mission has killed numerous civilians, many of whose deaths have been covered up. Billions of dollars have gone unaccounted for (Leigh 2010). "Mission creep" also set in early in Obama's presidency, with the United States' alleged ally Pakistan supporting the Afghan insurgency. Adopting the expanded presidential powers and logic of a frontless "war on terror," outlined under the Bush Justice Department (Mayer 2009), Obama has expanded the scope of the war with little oversight from Congress and little pushback from the American people. His "Af-Pak" war falls in line with a long tradition of American exceptionalism. While, in 2008, the discussion was over the precise date on which we would be pulling out of Iraq and Afghanistan, the view from 2013 looks much more pessimistic. Despite the media accounts claiming that the United States will soon leave Afghanistan, there has been continued pressure on Hamid Karzai to accept a U.S. presence there for at least another ten years (Farmer 2011; Ackerman 2013).

In Afghanistan, we also first saw what has become representative policy for Obama's government: the overt and covert use of drones throughout the world, carrying out targeted strikes (with questionable accuracy—see Linebaugh 2013). Obama had conducted more predator strikes in Afghanistan by 2010 than Bush did in eight years in office (Ali 2010, 108). Obama's increased

use of drones in Afghanistan has also flowed across the porous border with Pakistan to kill numerous Pakistani civilians (Mitchell 2011; Woodward 2010; Khan 2011).[5] Borders count only for other countries, whereas the United States can kill at will—with drone strikes in Afghanistan, Algeria, Iraq, Iran, Libya, Somalia, Pakistan, and Yemen (McKay 2013). In Obama's first three years as president, he approved at least 239 covert drone strikes, compared to forty-four during Bush's administration (Rohde 2012). This is part of Obama's policy shift to relying more heavily on the CIA than on the military for his foreign incursions, moving to swift strikes rather than full-scale invasions, but with even less oversight than in Bush's wars. As part of this shift, Obama has added extrajudicial killings to the president's powers by keeping a "kill list" of alleged terrorists who are now simply killed rather than being captured and tortured, as they were under Bush (Becker and Shane 2012). In an apparent constitutional violation, drone strikes have killed at least one American child without due process (ACLU 2013). While basing guilt of "terrorism" on matrices of behavior and affiliation, Obama's administration also systematically undercounts civilian deaths from drone strikes—any male victim of a drone strike over fourteen years old is automatically counted as a "combatant" (Becker and Shane 2012). Furthermore, the United States has been building secret drone bases in various locations in Africa (Harper 2011), with surveillance drones known to be flying over Niger, Mali, Mauritania, South Sudan, and the Sahara (Schmitt 2013; *Washington Post* 2013). The United States is also apparently sending drones with bombing capacities, no longer needed in Afghanistan, to do unspecified work in the formerly *"underserved"* region of Latin America (Ackerman 2012). The surveillance and "hunter-killer" drones in Africa, Asia, the Middle East, and Central and Latin America are signs in the sky that the United States claims this space, claims the authority to watch, name, judge, and kill any other being in any country. The global unpopularity of drones, and the political blowback from their extended use, has only begun to be felt. But Obama's systematic use of drones to watch and kill whomever he chooses is an extreme example of the belief that the United States is the world's policeman. As Du Bois noted a century ago, "It is curious to see America, the United States, looking on herself, first, as a sort of natural peacemaker, then as a moral protagonist in this terrible time. No nation is less fitted for this role" (Du Bois 1920, 50).

While he has claimed credit for ending the Iraq War and winding down in Afghanistan, Obama is not hesitant about involving our troops and our bombs in numerous other conflicts—as long as U.S. interests demand it. Since 2011,

we have seen an outpouring of popular movements in the Arab Spring across the Middle East and Turkey, shaking and sometimes overthrowing the leadership in Tunisia, Egypt, Yemen, Syria, Bahrain, and Libya. Obama and his cabinet have tailored their responses to each country, depending on their relationship with the respective despot. In Egypt, for example, where Obama and Israel both relied on Egyptian support to maintain their siege of Gaza, Obama was slow to call for Mubarak to leave. When governments cracked down violently on protesters in Bahrain, Syria, and Yemen, Obama first called for calm on both sides. In Syria, the Obama administration considered arming General Idriss, commander of the opposition's Supreme Military Council, as well as military strikes (Baker et al. 2013), before eventually backing off this plan. But the moment that Qaddafi's Libyan military began to strike protesters (with American weapons), Obama's advisors advised military intervention, which African states did not condone. And the Arab League was less than thrilled with the outcome of the no-fly zone in Libya, its members claiming that they supported the prevention of civilian casualties, not the intensive bombings (Cody 2011). Notably, while the wars in Afghanistan and, to a larger extent, Iraq encountered liberal resistance (although many liberal intellectuals, including Michael Ignatieff and Peter Beinart, approved of the Iraq War for humanitarian reasons), the bombing campaign in Libya was unquestionably conceived of, supported, and implemented by liberals (Dreyfuss 2011; Cole 2011). Obama's White House may also have purposely omitted intelligence on the use of nerve gas by both sides in the conflict when he was making a humanitarian case for a military strike against Syrian leader Assad in 2013 (Hersh 2013; Giraldi 2013).

As for American interests outside the Middle East, Obama's policies fall short there, too. Adopted intact from the Bush administration, Obama's policies in Africa effectively militarize humanitarianism (Besteman 2008). The formation of "AFRICOM," a supposedly benign command post that will aid African countries in fighting homegrown terrorists, hasn't fooled the African people (Fancher 2013a, 2013b). Obama was forced to locate the primary AFRICOM base in Germany, as no country except Liberia was willing to allow this base on its soil. This resistance is based partially on Africans' understanding of the naked quest for oil behind the alleged humanitarianism, and their memory of Africa's history of colonial subordination. The United States is increasingly reliant on oil from this area and fears competition from China for the resource.

Across East Asia, the United States remains engaged in a host of imperial projects, as exemplified in our relationship with Japan. According to Gavan

McCormack (2010), the Obama administration's stance on the U.S. base in Okinawa overrode the democratic will of the Japanese people. Key to recent political changes in Japan were promises to renegotiate the base, which residents of the island resent for the pollution, violence, sexual assault of locals, and general denigration represented by having a foreign base in a sovereign country (Inoue 2007). With imperial hubris, the then-secretary of defense Robert Gates said that the bases were nonnegotiable and warned that Japan would face consequences if it continued pushing for a transformation of the relationship (McCormack 2010). Ultimately, the United States refused any compromise, leading to the humiliating downfall of the center-left prime minister, Yukio Hatoyama, who resigned as the United States forced him to back down on key campaign promises.

In both Asia and Latin and Central America, Obama's policies have also furthered narrowly defined U.S. interests. This includes his support of neoliberal policies of free trade and structural adjustment, which always seek to maintain U.S. advantage at the cost of others. For instance, while Obama called NAFTA "'devastating' and 'a big mistake'" on the campaign trail, and said that NAFTA would need reform to protect labor and environmental rights, he backed off this position before he was elected (Easton 2008). By late 2013, Obama was spearheading the creation of a NAFTA-like Trans-Pacific Partnership; while the negotiations of this deal are secret, opponents are concerned that it will expand corporate power and deregulation (Balkhy 2013). This partnership is intended to marginalize China by providing trade advantages for many of its neighbors, and could have major political fallout by antagonizing the superpower.

Obama has also continued the time-honored American practice of organizing or supporting Latin American coups when the current leader is not amenable to U.S. desires, while singing the same old democracy song. Several Latin American governments have moved leftward in the past few years, nationalizing industry, forming an alternative fair trade bloc, the Bolivarian Alliance for the Americas (ALBA), and being generally uncooperative with corporate ambitions for their resources. Coups and attempted coups in Honduras, Ecuador, Bolivia, and Venezuela followed years of U.S. aid to political dissident groups, in the name of "democracy promotion" (Madsen 2010; Burron 2012). For instance, a WikiLeaks cable showed that by 24 July 2010, the State Department had "no doubt" that the Honduras coup of 28 June was illegal (Mitchell 2011). Despite this, the White House continued to claim publicly that the facts were fuzzy and that the coup's illegality could not yet be determined, allowing our government to keep funding the illegal govern-

ment (Honduras is the hub for the U.S. military's operations in Central America). After the postcoup election of Porfirio Lobo, which regional heads of state and international observers would not recognize, the United States congratulated Lobo for "restoring democracy" (Frank 2012). In Bolivia, the aborted coup against Evo Morales, which mustered white racist sentiment against Bolivia's first indigenous president, was publicly backed by the U.S. ambassador (Fuentes and Munckton 2008). And in October 2013, Hugo Chávez's successor to the Venezuelan presidency, Nicolás Maduro, expelled three U.S. diplomats, alleging that they were conspiring with right-wing opposition members to sabotage the Venezuelan economy (Robertson 2013). (Maduro also called Obama "the grand chief of devils" in a May 2013 interview [AFP 2013].)

Closer to home, Obama's stance on immigration *worsens the plight of people of color coming to the United States to find work*. Despite touting the differences with Bush-era policies, the militarization of the border and the terrorizing of families of color continue apace under the new administration. During the campaign, Obama recognized the state terror inherent in the Bush-era Immigration and Customs Enforcement (ICE) raids, claiming, "The system isn't working when . . . communities are terrorized by ICE immigration raids. . . . When all of that is happening, the system just isn't working, and we need to change it!" (Obama 2008). If this were only empty rhetoric, it would be tragic. Farcically, however, deportations under Obama have actually increased: he presided over the "greatest number of deportations in any two-year period in the nation's history" (Vedantam 2010), and is on track to deport more people in six years than Bush deported in eight (Golash-Boza 2013b). In addition, almost half a million immigrants are kept in detention centers each year (Noorani 2013), nearly half of them in privately owned centers with financial incentives to push for more detentions and deportations (Mason 2012). The terrorism has become more covert, but no less real for the families torn apart as the administration has moved away from high-profile ICE raids to enforcement through more effective electronic tracking and enforcement measures. This, however, does not mean that the administration has totally backed off the hypermasculine, made-for-TV enforcement measures that so titillate the Right. In 2010, Obama sent twelve hundred National Guard troops to police the Mexican border, and gave local law enforcement the power of federal agents in immigration enforcement (Booth 2011). Beyond this, unmanned predator drones, used to launch "Hellfire" missiles into Pakistani weddings, are now used to police border crossings (Booth 2011). These drones are unarmed for now, but as Mike Davis (1990)

points out, military hardware developed for policing racialized populations abroad often becomes central to arsenals aimed at domestic "Others."

This long list of Obama's policies is meant to convey the continuity between his presidency and those of his predecessors. And yet, as bombs drop in an ever-growing number of countries, protests against the continuation of these wars are virtually nonexistent (Heaney and Rojas 2011). This, we argue, is the most dangerous aspect of "multicultural white supremacy": the silencing of people on the left who would probably be speaking out against these policies if a (white) conservative politician were enacting them.

Ending the Farce: Silence or Resistance?

Over the past century of U.S. wars, there has been a consistent thread of black protest against involvement in imperialist conflicts, given blacks' own tenuous connection to and oppression by the same government enlisting their help in killing "other 'foreign' racialized bodies" (Mirabal 2005, 193). Mirabal documents the debate on this theme in black newspapers during the 1895–98 Cuban War of Independence. Black intellectuals then critiqued each succeeding war's imperialism and frequently invoked the irony of black participation in these wars. Du Bois's essay "The Souls of White Folk" was inspired by his disgust with World War I (after his initial support). Frantz Fanon and James Baldwin both wrote about black participation in World War II. Dr. King, Malcolm X, and Muhammad Ali all spoke out against the Vietnam War. After his one meeting with Dr. King in 1967, Ali said to a reporter, "Why should they ask me to put on a uniform and go 10,000 miles from home and drop bombs and bullets on Brown people in Vietnam while so-called Negro people in Louisville are treated like dogs and denied simple human rights? No, I'm not going 10,000 miles from home to help murder and burn another poor nation simply to continue the domination of white slave masters of the darker people the world over. . . . The real enemy of my people is here" (quoted in Zirin 2004).

Given this history, the lack of a similarly strong debate on the current imperialist wars (and black involvement in them) is striking. It is the result, we argue, of the success of multicultural white supremacy: in screening its own intentions, the white-led regime can elicit black support and complicity in its policies. The symbolic inclusion of (some) blacks in the public sphere is a double-edged sword, as blacks and other people of color are now them-

selves implicated in the United States' imperialist ambitions (while still being largely denied the spoils).

In the post–civil rights era, the United States' traditionally "racist" rhetoric has been eclipsed by subtle racism, but systemic white privilege remains. The "empire state" continues unabated, waging wars of choice against the "darker nations" (Prashad 2007). The highly public success of some blacks helps hide the fact that our institutions, policies, ceremonies, and national symbols are still largely governed by white power and white prerogatives. More sinisterly, incorporated minorities like Obama justify the continuation of imperial ventures. The process of unpacking the imperialist knapsack begins with recognizing the imperial roots of white privilege and the ability of racial regimes to co-opt dissent. The continued relevance of whiteness studies depends upon understanding the changing "phenotype" (Rodríguez 2009) of those in charge of reproducing white privilege. Only then will scholars and activists be well prepared to dismantle white supremacy.

As scholars of race and individuals opposed to both Bush's and Obama's wars, we have been deeply concerned by the dissipation of antiwar activism since Obama's election, as well as by the stagnant mainstream debate on race. The now theatrical performance of recognizing one's own "white privilege" is insufficient to address the structural conditions of global inequality that are consistent with our colonial past. The civil rights movement of the 1960s had important resonance and cross-fertilization with global anticolonial struggles, but domestic and foreign concerns have become decoupled because of the revolutionary potential of such connections. Even within academia, discussions of race tend to focus on the plight of racial minorities within the United States. We rarely discuss the impact of racism on current economic, political, and military foreign policy, nor do we regularly discuss the current military interventions in the historical context of imperialism, colonialism, and genocide. By looking at the impact of whiteness and white privilege on the global stage, as Du Bois did more than a century ago, we can carry out the important work of critiquing today's "postracial" society and politics and its still racialized effects across the globe.

Notes

1. Elsewhere, we have written much more about the Obama phenomenon and the "new racism." While we are focusing here on a new aspect of Obama's presidency, small sections of this chapter appeared in prior works by the lead author. For the full version, see Bonilla-Silva and Seamster 2011.

2. This is a paraphrase of a statement by V. I. Lenin, who said, "A democratic republic is the best possible political shell for capitalism, and, therefore, once capital has gained possession of this very best shell . . . it establishes its power so securely, so firmly, that no change of persons, institutions or parties in the bourgeois-democratic republic can shake it" (Lenin 1987, 279).

3. In the fall of 2013, Obama's proposed budget included cuts in Social Security's cost-of-living increases, amounting to $130 billion over a decade, and cuts in Medicare spending by $371 billion over ten years (Przybyla 2013).

4. Our brief review of Obama's foreign policy should be taken as partial, since even as we write multiple situations are evolving rapidly.

5. Of course, the ambivalent U.S.-Pakistan relationship was crystallized when U.S. special forces secretly entered Pakistan and assassinated bin Laden.

References

Ackerman, Spencer. 2012. U.S. military wants drones in South America, but why? *Wired*, 12 June. http://www.wired.com/dangerroom/2012/06/drones-south-america/?utm_source=twitter&utm_medium=socialmedia&utm_campaign=twitterclickthru.

———. 2013. Pentagon urges Afghanistan to sign agreement on US military presence. *Guardian*, 30 December. http://www.theguardian.com/world/2013/dec/30/pentagon-afghanistan-agreement-us-troops.

ACLU (American Civil Liberties Union). 2013. Targeted killings. http://www.aclu.org/national-security/targeted-killings.

AFP (Agence France-Presse). 2013. Venezuelan President Nicolas Maduro blasts "devil" Obama. 5 May. http://www.rawstory.com/rs/2013/05/05/venezuelan-president-nicolas-maduro-blasts-devil-obama/.

Ali, Tariq. 2010. President of cant. *New Left Review* 61 (January–February). http://newleftreview.org/II/61/tariq-ali-president-of-cant.

Alterman, Eric. 2011. *Kabuki democracy: The system vs. Barack Obama*. New York: Perseus Books.

Andersen, Margaret. 2003. Whitewashing race: A critical perspective on whiteness studies. In *White out: The continuing significance of racism*, ed. Ashley W. Doane and Eduardo Bonilla-Silva, 21–33. New York: Routledge.

Baker, Peter, Mark Landler, David E. Sanger, and Anne Barnard. 2013. Off-the-cuff Obama line put U.S. in bind on Syria. *New York Times*, 4 May. http://www.nytimes.com/2013/05/05/world/middleeast/obamas-vow-on-chemical-weapons-puts-him-in-tough-spot.html?pagewanted=all.

Balkhy, Ibrahim. 2013. Obama's Trans-Pacific Partnership may undermine public health, environment, internet all at once. *Huffington Post*, 9 December. http://www.huffingtonpost.com/2013/12/09/obama-trans-pacific-partnership_n_4414891.html.

Becker, Jo, and Scott Shane. 2012. Secret "kill list" proves a test of Obama's principles and will. *New York Times*, 29 May. http://www.nytimes.com/2012/05/29/world/obamas-leadership-in-war-on-al-qaeda.html?pagewanted=all.

Besteman, Catherine. 2008. "Beware of those bearing gifts": An anthropologist's view of AFRICOM. *Anthropology Today* 24, no. 5: 20–21.

Bobo, Larry, James Kluegel, and Ryan Smith. 1997. Laissez-faire racism: The crystalli-
zation of a "kinder, gentler" anti-black ideology. In *Racial attitudes in the 1990s:
Continuity and change*, ed. Steven A. Tuch and Jack K. Martin, 15–43. Westport,
Conn.: Praeger.

Bonilla-Silva, Eduardo. 1997. Rethinking racism: Toward a structural interpretation.
American Sociological Review 62, no. 3: 465–80.

———. 2013. *Racism without racists*. 4th ed. New York: Rowman and Littlefield.

Bonilla-Silva, Eduardo, and Louise Seamster. 2011. The sweet enchantment of color
blindness in black face: Explaining the "miracle," debating the politics, and
suggesting a way for hope to be "for real" in America. In *Rethinking Obama*,
ed. Julian Go, 139–75. Political Power and Social Theory, vol. 22. New York:
Emerald Group.

Booth, William. 2011. More predator drones fly U.S.-Mexico border. *Washington Post*,
21 December. http://www.washingtonpost.com/world/more-predator-drones-fly
-us-mexico-border/2011/12/01/gIQANSZz8O_story.html.

Brodkin, Karen. 1996. *How Jews became white folks and what that says about race in
America*. New Brunswick: Rutgers University Press.

Burron, Neil. 2012. Unpacking U.S. democracy promotion in Bolivia: From soft tactics
to regime change. *Latin American Perspectives* 39, no. 1: 115–32.

Carmichael, Stokely, with Ekwueme Michael Thelwell. 2005. *Ready for revolution: The life
and struggles of Stokely Carmichael (Kwame Ture)*. New York: Simon and Schuster.

Cody, Edward. 2011. Arab League condemns broad Western bombing campaign in
Libya. *Washington Post*, 20 March. http://www.washingtonpost.com/world/arab
-league-condemns-broad-bombing-campaign-in-libya/2011/03/20/AB1pSg1
_story.html.

Cole, Juan. 2011. An open letter to the Left on Libya. *Nation*, 27 March. http://www
.thenation.com/article/159517/open-letter-left-libya.

Davis, Angela. 2005. *Abolition democracy*. New York: Seven Stories Press.

Davis, Mike. 1990. *City of quartz*. New York: Verso.

DeSante, Christopher. 2011. How Americans evaluate applicants for welfare. Paper presented at the Center for the Study of Race, Ethnicity, and Gender in the Social
Sciences, Duke University.

Dovidio, John F. 2001. On the nature of contemporary prejudice: The third wave. *Journal
of Social Issues* 57, no. 1: 829–49.

Dreyfuss, Bob. 2011. Obama's women advisers pushed war against Libya. *Nation*, 19
March. http://www.thenation.com/blog/159346/obamas-women-advisers-pushed
-war-against-libya.

Du Bois, W. E. B. 1920. *Darkwater: Voices from within the veil*. New York: Harcourt,
Brace and Howe.

Easton, Nina. 2008. Obama: NAFTA not so bad after all. MoneyCNN.com, 18 June.
http://money.cnn.com/2008/06/18/magazines/fortune/easton_obama.fortune
/index.htm.

Fancher, Mark P. 2013a. Expected budget cuts won't cure the deadly AFRICOM disease.
Black Agenda Report, 17 December. http://blackagendareport.com/content
/expected-budget-cuts-won't-cure-deadly-africom-disease.

———. 2013b. The U.S. military's mind games in Africa: No bullets, but lethal. *Black
Agenda Report*, 27 July. http://blackagendareport.com/content/us-military%E2
%80%99s-mind-games-africa-no-bullets-lethal.

Fanon, Frantz. 1967. *Black skin, white masks*. New York: Grove Press.

————. 1968. *The wretched of the earth.* New York: Grove Press.

Farmer, Ben. 2011. US troops may stay in Afghanistan until 2024. *Telegraph,* 19 August. http://www.telegraph.co.uk/news/worldnews/asia/afghanistan/8712701 /US-troops-may-stay-in-Afghanistan-until-2024.html.

Feagin, Joe. 2000. *Racist America.* New York: Routledge.

Frank, Dana. 2012. Honduras: Which side is the U.S. on? *Nation,* 22 May. http://www .thenation.com/article/167994/honduras-which-side-us#.

Fuentes, Federico, and Stuart Munckton. 2008. Bolivia: Fascist right launches "civic coup." *Green Left,* 13 September. http://www.greenleft.org.au/node/40311.

Giraldi, Philip. 2013. Quitting over Syria. *American Conservative,* 13 November. http:// www.theamericanconservative.com/articles/quitting-over-syria/.

Golash-Boza, Tanya. 2013a. The problems with white allies and white privilege. *Al Jazeera,* 20 September. http://www.aljazeera.com/indepth/opinion/2013/09 /2013920103353832487.html.

————. 2013b. The real deal on Obama's deportation record. *Counterpunch,* 19 December. http://www.counterpunch.org/2013/12/19/the-real-deal-on-obamas -deportation-record/.

Hall, Stuart. 1980. Race, articulation, and societies structured in dominance. In *Sociological theories: Race and colonialism,* ed. UNESCO, 305–45. Paris: UNESCO.

Hanly, Ken. 2013. Op-ed: The new Guantanamo at Bagram Afghanistan. *Digital Journal,* 25 December. http://digitaljournal.com/news/world/op-ed-the-new-guantanamo -at-bagram-afghanistan/article/364629.

Harper, James L., Jr. 2011. U.S. building secret drone bases in Africa, Arabian Peninsula, officials say. *Washington Post,* 20 September. http://www.cbsnews.com /news/us-building-secret-drone-bases-in-africa-arabian-peninsula-officials-say/.

Heaney, Michael T., and Fabio Rojas. 2011. The partisan dynamics of contention: Demobilization of the antiwar movement in the United States, 2001–2009. *Mobilization: An International Journal* 16, no. 1: 45–64.

Herbert, Bob. 2007. The ugly side of the GOP. *New York Times,* 25 September. http:// www.nytimes.com/2007/09/25/opinion/25herbert.html.

Hersh, Seymour M. 2013. Whose sarin? *London Review of Books,* 19 December. http:// www.lrb.co.uk/v35/n24/seymour-m-hersh/whose-sarin.

Hutchings, Vincent L. 2009. Change or more of the same? Evaluating racial attitudes in the Obama era. *Public Opinion Quarterly* 73, no. 5: 917–42.

Inoue, Masamichi S. 2007. *Okinawa and the U.S. military: Identity making in the age of globalization.* New York: Columbia University Press.

Johnston, David. 2009. For Holder, inquiry on interrogation poses tough choice. *New York Times,* 21 July. http://www.nytimes.com/2009/07/22/us/22holder.html?_r=1.

Jung, Moon-Kie. 2011. Constituting the U.S. empire-state and white supremacy: The early years. In *The state of white supremacy: Racism, governance, and the United States,* ed. Moon-Kie Jung, Joao H. Costa Vargas, and Eduardo Bonilla-Silva, 1–25. Stanford: Stanford University Press.

Khan, Akbar Nasir. 2011. The U.S.'s policy of targeted killing by drones in Pakistan. *IPRI Journal* 11, no. 1: 21–40. http://harvard.academia.edu/AkbarNasirKhan /Papers/157952/U.S._Policy_of_Targeted_Killing_by_Drones_in_Pakistan.

Knowles, Eric D., Brian S. Lowery, and Rebecca L. Schaumberg. 2009. Anti-egalitarians for Obama? Group-dominance motivation and the Obama vote. *Journal of Experimental Social Psychology* 45, no. 4: 965–69.

Kuhn, David Paul. 2008. Obama shifts affirmative action rhetoric. *Politico,* 10 August. http://www.politico.com/news/stories/0808/12421.html.

Leigh, David. 2010. US embassy cables leak sparks global diplomatic crisis. *Guardian*, 28 November. http://www.guardian.co.uk/world/2010/nov/28/us-embassy -cable-leak-diplomacy-crisis.

Lenin, Vladimir I. 1987. *Essential works of Lenin.* Ed. Henry Christman. New York: Dover Publications.

Linebaugh, Heather. 2013. I worked on the US drone program: The public should know what really goes on. *Guardian*, 29 December. http://www.theguardian.com /commentisfree/2013/dec/29/drones-us-military.

Lutz, Catherine. 2006. Empire is in the details. *American Ethnologist* 33, no. 4: 593–611.

Madsen, Wayne. 2010. Obama authorizes covert economic war against Venezuela. *Center for Research on Globalization*, 19 January. http://www.globalresearch.ca /index.php?context=vaandaid=17072.

Marable, Manning. [1983] 2000. *How capitalism underdeveloped black America: Problems in race, political economy, and society.* Cambridge, Mass.: South End Press.

Marx, Karl. [1852] 1978. The eighteenth Brumaire of Louis Bonaparte. In *The Marx-Engels reader*, ed. Robert C. Tucker, 594–617. New York: W. W. Norton.

Mason, Cody. 2012. Dollars and detainees: The growth of for-profit detention. *The sentencing project*, July. http://sentencingproject.org/doc/publications/inc_Dollars _and_Detainees.pdf.

Mayer, Jane. 2009. *The dark side: The inside story of how the war on terror turned into a war on American ideals.* New York: Random House.

McCormack, Gavan. 2010. Obama vs. Okinawa. *New Left Review* 64 (July–August): 5–26.

McIntosh, Peggy. 1989. White privilege: Unpacking the invisible knapsack. *Peace and Freedom*, July–August, 10–12.

McKay, Tom. 2013. Guess which 8 countries the U.S. is waging secret drone campaigns against? *Policymic*, 20 January. http://www.policymic.com/articles/23708/guess -which-8-countries-the-u-s-is-waging-secret-drone-campaigns-against.

Mills, Charles M. 1997. *The racial contract.* Ithaca: Cornell University Press.

Mirabal, Nancy Raquel. 2005. Scripting race, finding place: African Americans, Afro-Cubans, and the diasporic imaginary in the United States. In *Neither enemies nor friends: Latinos, blacks, Afro-Latinos*, ed. Anani Dzidzienyo and Suzanne Oboler, 189–207. New York: Palgrave Macmillan.

Mitchell, Greg. 2011. *The age of WikiLeaks: From collateral murder to Cablegate (and beyond).* New York: Sinclair Books.

Montejano, David. 1987. *Anglos and Mexicans in the making of Texas.* Austin: University of Texas Press.

Nagourney, Adam. 2008. Obama elected president as racial barrier falls. *New York Times*, 4 November. http://www.nytimes.com/2008/11/05/us/politics/05elect.html.

Noorani, Ali. 2013. Detention costs convey immigration reform's urgency. *Huffington Post*, 22 August. http://www.huffingtonpost.com/ali-noorani/detention-costs -immigration-reform_b_3792497.html.

Norton, Michael I., and Samuel R. Sommers. 2011. Whites see racism as a zero-sum game that they are now losing. *Perspectives on Psychological Science* 6:215–18.

Obama, Barack. 2008. Speech at the 79th National Convention of the League of United Latin American Citizens, Washington, D.C., 8 July.

Oliver, Melvin L., and Thomas M. Shapiro. 2006. *Black wealth/white wealth: A new perspective on racial inequality.* New York: Routledge.

Omi, Michael, and Howard Winant. 1994. *Racial formation in the United States: From the 1960s to the 1990s.* New York: Routledge.

Parks, Gregory, and Matthew Hughey. 2011. *The Obamas and a (post) racial America?* New York: Oxford University Press.

Payne, Charles. 2007. *I've got the light of freedom: The organizing tradition and the Mississippi freedom struggle.* 2nd ed. Berkeley: University of California.

Pettigrew, Thomas F. 2009. Post-racism? Putting President Obama's victory in perspective. *Du Bois Review* 6, no. 2: 279–92.

Prashad, Vijay. 2007. *The darker nations: A people's history of the third world.* New York: New Press.

Priest, Dana, and William M. Arkin. 2011. "Top Secret America": A look at the military's Joint Special Operations Command. *Washington Post*, 2 September. http://www.washingtonpost.com/world/national-security/top-secret-america -a-look-at-the-militarys-joint-special-operations-command/2011/08/30 /gIQAvYuAxJ_story.html.

Przybyla, Heidi. 2013. Republicans' debt-ceiling strategy relies on Obama budget. *Bloomberg News*, 24 September. http://www.bloomberg.com/news/2013-09-24/ republicans-debt-ceiling-strategy-relies-on-obama-budget.html.

Reed, Adolph. 2001. *Class notes: Posing as politics and other thoughts on the American scene.* New York: New Press.

Reuters. 2010. U.S. drones to watch entire Mexico border from September 1, 30 August. http://www.reuters.com/article/2010/08/30/us-usa-immigration-security -idUSTRE67T5DK20100830.

Richomme, Olivier. 2012. The post-racial illusion: Racial politics and inequality in the age of Obama. *Revue de Recherche en Civilisation Américaine* 3. http://rrca.revues .org/index464.html.

Robertson, Ewan. 2013. Nicolas Maduro expels three US diplomats from Venezuela for alleged conspiracy. Venezuelanalysis.com, 30 September. http://venezuela nalysis.com/news/10054.

Rodríguez, Dylan E. 2008. Inaugurating multiculturalist white supremacy. *Colorlines*, 10 November. http://colorlines.com/archives/2008/11/the_dreadful_genuis_of _the_oba.html.

———. 2009. *Suspended apocalypse: White supremacy, genocide, and the Filipino condition.* Minneapolis: University of Minnesota Press.

Roediger, David. 1991. *The wages of whiteness: Race and the making of the working class.* New York: Verso.

Rohde, David. 2012. The Obama doctrine: How the president's drone war is backfiring. *Foreign Policy*, 27 February. http://www.foreignpolicy.com/articles/2012/02/27 /the_obama_doctrine.

Rosenberg, Carol. 2014. "Transparent" detention at Guantánamo? Not anymore. *Miami Herald*, 4 January. http://www.miamiherald.com/2014/01/04/3852565 /transparent-detention-at-guantanamo.html.

Ross, Sonya, and Jennifer Agiesta. 2012. Racial views: Poll shows majority harbor prejudice against blacks. *Huffington Post*, 27 October. http://www.huffingtonpost .com/2012/10/27/racial-views-new-polls-sh_n_2029423.html?utm_hp_ref =fb&src=sp &comm_ref=false.

Schmitt, Eric. 2013. Drones in Niger reflect new U.S. tack on terrorism. *New York Times*, 10 July. http://www.nytimes.com/2013/07/11/world/africa/drones-in -niger-reflect-new-us-approach-in-terror-fight.html?_r=0.

Shane, Scott, and Mark Lander. 2011. Obama clears way for Guantánamo trials. *New York Times*, 7 March. http://www.nytimes.com/2011/03/08/world/americas/08guantanamo.html.

Smith, Andrea. 2005. *Conquest: Sexual violence and American Indian genocide.* Cambridge, Mass.: South End Press.

———. 2012. Unsettling the privilege of self-reflexivity. In *Geographies of privilege*, ed. France Winddance Twine and Bradley Gardener, 263–79. New York: Routledge.

Smith, Robert C. 1995. *Racism in the post–civil rights era: Now you see it, now you don't.* Albany: SUNY Press.

Street, Paul. 2009. *Barack Obama and the future of American politics.* Boulder, Colo.: Paradigm.

Tesler, Michael, and David O. Sears. 2010. *Obama's race: The 2008 election and the dream of a post-racial America.* Chicago: University of Chicago Press.

U.S. Department of Homeland Security. 2009. *Rightwing extremism: Current economic and political climate fueling resurgence in radicalization and recruitment.* Washington, D.C.: U.S. Government Printing Office.

Vedantam, Shankar. 2010. Defeat of immigration measure reveals failed White House strategy, advocates say. *Washington Post Online Edition*, 18 December. http://www.washingtonpost.com/wp-dyn/content/article/2010/12/18/AR2010121801679.html?hpid=topnews.

Washington Post. 2013. Drones and spy planes over Africa and Arabian Peninsula. 29 January. http://www.washingtonpost.com/wp-srv/special/national-security/drones-and-spy-planes-over-Africa/index.html.

Winant, Howard. 2001. *The world is a ghetto: Race and democracy since World War II.* New York: Basic Books.

Woodward, Bob. 2010. *Obama's wars.* New York: Simon and Schuster.

Zirin, Dave. 2004. Revolt of the black athlete: The hidden history of Muhammad Ali. *International Socialist Review* 33 (January–February). http://www.isreview.org/issues/33/muhammadali.shtml.

4

Other Perspectives on
White and Western Privilege

11

Whiteness and Africana Political Economy

Paget Henry

In an earlier paper, I examined the problem of whiteness from the perspective of the discourse of Africana phenomenology (Henry 2004). In this chapter, I shift my focus and look at the problem of whiteness from the perspective of the discourse of Africana political economy. From this latter perspective, I revisit Cedric Robinson's notion of racial capitalism in an effort to make explicit the racial foundations upon which capitalism as a global system has rested for so long. After outlining these racial underpinnings of global capitalism, I take up the impact of the Great Recession of 2008 on the racial codes that have been vital sources of order and support for this economic system. In particular, I argue that the recession will produce a significant weakening of the system's yellow, brown, and mongrel codes as a result of the performances of the Chinese, Indian, and Brazilian economies during this period. Its black codes have been affected by the election, and subsequent re-election, in the United States of President Barack Obama. However, I also argue that the specific long-term results of the changes in these codes are still working themselves out.

Africana Phenomenology and Africana Political Economy

Between Africana phenomenology and Africana political economy there are a number of important continuities and discontinuities of which we should

be aware. Here I will make note of three continuities and also three disconti-nuities that are vital for grasping relations between these two subfields. The first continuity is clearly the fact that both Africana political economy and Africana phenomenology address the negrification of African identities within the systems of empire that imperial Europe established in Africa and in "the New World." Both of these discourses converge on this terrain of negrification, even as they diverge in different disciplinary directions. Our second important continuity is that Africana political economy and Africana phenomenology share a number of important thinkers, among them W. E. B. Du Bois, C. L. R. James, Frantz Fanon, Aimé Césaire, Richard Wright, Sylvia Wynter, Lewis Gordon, and Charles Ephraim. Third and finally, both Africana phenomenology and Africana political economy are subfields of that larger field that Cedric Robinson has called "the black radical tradition." The fact that Robinson frames his classic account of this tradition around the figures of W. E. B. Du Bois, C. L. R. James, and Richard Wright is indeed one of the most telling reminders we have of the need to keep the continuities between these two subfields constantly in view.

But in spite of these substantive continuities, there are also definite dis-continuities between these two subfields. The first is the fact that Africana phenomenology and Africana political economy are addressing different sides of the same Africana phenomenon: the responses of people of African descent to their racial domination and economic exploitation within the empires of imperial Europe. Africana phenomenology has focused on the subjective and experiential aspects of this encounter, while Africana political economy has directed its gaze at the objective or productivist aspects of this encounter with imperial Europe.

The second important discontinuity between these two fields is the fact that the aspects and images of the Africana self that have accompanied the knowledge-producing practices of these two discourses have consistently been quite different. In Africana phenomenology, the correlated aspects and conceptions of the Africana self have been those thoughtful and awak-ened moments in which the Africana subject has attempted to grasp, self-reflectively, the experience of its racialization as "a Negro." In Africana political economy, the accompanying conceptions of the self have been those moments in which the Africana subject attempted critically and empirically to grasp its commodification as "Negro labor" within European systems of economic production.

Our third and final discontinuity is the discursive/disciplinary nature of the distance between these two conceptions of the racialized Africana self.

Because of the many twists and turns on the route between the two—moving from specific locations within politics and economics to specifically phenomenological sites within philosophy—it has often been difficult to keep these two conceptions of the Africana self, and the connections between them, in view. But, in spite of these difficulties, their deeper unity must be kept experientially accessible and theoretically in view.

Africana Political Economy

The field of Africana political economy has its roots in the impulses of Africans to resist their commodification as "Negro slaves" and "Negro workers" in European-owned economies and related attempts to fashion economies of their own. The first signs of these impulses were seen in the economic practices of ex-slave Maroon communities, in major uprisings such as the Haitian Revolution of 1791, and in the labor and independence movements of Africa and the Caribbean that extended from the 1930s to the 1960s. However, the systematic examination of the highly oppressive condition of being a "Negro laborer" began with the writings of Africans in the colonial societies of the Americas. It is in these eighteenth-century texts that we find the earliest of the Africana political writers, such as Ottobah Cugoano, Olaudah Equiano, and Lemuel Haynes. In Cugoano, the norms of precolonial African political economy are still very much alive and, along with Christianity, provide one of the important bases for critiquing the racial and economic practices of Western capitalism (1999, 22–28). In the works of Haynes, a fighter in the American Revolution of 1776, we see the formulation of a black republicanism that was critical not only of slavery but also of the proposal to send free African Americans back to Africa. This opposition resulted in Haynes's open challenges to George Washington, Thomas Jefferson, and James Madison—the key founders of the new American Republic—who had been in support of this proposal (Saillant 2003, 47–82).

In the United States, this politico-economic opposition continued in the nineteenth-century texts of figures like David Walker, Maria Stewart, Hosea Easton, Frederick Douglass, and Anna Julia Cooper. In the twentieth century, this discourse of Africana political economy continued in the writings of W. E. B. Du Bois, Hubert Harrison, Marcus Garvey, Claudia Jones, and on into the period of the civil rights and black power movements. During this latter period, the stream of Africana political economy was joined even more intensely by contributions from Africa and the Caribbean. Particularly

important in this regard are the figures of Arthur Lewis, Eric Williams, Lloyd Best, Walter Rodney, Clive Thomas, Norman Girvan, and Samir Amin. This brief outline is the subfield of Africana political economy.

Africana Political Economy and Whiteness

Although Africana political economists and phenomenologists explain whiteness differently, they converge in their views on the key features of whiteness and the problems that it has created for people of African descent. Both groups of Africana scholars have portrayed whiteness as a deeply rooted compulsive drive for global domination in economics, politics, culture, and identity, one that necessitates the excessive inflating and normativizing of the European subject. This inflating of the European subject has as its correlate the deflating, dehumanizing, and economic exploitation of non-Europeans, including the negrifying and making of Africans into a slave labor force. Thus W. E. B. Du Bois summed up the problem of whiteness in the following way: "I am given to understand that whiteness is the ownership of the earth forever and ever, Amen!" (1999, 18). Consequently, for both groups of scholars, whiteness as we know it today emerged during the course of the sixteenth-century encounters between an expanding imperial Europe and the nonwhite peoples of Africa, Asia, and the Americas. Distortions of identity, cultural misrepresentation, and historic erasures of major proportions grew out of this fateful encounter that transformed both Europeans and non-Europeans.

As a result of these dramatic shifts in group representation, Europeans emerged from these encounters more as "whites" than as the Christians they were at the start of this imperial project. Africans emerged more as blacks and Negroes and less as the Yoruba, Akan, or Fulani they were before this encounter with Europeans. The people of India were racialized into browns and coolies rather than the Hindus and Muslims they had been for so long. In relation to whiteness, the people of China would be racially transformed into yellows and coolies, which displaced their Buddhist and Taoist identities. Finally, throughout the Americas and the Caribbean, the indigenous population became reds and Injuns rather than the Tainos, Arawaks, Mayans, Navahos, or Cherokees that they were before their encounter with imperial Europe. In short, racial changes in identity of great inner depth and major outer proportions accompanied the rise and global expansion of European capitalism, and whitened its identity. This is the phenomenon of whiteness

and the imperial context in which Africana political economists and Africana phenomenologists have located it, even though their approaches to the rise of whiteness differ significantly.

Among Africana phenomenologists such as Lewis Gordon and Charles Ephraim, the phenomenon of whiteness is seen as an eruption of ontological desire from the deep existential structures that frame and support, or fail to support, the efforts of the European subject to establish itself in the world. For example, Gordon links the emergence and practice of whiteness as a project of global supremacy to the set of bad-faith practices through which Europeans and peoples of European descent have been able to relieve, evade, or compensate for feelings of a lack of full determinacy (nonbeing) that flow necessarily from the nature of human freedom. One way of getting rid of these negative and undesirable feelings is to externalize them and project them onto non-European groups, while at the same time denying the true origins of these feelings. Following Jean-Paul Sartre, Gordon defines bad faith as lying to oneself and believing the lie (1995, 8). As a designated carrier of these projected negativities, "the Negro," or worse, "the nigger," became that part of the white psyche that it hated the most, and thus rejected and excluded from its idealized self-image as the supreme realization of humanity. Gordon suggests that by using this strategy, Europeans have been able to maintain not only the lie of white supremacy but also that of black inferiority.

In Ephraim's view, the white European's need to inferiorize, dehumanize, and exploit Africans is linked very directly to what he calls "an obsessive need for self-aggrandizement" (2003, 2). This is a deep libidinal drive that motivates and sustains practices of white racism, which is both a symptom of and a cover for this pressing drive for self-inflation. Behind this drive and the racism it produces lies an even more deeply hidden lack that produces in the European an attitude of *ressentiment* against the world (67–70). For Ephraim, this *ressentiment* toward the world is the deepest layer of the inflated posture of whiteness and its discriminatory and dehumanizing practices. Drawing on Nietzsche, Ephraim argues that *ressentiment*, with its desire for vengeance or a will to power against a harsh world, must be rooted in a set of life-threatening experiences that left the European subject feeling weak, vulnerable, and exposed. These would be the categorical equivalent of the negative feeling arising from the experience of ontological lack, in Gordon's terms. In short, for Ephraim, the eruption of racially potentiated whiteness was one manifestation of a compulsive drive for self-aggrandizement that in turn was driven by an underlying attitude of *ressentiment* that grew out of earlier experiences that exposed the weakness of the European subject. Both Gordon's

and Ephraim's accounts of the phenomenon of modern whiteness reflect elements of Fanon's account. If these existential approaches to whiteness are correct, then from an intentional perspective it becomes possible to argue that capitalism is fundamentally a mobilizing of the capabilities of human societies for a war against poverty, human weakness, and nature—the last being the source of human poverty by withholding its secrets, and at the same time the great exposer of human weakness.

In contrast to these two existentially based explanations of the phenomenon of whiteness is the sociohistorical account of Cedric Robinson, which is very representative of the accounts found in Africana political economy. However, it is important to note that the unusual brilliance of Robinson's *Black Marxism* lies in the author's ability to carry out phenomenological analyses of social forms such as relations of production, concepts of nations, and state formation as exercises that complement his detailed historical, political, and black-laborist analyses. In short, although he is primarily a political analyst, like Fanon, Robinson succeeds in bringing together the contributions of both Africana political economy and Africana phenomenology.

Cedric Robinson, Africana Political Economy, and Whiteness

Cedric Robinson approaches the problem of whiteness through a brilliant critique of European Marxism, the European discourse that has most profoundly influenced Africana political economy. Robinson's critique, which is simultaneously phenomenological and black-laborist, deconstructs (before the rise of deconstruction) the universalist claims and metaphysical hierarchies of European Marxism to expose its whiteness. It is this whiteness of Marxism that he identifies as the primary source of the discomfort that many people of African descent have experienced with this revolutionary European discourse. The primary thrust of Robinson's critique is his demonstration of the importance of the racial, ethnic, nationalist, and other sociological dimensions that Marxism inherited from European feudalism.

Robinson traces the roots of contemporary whiteness, including that of Marxism, along with their metaphysical justifications, all the way back to the racial categories and hierarchies that modern capitalism inherited from feudalism. This is the major reason why modern capitalism is, for him, racial capitalism. He begins this history of the phenomenon of whiteness with the binary categories Romans/barbarians, "barbarian" being a term that the ancient Romans used to distinguish themselves from other peoples, including

Visigoths, Vandals, Franks, and other Europeans. From these beginnings, Robinson moves to the ninth-century conception of Europe created by the Carolingian dynasty. After the collapse of that dynasty around 899, the idea of Europe ceased to be a political one and took the religious form of Christendom. In both of these post-Roman incarnations, the Roman category of the barbarian persisted, with its new binary opposite being significantly Christianized. Within these three systems of rule, the Roman, the Carolingian, and the Christian, Robinson points out that barbarians were not primarily conquerors but immigrants looking for work. These "barbarian" immigrants were assimilated into these multicountry systems "primarily as a slave labor force" (2000, 11). Thus in these three cases, we have ethnic groups that were othered, barbarianized, enslaved, and exploited—practices that came with elaborate ethnic discursive justifications.

The next important phase in Robinson's account of the racist practices that capitalism inherited from feudalism is the rise of the European bourgeois classes in the twelfth century within the interstices of the feudal economy. Born at a time of population growth and stagnant agricultural output, the European bourgeoisie emerged as rich merchants who were able to capitalize on increasing outbreaks of famine by transporting produce from regions with surpluses to those that were in crisis. From these humble beginnings, these merchants were able to revive regional and long-distance trading, which had collapsed with the fall of Rome and the rise of the Islamic empire. In spite of this revival of trade in agriculture and textiles, Robinson notes, "the most precious cargo of the Mediterranean tradesmen was slaves" (16). He goes on to suggest that this early use and sale of barbarian slave labor by early bourgeois groups served as a model for the Atlantic African slave trade that later bourgeois groups would initiate in the sixteenth and seventeenth centuries. In short, modern capitalism inherited from feudalism an intra-European set of ethno-national hierarchies that were discursively elaborated in such a way as to justify the enslavement and economic exploitation of groups occupying the lower ranks of these hierarchies.

As it came into its own, European capitalism not only made increasing use of this intra-European and slavery-justifying ethno-national discourse but also projected it overseas to Africa, India, China, and the Americas. Robinson suggests that at home this hierarchical ethno-national discourse led to its *Herrenvolk* formulation, which "explained the inevitability and naturalness of the domination of some Europeans by other Europeans" (27). Abroad, capitalism racialized this inherited feudal discourse to produce the negrification of Africans, the injunizing of Native Americans, the coolietizing of Asians,

and the Anglo-Saxonizing and whitening of the earlier Roman and Christian identities of some Europeans. It is on account of this expanding system of racial categories that capitalism inherited from its feudal past what Robinson insists on calling racial capitalism, and not just capitalism, as Marx called it. In short, for Robinson, whiteness and its related practices of domination and exploitation are the categorical and discursive underpinnings of European systems of production that date back to the feudal period.

What are we to make of the differences in these accounts of whiteness provided by Gordon and Ephraim on the one hand and Robinson on the other? Do they complement each other, or do they cancel each other out? I think the former, especially in the case of Ephraim, who suggested that the roots of European *ressentiment* must be found in experiences that exposed the weakness and vulnerability of the late medieval European subject. However, Ephraim did not specify what precisely those experiences were. It is at this point that Robinson can be helpful. He notes that a series of extremely traumatic events of the fourteenth and fifteenth centuries devastated Europe and interrupted the bourgeois formation of capitalism. Robinson further suggests that "the consequence of those events were [sic] to determine the species of the modern world: the identities of the bourgeoisies that transformed capitalism into a world system" (17).

These traumatic events were persistent periods of famine in which many died, the Black Death (bubonic plague) of the mid-fourteenth century and subsequent years, the Hundred Years' War (1337–1453), and the many rebellions of peasants and artisans. It was in this brutal context of famine, decimation by plague, and destruction by war and class uprisings that the modern European bourgeoisie was forced to secure its survival and fight its way to the top. Together, these events could easily be the set of life-threatening and overpowering circumstances that left Europeans feeling weak and vulnerable, and thus bitterly resentful of existence for exposing their helplessness so dramatically.

In Gordon's view, such events could easily have aroused and brought to the surface feelings of nonbeing that existing strategies of bad faith had up until then been holding in check. When we consider the Protestant turn in European religion at the end of this period of trauma, we see that it is quite possible that old existential strategies of allaying anxieties and evading experiences of nonbeing had to be inflated and increased, producing the megalomaniacal proportions of white identities and their world-dominating practices. These are just two of the ways in which the explanations of modern whiteness provided by Africana phenomenology and Africana political economy

can complement each other. Together, they have produced some of the leading accounts of whiteness to come out of the black radical tradition.

Theorizing Racial Capitalism

In addition to being a response to the white supremacist ideology of Anglo-Saxonism, the concept of racial capitalism, as developed by Cedric Robinson, emerged out of the categorical history of the discourse of Africana political economy. Racial capitalism has been an intrusive imperial presence in Africana societies and communities, constraining local economic activities, and was therefore both a target of resistance and a motivating force behind the search for alternative political economies. In Robinson's view, the roots of the black radical tradition, and thus of Africana political economy, are to be found in the distinct strategies and histories of African peoples' resistance to their enslavement in the European world economy. These strategies have included rebellions on slave ships, marronage, calling on the ancestors and nature deities, slave uprisings, political agitation, and the writing of critical and historical texts, to name a few. It was the distinctness of these struggles that the whiteness of European Marxism failed to capture adequately.

With regard to Africana political economy, its systematization began in settings in which Africans regained some measure of sovereignty and were thus responsible for their own production of material goods and services. Among the earliest instances were the Maroon societies of the Caribbean and Brazil (*quilombos*) that emerged in the seventeenth century. The political economies that informed the organizing of these Maroon communities were based primarily on a number of African models. For example, political institutions were based on Akan and Congo models of monarchies and chieftaincies, while economic production was based on the adaptation of African farming practices to the conditions and resources of "New World" environments. In short, this first phase in the history of Africana political economy we can call neo-African, as it gave rise to kingdoms and communities of independent peasants that resembled African ones.

The second important phase in the development of Africana political economy was produced by the governance and productive demands of the Haitian Revolution of 1791. Unlike the Maroon communities, the leaders of this revolution inherited an entire national economy from the French colonizers. Because of its colonial history, the dominant sector and major foreign exchange earner of this new postcolonial economy was the European-created

sugar plantation system. Consequently, Toussaint and his administration had to decide whether to keep this dominant plantation sector, or, like the Maroon communities, pursue the strategy of a neo-African political economy. The leaders opted for the former route, while the Haitian masses pursued the latter in practice. The result was a divided political economy that contributed very significantly to Haitian economic stagnation. But in spite of this outcome, the ideas and policy positions of postcolonial Haiti remain a very important moment in the formation of Africana political economy.

The third important chapter in the development of Africana political economy takes us to the postslavery Reconstruction period (1860–80) in the United States. This was a short but distinct era that followed the American Civil War—a conflict in which two hundred thousand African American men fought with the forces of President Abraham Lincoln to end slavery and preserve the Union. During Reconstruction, because they were the majority in many counties in southern states, African Americans became members of both state and federal legislatures. However, unlike the Haitians, they came to power not by themselves but in alliances with northern investors who were eager to penetrate the South, led by Radical Republicans like Thaddeus Stevens, who wanted to break up the southern plantation system, and with the occupying military forces of the North. Needless to say, there were a lot of tensions within this alliance. But in spite of the tensions, this alliance created what W. E. B. Du Bois called "a dictatorship of labor" (1998, 185) that unsuccessfully attempted a reconstruction of democracy and economy in postslavery America.

The primary failure of this alliance was its inability to break up the large plantations and redistribute the land to black and white farmers. On the contrary, as in the case of Haiti, its members ended up restoring much of that system. However, within the constraints of this alliance, African American legislators were able to pursue "civil and political rights, education, and land" for their black constituencies (Du Bois 1998, 239). Thus it was during this period that African American universities such as Howard and Atlanta were started. In several states, there was the beginning of black labor movements, and the passage of legislation in support of the rights of sharecroppers. It has indeed been the great achievement of Du Bois's classic text, *Black Reconstruction in America*, to show the positive outlines of African American political and economic thinking before this historic alliance collapsed and Reconstruction came to an end.

The next important moment for the discourse of Africana political economy that I will note here takes us to a different period in U.S. history, the era

With the antisystemic push from the periphery contained, the socialist world in retreat, Japanese economic growth slowed, and Iraq invaded, the further expansion of American-style capitalism appeared unstoppable to many. Echoing this triumphalist euphoria were the works of authors such as Francis Fukuyama (1992) and Samuel Huntington (1996). However, this new imperialist posture concealed many structural weaknesses in the United States and other Western economies, and gross miscalculations in the new drive for imperial expansion in the Middle East, primarily to secure the sources and routes of U.S. oil supplies. Toward the end of the first decade of the twenty-first century, these new policies of deregulation, globalization, financialization, expansion into the Middle East, etc., led to the Great Recession of 2008. This chain of events did not only burst the triumphalist bubble but, together with the rise of China, India, and Brazil, it has also profoundly shaken Western economic self-confidence, weakened its economic image abroad, and further destabilized the current hierarchy of racialized human value that undergirds this global economic system.

From the perspective of Africana political economy, three crucial questions emerge immediately. The first concerns the nature of the crisis. The second has to do with how this crisis and its aftermath will affect the underlying *pieza* framework of human value by which Western capitalism has racialized itself and others. The third addresses the prospects for substantive change in Africana political economies in the postcrisis years.

The Nature of the Crisis of 2008

The Great Recession of 2008 began with the bursting of a bubble that had developed in the American housing and financial markets, and from these locations spread with amazing rapidity to the rest of the American economy and to financial markets across the globe. The speed and intensity with which this financial explosion spread a fire that engulfed the global economy was both frightening and devastating, as its flames destroyed tens of trillions of dollars' worth of wealth in so many of its member countries. To grasp clearly the nature and structural dimensions of this crisis, we must immediately take note of a number of new trends that had emerged in the American economy. The most important of these were (1) the continued off-shoring of the American industrial sector; (2) the rise of new information and communications technologies; (3) financialization, or the emergence of the financial sector as the leading sector of the economy, replacing industrial production;

and (4) repeated attempts to build a postindustrial economy around services that would be empowered and made highly competitive by the new information and communications technologies. The still unrealized goal of these attempts at a "new economy" I have called the "informatic" phase of American capitalism (Meeks and Girvan 2010, 172–205).

The crisis of 2008 was the third failed attempt by American capitalists to establish the long announced "new economy." The first of these attempts consisted of the "dot-com" companies that collapsed in 2001. The second failed attempt was the model of the high-tech energy and high-tech infrastructure companies led by Enron, WorldCom, and Cisco. The collapse of Enron and WorldCom released telling hints about the new practices of greed, fraud, and corruption that the new systems of management incentives were encouraging. In spite of the 2002 Sarbanes-Oxley Act of managerial reform, these corrupt practices exploded a thousand times over as the crisis of 2008 unfolded and the third attempt at a "new economy" for America was consumed in its flames.

The greater intensity of the collapse of this third attempt at a new American economy I attribute to the fact that it rested on at least three novel trends that were more global and more risky in nature: (1) the neoliberal globalizing of financial markets; (2) a drive to make the financial sector the replacement of the increasingly off-shored industrial sector; and (3) the rise in importance of "shareholder value" in models of corporate governance, along with its new systems of managerial incentives, which made managers into shareholders. From the perspective of the crisis of 2008, probably the most important of these was the developmental strategy of replacing the outgoing industrial sector with finance, which has come to be known as the financialization of the American economy.

This process of financialization was the result of revolutionary changes in the banking system over the past twenty-five years that the new information and communications technologies have made possible. In the broadest terms, the new technologies made possible what Marx would probably have called the full commodification of financial transactions. Prior to the present period, financial transactions were largely contractual in nature and bank centered. Banks in turn were closely regulated by central and local governments with the goal of minimizing competition between these institutions and also insulating them from the ups and downs of the market. This older order of minimal commodification of financial transactions is precisely what the new information and communications technology has made obsolete. As mechanical technologies made possible the commodification of material

transactions, so the new information technologies have made possible the commodification of financial transactions on a global scale. This accounts for the significant growth in the number of stock markets around the world in the past twenty years, including those of tiny islands in the eastern Caribbean.

One important way in which the new technology facilitated this process of the full commodification and globalization of finance was by making instantly and widely available reliable information on firms from a variety of centralized sources, such as Standard and Poor's or Dunn and Bradstreet. These sources provide banks and investors with information on company earnings, credit records, accounting data, and so on, and also similar information on individuals. With this kind of "hard" information readily available, it became much easier for banks to make loan decisions to distant customers without face-to-face meetings. This new ability expanded and globalized access to capital.

Greater access to capital from several places across the globe was also facilitated by policies of deregulation, which helped to clear the way for banks to operate in marketized as opposed to contractual spaces. Further, this combination of new technology and deregulation also made possible the rapid growth of new financial institutions and corresponding changes in the nature and functioning of banks. Consequently, the recent period has seen the rise of private equity firms, hedge funds, sovereign wealth funds, and banks, mixing their old contractual practices with the new market-based transactions. As a result, traditional banks are no longer at the center of the Western financial system, even though they remain significant players. Investors may now enter these growing financial markets through hedge funds, mutual funds, corporate bonds, stocks, and a growing number of alternatives to traditional bank offerings.

One important consequence of this growth in nonbank financial institutions has been the standardization of the contractual terms for loans. This standardization facilitated the selling of loans, by making it possible for them to be packaged into diverse bundles for sale to investors with different interests, tastes, and appetites for risk. This process of packaging loans whose contractual terms have been standardized has come to be known as "securitization" (Faber 2009, 44). Along with these securitized loans came new financial products, such as credit default swaps and credit derivatives—all terms that were added to the economic vocabulary of the public by the unfolding of the major crisis that started in 2008 (Morris 2008, 59–79).

With these significant changes of the past twenty-five years in the financial sector, it is easy to see why it emerged as a primary candidate for the role

of the "leading sector" that would be the basis for the "new economy" of America. However, for this new leading sector to grow and dynamize other sectors of the economy, it would need demand—trillions of dollars' worth of demand. Consequently, it would have to capture the financial needs of all and sundry or create new forms of indebtedness that it would then proceed to finance. First, the new leaders of global finance moved to replace or minimize the role of direct government participation in this sector. Thus loans to governments in developing countries and to students pursuing higher education in for-profit universities became new sources of demand for this sector. Many even suggested that Social Security and Medicare be placed under the control of this new leading sector. In the private sector, credit card financing and the "dot-com" companies were also important sources of demand for the rising sector. But by far its most important source of demand was the financial needs of the real estate market. The purchasing, securitizing, and selling of loans taken out by home buyers and real estate developers in the United States and abroad became the primary source of demand driving the growth of the new sector. However, as we shall see, this model of financialization was overtaken by levels of greed and corruption that made Enron and WorldCom look like junior high school operations. These practices created and fed the bubble that would increasingly enclose the high-tech sector and once again block the emergence of the struggling informatic phase as it burst and caught fire.

In the period immediately following the Al-Qaeda attack on the World Trade Center in September 2001, the Federal Reserve Bank lowered interest rates in an effort to calm the markets and to keep the American economy stimulated. The banks, in particular, took advantage of this cheap money to push mortgages. A lot of these mortgages were then sold to Freddie Mac and Fannie Mae, two government-supported enterprises (GSEs) that were the largest mortgage companies in the country. Indeed, they had introduced the practice of securitization and were the leaders in the making and selling of the new financial products to investors at home and abroad. However, in 2011, the leaders of Freddie Mac were brought up on charges of misrepresenting crucial numbers in the company's accounts, which caused many of their clients to lose confidence in them. Into the vacuum that was created by this collapse of confidence moved the major Wall Street banks—Goldman Sachs, J. P. Morgan, Lehman Brothers, and other financial institutions such as AIG, the insurance giant.

As the investment banks realized the potential of this business model for profits, they opened it up in a way that went miles beyond the practices of

Freddie Mac and Fannie Mae. They had far greater global connections than the GSEs and so were able to sell securitized mortgages to many more overseas investors. Further, confident that they now had the risks in these financial products mathematically calculated and under control, the investment banks began buying up all the mortgages they could get their hands on. This colossal demand for mortgages, together with the cheap money from the Federal Reserve, started the chain reaction that would inflate the bubble and eventually burst it.

A host of new institutions emerged to service these growing demands of the Wall Street bankers. These institutions benefited from the cheap credit that the Federal Reserve made possible after 2001 and used it to make loans of a wide variety, but particularly to home buyers. They then securitized the loans themselves or sold them to securitizers and then to the big investment banks. In many cases, the securitizers to whom these loans were sold purchased them with cheap money they had borrowed. Thus the bubble continued to inflate, and home prices continued to rise.

As the profits continued to roll in and more firms entered this booming market, competition forced the making of ever riskier loans. By this time, all the cautions of traditional banking practices had long since disappeared. Even cautions such as credit scoring were in many instances abandoned in this new context, where it was assumed that the risk in a bad investment could be countered by the mathematics of bundling them with good ones. It was in this context that subprime mortgages not only became marketable mortgages but parts of Triple A–rated securities. This of course required the cooperation and collusion of the rating agencies in the dramatic changing of the meaning of a Triple A rating. This scheme continued for several years, making a lot of money for Wall Street banks and again driving up home prices.

But a scheme like this could not go on for very long without a more substantial productive base. Further, the financial managers did not really have control over the risk factors in the mortgages they were securitizing. The first signs of trouble began with homeowners not being able to pay their prime and subprime mortgages. As these defaults moved from a trickle to a flood, the systems of risk management, including credit default swaps, began to fail in dramatic chain reactions. These chain reactions soon left several British banks and all of the major Wall Street investment banks short of cash and unable to meet their major obligations to investors. In other words, they were on the verge of bankruptcy. The first of these American banks to send out distress signals and seek assistance was Bear Stearns.

The federal government had to rescue it with a forced marriage to J. P. Morgan Chase and $29 billion in U.S. government financing. Next to implode were the two GSEs, Freddie Mac and Fannie Mae. They had to be rescued with $200 billion in U.S. government financing. Lehman Brothers was the next Wall Street giant to send out distress signals. However, because of growing taxpayer anger at the first three bailouts, then secretary of the Treasury Hank Paulson and Federal Reserve chair Ben Bernanke were under great pressure to find a private-sector solution. Barclays Bank and Bank of America expressed interest. However, when they were allowed to examine the books of Lehman Brothers, they found the latter's problems so severe that they both backed out. Lehman Brothers was allowed to fail.

The impact of the Lehman Brothers collapse was much greater than Paulson and Bernanke had anticipated. Because of the exposure of so many other major financial institutions to Lehman Brothers, it pushed many of them to the edge of collapse, including the entire money market and commercial paper sectors. Teetering on the edge, along with the companies in these two sectors, were such financial giants as Merrill Lynch, Goldman Sachs, Morgan Stanley, and AIG—the largest insurance company in the world and the major seller of credit default swaps. Others would soon follow, including General Electric, General Motors, Citibank, Bank of America, and Countrywide. Overseas, these dramatic slides were triggering similar collapses in Europe, particularly in England, Iceland, and, later, Ireland, Greece, Spain, and Portugal.

The avalanche of companies that were about to follow in the footsteps of Lehman Brothers triggered the U.S. government's Troubled Assets Relief Program (TARP) of $700 billion. The strategy here was to buy up some of the toxic assets on the balance sheets of these banks in the hope that this would restore their stability and credibility. However, the momentum of these falling companies was such that this strategy had to be replaced by one in which the U.S. government purchased large shares of equity in many of these companies, followed by passage of the Dodd-Frank Wall Street Reform and Consumer Protection Act of July 2010. Similar rescue programs were undertaken by the British and Chinese governments, with the aim of helping to stem this tide of financial collapse. Thus began a multigovernment effort to contain the collapse that many believe was on track to be another Great Depression. Fortunately, these combined efforts succeeded in steering the catastrophic financial situation into the Great Recession of 2008. Although these government interventions avoided a depression, they were unable to save the third attempt at launching the informatic phase of American capitalism.

Race and the Informatic Phase of Capitalism

The dramatic collapse of the financial core of American capitalism did not just delay once again the start of a new informatic phase that had been struggling to be born for some time. In addition, it forced both the United States and Europe to move in the state capitalist directions that they had explicitly rejected at the start of the neoliberal period in the 1980s. This unintended turn toward state capitalism converged with a turn away from socialism and toward state capitalism in China, Russia, and Eastern Europe. Consequently, the period from 2008 to the present has been one in which different forms of state capitalism have dominated the political economies of the major countries. In countries like the United States and Britain, the state has returned to playing a more central and Keynesian role in the economy, while in countries like China, Russia, and Vietnam, the markets have come to play a much more central role in the economy than their earlier socialist positions had stipulated. At the same time, the different shifts in the direction of state capitalism have produced major shifts in the balance of power within the world economy, including the possibility of the emergence of a new center for this global economic system. Thus, to make explicit the implications of these power shifts for the racial schema of value that supported the period of American dominance, we must first think through the likely shape of the world economy in the postcrisis period.

First, we can expect the United States to terminate its current period of state capitalism and make a fourth attempt at launching its informatic phase on more liberal and private-sector-led foundations. This was very clear in President Obama's speech of 21 January 2011, in which he appointed Jeffrey Immelt, the CEO of General Electric, to chair his Council on Jobs and Competitiveness. The president noted that the past two years had been spent pulling the economy back from the brink and that the next two must be spent in getting this giant economic machine into overdrive. At the center of Obama's model of development is the high-tech clean-energy sector on which he campaigned. This model is a green version of the high-tech energy/high-tech infrastructure model that had been pushed by companies like Cisco and the now defunct Enron and WorldCom. In addition to its green features, the Obama model differs from its predecessor in that it is being led by government, suggesting that the phase of state capitalism may be around much longer than many would like. Whatever the time horizon, this is now the most likely view of the new informatic American economy of the future.

If Japan is able to resolve its long-standing financial crisis, it could also be a locus for the emergence of the informatic phase of the world economy, as many in the 1980s thought that it would be. It certainly has the productive base and the technological capabilities for fulfilling this role. However, Japan's postcrisis political economy would be quite different from that of the United States, given its different perceptions of and attitude toward the role of the state in the economy.

At present, given China's remarkable rate of economic growth, many are of the view that China will become the new center of the global economy. Having recently surpassed Japan, China is now the world's second-largest economy and could overtake the United States in fifteen to twenty years. Because of its growing pollution problems and the ecological challenges raised by the prospects of China's future growth, its leaders have been investing heavily in high-tech infrastructure and the transition to green or low-carbon energy production. Indeed, General Electric, the leading American company in green energy, whose CEO is now Obama's point man in this area, has most of its green investments in China. In fact, one of the most striking features of the emerging global economic order is the deeply symbiotic relationship that has developed between the American and Chinese economies. Thus the term "Chimerica" has been coined to mark the deepening ties that now bind these two economies (Karabell 2009, 3). There is a lot of cooperation and competition in this relationship and thus some growing tensions. I will return to the significance of this U.S.-China relationship for Africana political economy in the final section of this chapter. Even more than Japan, China's postcrisis political economy is likely to be very different from that of the United States. It could easily be a continuation of the present order, which has been described as both state capitalist and market socialist.

Coming up rapidly behind China is India. The latter's high-tech infrastructure will certainly make it a major player in the launching of the informatic phase of the world economy. Finally, there is Brazil, whose recent economic performance, first under the leadership of President Luiz Inácio Lula da Silva and now under President Dilma Rousseff, has made it a major player in the world economy. In the three years immediately following the crisis of 2008, China, India, and Brazil surpassed the United States as desirable sites for investors. With these nonwhite territories, the United States and Europe could be confronted with the prospect of an informatic global economy led by former coolies and mongrels. Such a global economic order would clearly be at odds with the racial schema of human exchange value in which Anglo-Saxon whiteness was a primary marker of economic supremacy and leadership.

In addition to posing these "yellow," "brown," and "mongrel" challenges to the racial codes of the America-dominated period of the world economy, the crisis of 2008 also brought with it at least three important black challenges to American capitalism. The first was the resistance of African Americans to the attempts of many white conservatives to make them into subprime scapegoats and thus the cause of the Great Recession of 2008. Second, in spite of great doubt and fear, the leaders of American capitalism had to accept the election of Barack Obama, who became the country's first African American president. This election made explicit many of the racial codes that still undergirded the American political system. The third and final challenge was the very real but hardly surprising higher rate of unemployment and overall economic contraction in the economies of African American communities. Two and a half years after the onset of the Recession, the official national unemployment rate hovered around 9 percent, while the rate among African Americans was 15 percent. In its 2010 *State of Black America* report, the National Urban League estimated this rate to be 16.5 percent, "the highest for any racial or ethnic group" (Solis 2010, 68). However, starting in March 2011, the official unemployment rate began to drop slowly, reaching 8.8 percent by the end of that month and continuing to decline. Approaching five years after the onset of the Great Recession (May 2013), official unemployment was stagnating at around 7.6 percent, and African American unemployment stood at 13.5 percent. Thus, in contrast to the challenges from China, Brazil, and India, the challenges from the black world, whether Africa, the Caribbean, or Afro-America, did not include the dramatic economic performances that shattered the racially prescribed levels of capability in these productive areas. I will return to this economic dimension of black resistance after examining the significance of the more visible political dimensions of our resistance to our place in the current world economy.

In the responses of white elites to the three postcrisis challenges from Afro-America, we can observe some of the continuities and discontinuities in the racial codes of the American political economy. The controversies that surrounded the election of President Obama, from the many death threats to the outrageous statements by Geraldine Ferraro of the Hillary Clinton camp, made quite clear the Republican promise of the American political imaginary and the racial restrictions in which it is still inscribed. The controversies over the subprime mortgage scapegoating of African Americans further demonstrated the power and persistence of the antiblack codes that inform American economic and political thinking. In the higher rates of unemployment and other indicators of economic decline, we see the persistence of old

structural and normative patterns that have sustained the ghettoization of African American economies and practices of job discrimination against African Americans.

Obama's presidency has been a lightning rod for the ambivalent responses that have consistently flowed from the racialized Republican codes of the American political imaginary. The millions of white Americans who voted for Obama clearly indicated significant shifts in the racial coding of their political activities. Until that moment, this would have been a code-prohibited act for many whites. However, what exactly this weakening of racial codes will mean for the future is still working itself out, as it has to contend with their strengthening among millions of conservatives and groups on the Far Right. The strengthening of racial codes among these groups has been a noticeable trend since the official break with the civil rights era inaugurated by the Reagan administration in the early 1980s. This break was also the start of the so-called color-blind era, as color blindness became the official policy of the Reagan administration. But the rise of racial hatred on the right signaled otherwise. Carol Swain has carefully documented the rise of white supremacist groups in her book *The New White Nationalism in America* (2002). At the same time, Eduardo Bonilla-Silva has shown that color-blind America has racial codes of its own that lead to what he calls "color-blind racism" (2010, 25). In its 2009 report on right-wing extremism, the U.S. Department of Homeland Security noted that "rightwing extremists have capitalized on the election of the first African American president, and are focusing their efforts to recruit new members, mobilize existing supporters, and broaden their scope and appeal through propaganda, but they have not yet turned to attack planning" (2009, 2). This rising effort on the right to reestablish the racial codes of the pre–civil rights era within the spaces of the new color-blind policy was the countercurrent that Obama's bid for the presidency encountered head-on.

For these conservative and Far Right groups, Obama's presidency has been the occasion for a variety of antiblack projections, based on bad faith or *ressentiment*, and efforts to reinforce the old Anglo-Saxon codes. Thus President Obama has been the target of death threats and of racist judgments, both covert and explicit, including the view of millions who refuse to believe that he is an American. To give just one example, of countless others, there was the case of a military officer who refused to obey an order to serve in Afghanistan on this basis. Further, President Obama has been the target of what Richard Hofstadter (1967) has called "the paranoid style" in American politics. Dating all the way back to the revolutionary period, this paranoid

frame of mind points obsessively to conspiratorial external threats to destroy American freedoms. In being labeled a dictator, a Nazi, a socialist, or a Muslim during the debates over his proposed health-care reforms, Obama became the target of these paranoid codes of the American political imaginary. He became a threatening and freedom-devouring figure from whom conservative Americans had to "take back our country."

The postcrisis black challenges to the racial codes of America must be added to those from China, India, and Brazil. Each in its way poses significant delegitimating threats to the color-blind racial order that marked the past thirty years of U.S. hegemony over the world economy. It is too soon to say precisely what the outcome of these challenges will be, as their complex dynamics and counterdynamics are still working themselves out. However, it seems reasonable to expect that from whatever point or points the transition to the informatic phase of the world economy is eventually launched, the racial legacy of Western dominance will be with us for a while.

Informatic Capitalism and Africana Political Economy

The race to launch the informatic phase of the world economy in the years ahead will have many important implications for the discourse of Africana political economy. In the final section of this chapter, let us look at just two of these implications: first, the widespread turn to state capitalism, in both socialist and capitalist economies, that has followed the financial meltdown of 2008; and second, the significance of the higher rates of economic decline that the financial crisis brought to Afro-America, and the prospects for moving into the new informatic global economic order that lies ahead. These issues will make clear the value of contributions made by Africana political economy, and the challenges it must now confront in dealing with the problems of economic growth in black economies around the globe.

With regard to the first issue, we can begin by noting that within the tradition of Africana political economy, the term "state capitalism" immediately calls to mind the works of C. L. R. James, in particular, texts like *State Capitalism and World Revolution* and *The Invading Socialist Society*. In these works, James developed the view that state capitalism was a fallback position from the crisis tendencies of both liberal capitalism and authoritarian socialism. In the tendency of these two systems to move toward state capitalism, James, writing in the 1940s, envisioned the dark possibility of a coinciding of interests between the USSR and the United States based on containing the rising

demands of workers in the advanced countries for direct democracy and economic self-management (1972, 8). As these demands posed similar threats to the accumulation process in both authoritarian socialist and liberal capitalist countries, James saw state capitalism as a compromise position that would allow the ruling elites of both countries to ease the polarization between them, and to assist each other in continuing their different models of extracting surplus value from their subordinated but increasingly insurgent working classes. It was in this possibility of helping each other to contain the growing working-class contradictions inherent in their models of accumulation that James perceived the biggest threat to working-class liberation. However, in this convergence of interests between authoritarian socialism and liberal capitalism, James saw the former as having to absorb and contain more of the working-class demands, as liberal capitalism was the stronger of the two systems.

How relevant is this Jamesian theory of the 1940s to our current situation? There are many ways in which this theory continues to be relevant, but I will mention only two. First, it helps us understand why the crisis of authoritarian socialism has produced such a wide variety of state capitalist formations and not a single case of proletarian socialism. In Russia and Eastern Europe in particular, we have seen the emergence of corrupt and not very dynamic forms of state capitalism. In China and Vietnam, we have seen the emergence of state capitalism that so far has been very dynamic and productive of growth. The most recent turn to state capitalism in an authoritarian socialist country is seen in the recent reforms of the Cuban economy under President Raul Castro. Even here, however, unsolved economic problems have stood in the way of a transition to proletarian socialism.

The second way in which James's theory of state capitalism is relevant to the dominant trends of our time is the already noted convergence between the accumulative logics of the Chinese and American economies, particularly in the period following the crisis of 2008. Although James did not get the specific country right, the idea that state capitalist solutions to crises of accumulation could lead to a convergence of interests between authoritarian socialism and liberal capitalism is clearly one that not only marks but also sheds great light on our present situation. Indeed, this "Chimerican" convergence of interests around issues of capital accumulation has gone even further than James imagined. In the view of former British prime minister Gordon Brown, the way out of the crisis lies in China's middle class growing at a faster rate than it currently projects, so that it can consume knowledge-based products produced in and exported by the West (Brown 2010, 209–31).

As James anticipated, in this symbiotic relationship with the West, China has already had to absorb more of the contradictions in the American model of capital accumulation, as it has been the weaker of the two countries. Thus, in spite of being nominally a workers' state, since the late 1970s China has made its "communist" working class available to American and European capitalists for purposes of surplus extraction at rates that have allowed them to contain the upward push of American and European workers by sending jobs overseas and weakening labor unions. In exchange, American and European capitalists have been supplying China with needed investment capital, technology, and entrepreneurial expertise that have greatly expanded its accumulative capabilities. The growth dynamics of Chimerican exchange relations will probably determine who will lead the world economy in the future. In what began as a typical Western imperial penetration of a Third World economy, China, by insisting on 51 percent partnerships with major Western corporations, has quite rapidly and strategically turned that penetration to its advantage and, since the crisis of 2008, has become the greater beneficiary of this historic convergence. But whatever the outcome, James's theory of state capitalism gives us a solid grasp of this peculiar convergence, and thus a vital hold on a major politico-economic formation that has become central to our current conjuncture.

As noted above, in spite of strenuous efforts, there were no dynamic transformations in the political economies of black nations or communities to rival the growth performances recorded in China, Brazil, and India. Rather, for the entire postwar period of American hegemony, these economies have not been able to break out of the racialized patterns of neocolonial economic dependence. In other words, they have not been able to mobilize sufficient power, capital, and entrepreneurial ability to overcome the negatives in their specific situations or turn them into positives. This is in part the meaning of the higher rates of unemployment and decline in the economies of African American communities as compared to the American nation as a whole. The persistence of these differences has raised once again an old question for Africana political economy: have past and existing racial codes created one or two American economies? More often than not, scholars tend to assume the existence of one national (white) economy into which African Americans have been incorporated as cheap "Negro" labor. Consequently, the persistent poverty and divergent economic indices have been assumed to follow from related practices of exclusion and job discrimination.

However, I have argued that, given the separatist effects of past segregationist and current color-blind racial codes, a more accurate conceptualization

would indeed be that of two separate economies—as separate as black and white churches, black and white colleges, or black and white residential neighborhoods. In other words, the institutional dualism produced by the long history of American racial codes has left its divisive imprint on the American economy as much as it has on the American church or the American academy. Thus the attempt to study carefully the nature and developmental problems of these racially separated and ghettoized economies has been another of the important contributions of Africana political economy. As a part of this larger effort, I have suggested that the economies of African American communities can usefully be viewed as white-owned peripheral formations from which the major export to the white centers has been cheap "Negro" labor. In short, African American communities have been and still are primarily labor-exporting economies rather than producing ones.

The first exports from these externally controlled economies took the form of slave labor on white-owned plantations. Then came the labor of sharecroppers on white-owned land, and finally wage labor in white-owned industrial factories. Payment for these labor exports has been the major source of income for African American economies, and the largest contributor to their GDP.

Complementing this labor-based export sector has been an internal or community-based sector that produces goods and services for customers within these African American communities. For much of its history, and still, for the most part, today, the most lucrative enterprises of this internal sector, real estate and retail, were owned by whites. These white owners did not live in the communities and thus took the surplus generated in these businesses outside African American communities. Thus the cycle of capital accumulation and reinvestment that produces economic growth and wealth was fatally broken. Further, as "redlined" districts, African American communities until recently lacked adequate banking services to support the entrepreneurial and investment activities that are vital for economic growth. Consequently, when we add together the practices of white purchases of cheap "Negro labor," white control of the most lucrative enterprises of the community-based sector, the breaking of the capital-investment cycle, and the redlining of black economies by white banks, we get some of worst cases of economic exploitation on record. The poverty in these African American communities cannot be separated from those extremely high levels of surplus value extraction.

Also important for grasping the overall structure of the economies of African American communities are the black-owned enterprises of the internal

or community-based sector. These are primarily service enterprises such as barbershops, restaurants, beauty shops, funeral parlors, nightclubs, and sports clubs. They are clearly businesses that whites have little desire to frequent, given the close contact with blacks that they require. Income from these businesses constitutes the economic foundations of the black middle class. Their cycles of capital accumulation, investment, and expansion have been quite restricted, given the constraints under which they must operate. The newest form of these restrictions by and subordination to external white capital can be seen in the Empowerment Zone projects for the development of Harlem and the "inner-city areas" of Atlanta, Baltimore, Detroit, and Philadelphia that President Clinton announced in 1994. These projects have dramatically increased white ownership of the retail and real estate sectors of the black communities in question, and have thus reinforced old patterns of surplus extraction. Thus, if economic mobilization for growth via capital accumulation is white America's answer to the problem of poverty, then its concerted efforts to block such mobilization in African American communities must be a major part of the explanation for the higher rates of unemployment, poverty, and economic decline that have kept African American communities at Third World levels of economic development.

Conclusion

Given the results of past policies of black economic development, it is clear that Africana political economists have a lot of work to do. As the austerity measures of the postcrisis years begin to take effect, this work will only get more difficult. Having bailed out the big investment banks, federal and local governments must now cut back in major areas of spending if they are to get their balance sheets back in order. This pressure comes most immediately, of course, from their creditors and bondholders. Add to this pressure the fact that private-sector off-shoring of jobs has not yet peaked, in spite of the failure to launch the "new economy," and we get a sense of the powerful countertrends against which new policies and strategies of black economic development will have to be pursued.

As I have shown elsewhere, the Caribbean cannot escape another round of dependent growth in relation to Western capital, as its attempts to launch new economies have nearly all collapsed. Similar collapses in Africa and Afro-America can only lead to similar results: new rounds of dependent growth within the global economy for their economies. Thus the challenge

for Africana political economists is to start planning now for the end of these new cycles of dependent growth. In my view, two key factors will determine the ending of these current cycles of slow growth that depend excessively on white capital: the first is the continued rise in the price of Chinese labor, which will increase until it reaches the point where it is significantly less attractive to Western capital; and the second is the return of solvency to the balance sheets of Western governments.

In my view, we must begin now to lay the foundations that will position black economies more independently and competitively in the coming informatic phase of the global economy. This will require, on the part of Africana people, higher levels of education, entrepreneurial performance, and investment in and ownership of black economies, as well as fighting job discrimination. In order to establish his own economic identity, Caliban must enter not only into regions Caesar never knew but also into entrepreneurial regions that Caesar knew very well. In the future, there will be new projects like the Empowerment Zones. This is the only way in which the accumulative logic of the white economic establishment can relate to the economies of black communities. Like the Chinese, we must prepare ourselves to turn such projects to our advantage.

Finally, this strategic orientation toward the postcrisis informatic era assumes that there will be no major Jamesian upsurges of popular creativity such as those that are currently unfolding in the Middle East and North Africa. I make this assumption because these major upsurges are extremely difficult to predict. If these upsurges arrive sooner than these plans make room for, of course, we must scrap them and engage those that will be acted out on the streets.

References

Bonilla-Silva, Eduardo. 2010. *Racism without racists: Color-blind racism and the persistence of racial inequality in the United States.* Lanham, Md.: Rowman and Littlefield.
Brown, Gordon. 2010. *Beyond the crash.* New York: Free Press.
Cugoano, Ottobah. 1999. *Thoughts and sentiments on the evil of slavery.* London: Penguin Classics.
Du Bois, W. E. B. 1998. *Black reconstruction in America.* New York: Free Press.
———. 1999. *Darkwater.* New York: Dover Publications.
Ephraim, Charles. 2003. *The pathology of Eurocentrism.* Trenton, N.J.: Africa World Press.
Faber, David. 2009. *And the roof caved in.* Hoboken: Wiley and Sons.
Fanon, Frantz. 1968. *The wretched of the earth.* New York: Grove Press.
Frazier, E. Franklin. 1957. *Black bourgeoisie.* New York: Free Press.

Fukuyama, Francis. 1992. *The end of history and the last man*. New York: Free Press.

Gordon, Lewis R. 1995. *Bad faith and antiblack racism*. Atlantic Highlands, N.J.: Humanity Books.

Henry, Paget. 2004. Whiteness and Africana phenomenology. In *What white looks like: African-American philosophers on the whiteness question*, ed. George Yancy, 195–210. New York: Routledge.

Hofstadter, Richard. 1967. *The paranoid style in American politics*. New York: Vintage Books.

Huntington, Samuel. 1996. *The clash of civilizations*. New York: Simon and Schuster.

James, C. L. R. 1972. *The invading socialist society*. Detroit: Bewick Editions.

———. 1986. *State capitalism and world revolution*. Chicago: Charles H. Kerr.

Karabell, Zachary. 2009. *Superfusion: How China and America became one economy and why the world's prosperity depends on it*. New York: Simon and Schuster.

Meeks, Brian, and Norman Girvan, eds. 2010. *The thought of new world*. Kingston, Jamaica: Ian Randle.

Morris, Charles. 2008. *The trillion dollar meltdown: Easy money, high rollers, and the great credit era*. New York: Public Affairs.

Robinson, Cedric. 2000. *Black Marxism: The making of the black radical tradition*. Chapel Hill: University of North Carolina Press.

Saillant, John. 2003. *Black puritan, black republican*. New York: Oxford University Press.

Solis, Hilda. 2010. Creating jobs for everyone. In *The state of black America, 2010*, ed. Stephanie Jones, 66–75. New York: National Urban League.

Swain, Carol. 2002. *The new white nationalism in America*. New York: Cambridge University Press.

U.S. Department of Homeland Security. 2009. *Rightwing extremism: Current economic and political climate fueling resurgence in radicalization and recruitment*. Washington, D.C.: U.S. Government Printing Office.

Wynter, Sylvia. 1992. Beyond the categories of the master conception: The counter-doctrine of the Jamesian poiesis. In *C. L. R. James's Caribbean*, ed. Paget Henry and Paul Buhle, 63–91. Durham: Duke University Press.

12

The Great White North: Failing Muslim Canadians, Failing Us All

Tracey Nicholls

I arrived in Canada, as an elementary school child, in 1975—after the old Canadian flag with the Union Jack on it had been replaced by the maple leaf design, after Prime Minister Lester B. Pearson's introduction of official bilingualism, after Trudeaumania, at the precise moment in Canadian history when the nation's formerly British-inflected identity was being rearticulated as a "cultural mosaic" of immigrants from all over the world. Indeed, I arrived in Montreal—in the very white, very middle-class, *very* anglophone suburb of Beaconsfield, to be precise—a mere five years after the FLQ crisis that saw Montreal placed under martial law, an experience that rankles the city's sovereigntists to this day. My family came to Canada from another British Commonwealth country, New Zealand, not driven by oppression or desperation but lured instead by the intangible check that, seemingly, middle-class adults everywhere seek to cash: upward mobility.

I lived in my adopted country for years, completely insulated and blinded by my white privilege, believing that the sphere of public life in Canada was

---

This chapter is dedicated to the memory of Somali youth Shidane Arone, whose death, on 16 March 1993, by torture at the hands of members of the Canadian Airborne Regiment stationed in Somalia continues to horrify me as a fellow human being and shame me as a Canadian. It is also dedicated to the Canadian diplomat Richard Colvin, in recognition of his courageous efforts to publicize—first to his superiors in the Canadian government and then to members of the public—his concerns about Canada's complicity in the torture of detainees that Canadian military personnel were handing over to Afghani security forces without obtaining adequate assurances of their safety.

truly a level playing field, until a series of chance encounters and government decisions finally enlightened me about the differential treatment of citizens. This chapter explores the question of the role that race appears to play in differential treatment, weaving together personal narratives of my coming to awareness about my own social privilege with analysis of a series of incidents in which Canadian citizens in trouble abroad have received unequal treatment at the hands of the government that is supposed to be protecting us all. In particular, I take up the guarantee, in the UN's Universal Declaration of Human Rights, of the right of a citizen to live in his or her country of citizenship and to enter or leave it at will, and I examine the extent to which that right was respected (or not) by the Canadian government in the cases of Amanda Lindhout, kidnapped and held hostage in Somalia in 2008 and 2009; Abousfian Abdelrazik, stranded in the Canadian embassy in Sudan between 2003 and 2009; and Suaad Hagi Mohamud, arrested in Kenya in 2009 at the apparent behest of the Canadian Department of Foreign Affairs. I use this examination of differential treatment to ground my speculations about the stunning silence of the Canadian public in the face of what seems to be Canadian complicity in war crimes.

Two decades after I arrived in Montreal, I found myself living in Vancouver, where, after years of working my way up through the ranks of clerical accounting, I was seized by a desire to leave the corporate world and study philosophy. To a great extent—greater than I realized for some time—my life as a thirty-year-old undergraduate recipient of Canada and British Columbia student loans was possible only because of my unrecognized social privilege, in this case, the implicit promise of creditworthiness that my whiteness and apparent middle-class status represented to the bank that held my loans. During my studies at the University of British Columbia, I found myself a work-study job as a peer tutor in the First Nations House of Learning (the Longhouse). It was a job I loved, not just a means to a paycheck but a chance to spend time in the company of highly focused students who all seemed to share a dark, dry sense of humor about the obstacles they faced and a generous willingness to support one another. It was also a profoundly uncomfortable place for me to be once I realized that these students I was working with had made the assumption that I too was First Nations. I wasn't, but I felt I couldn't tell people that. I simply didn't know how to correct their mistaken assumption without giving the impression that I was rejecting a socially despised identity. Instead, I stayed silent, and learned a firsthand lesson in the guilt and uneasiness that comes with knowing that

one is getting a privilege—in this case, unquestioning acceptance into these students' social circle—that one has not earned.

One of the students I worked with there was a young First Nations man I will call Joe. Joe gave me a ride home late one night because I had a textbook at home that he wanted to borrow so he could study for a test. I no longer remember what we talked about for most of the car ride, but I do recall vividly his reaction to a silly, unthinking comment I tossed out—a holdover from my conformist, British-inflected childhood—to the effect that "the police officer is your friend." Joe, this young man who had always engaged with me through his evident respect for my intelligence, looked utterly dumbstruck, as if he simply could not reconcile the remark he had just heard with the person he thought I was. Finally, he managed to observe tactfully that I obviously had not grown up on a reservation (an Indian reserve). I also no longer remember where the conversation went from that point, but I will always remember that as the moment that I first fully and completely realized that not all of my fellow Canadians experienced the policing of our society as the level playing field I thought it was.

Of course, I had realized this lack of parity already on a conscious level. I knew it was hard for people with criminal records to get jobs, and I knew that—even in hippie, pot-smoking Vancouver—it was a really good idea not to seem like a drug dealer if you wanted to avoid police harassment. I just honestly—I don't know how—didn't really realize that people's racial identities could generate different relations to the law-and-order personnel who were—I thought—supposed to be serving and protecting us all.

About five years after that moment of awakening, I was back in Montreal, my Canadian home, pursuing a doctoral degree in philosophy at McGill University, the last bastion of anglophone privilege in that mostly francophone city. One Thursday evening, I was walking home from the university after having spent the afternoon leading discussion groups for students in a course on the philosophy of law, on the importance of making sure that the people who enforced the law were also held to the same standards they apply to us. I was standing at the corner of Prince-Arthur and Saint-Laurent, making a mental list of things I needed at the grocery store and waiting for the light to change. The little pedestrian "walk" signal lit up and I stepped off the curb into the intersection, just as a police officer in a paddy wagon rolled through the intersection, running a red light. Dumbfounded—because *that* was exactly what I had spent my afternoon criticizing—I forgot that I'm not

supposed to talk to myself in public and said out loud, staring after him, "Hey, asshole, you can't do that!" But he had, and there was nothing I could do about it. So I crossed the street, fuming to myself, and headed for the grocery store. As I was walking toward the store, I became aware that someone was trying to get my attention, and I looked out past the parked cars to the street. There was the officer in the paddy wagon, slowed down to a crawl, and gesturing at me to come closer. I stepped off the sidewalk into the space between two parked cars, glared at him, and snapped, "What?" Slightly taken aback, he gestured to his rear-view mirror and said in Québécois-accented English, "I see in the mirror you call me 'asshole.'" Now, I had never for a single second, until that moment, entertained the possibility that police officers might be able to lip-read (a useful, entirely commonsensical skill for them to have, and one that I encourage the future law enforcement officers in my philosophy of law classes to acquire whenever I recount this story to them). Fortunately, this was one of those rare moments when my surprise at something utterly unexpected didn't throw me off my stride; I had the presence of mind to stare him down and say, "Yeah, so?" This aggressive attitude was clearly not what he was expecting as a response to what he must have considered a reprimand, and he asked me why I had called him an asshole. Astounded, I started to splutter. I could not fathom that he was unaware of his wrongdoing and my witnessing of it, so I assumed that he was trying to bluff his way out of it, thinking that he could intimidate or confuse me into believing that I was not entitled to hold him to account. I pointed back to the intersection and told him, "That was *my* light," to which he replied, "Oh, I thought it was mine." Outraged, I insisted that it wasn't, prompting a shrug on his part—that patronizing Gallic shrug that makes me want to put aside my otherwise steadfast commitment to pacifism and pick up a baseball bat—after which he drove off. Shaking with rage, I watched the paddy wagon disappear up Saint-Laurent, cursed myself for being so clueless as not to have made note of a badge number or a license plate, and then continued on to the grocery store, nursing my impotent rage. Thirty minutes later, I was juggling my briefcase full of textbooks and lecture notes against my shopping bags full of dinner and inserting my key into the lock of my apartment building's front door, when the penny dropped. Only then did I realize that I had flung attitude into the face of a member of a police force notorious for brutality and suspicious deaths of those in custody. Only then did it occur to me that this incident would have ended very differently if I had been a Haitian teenager in Montréal-Nord,[1] instead of a white, anglophone graduate student in the Plateau.

This was another "lightbulb" moment for me. Following my conversation with Joe, I had started to really try to take note of the social inequities in my environment, but this experience took me one step further. It revealed to me just how much I get away with on a daily basis: because of my race, because of the middle-class identity I can easily assume, because my primary language puts me in the category of historical colonizer—a status that continues to pay dividends in Montreal despite the cultural decolonization Quebec has undergone since the 1960s.

This gap between me and those of my fellow citizens who are not so socially privileged has become even more evident in the wake of news stories that testify to the differential treatment the Canadian Department of Foreign Affairs appears to habitually accord to the citizens it is supposed to serve equally. Prior to these stories, I had had an ambivalent view of the work that Foreign Affairs does in protecting Canadian citizens overseas. My partner had been visiting his family in Haiti during the 2004 Aristide "coup-napping," and my fears for his safety led me to contact Foreign Affairs with inquiries about what could be done to get him safely back to Canada.[2] The real live human beings who staff the 24/7 emergency telephone line in Ottawa were responsive, and as helpful as they could be, given that they were making evacuation plans from a great distance and in conditions of great political instability. Although it fortunately proved unnecessary—commercial flights between Port-au-Prince and Montreal were restored quickly enough that he was able to fly home on his original airline ticket—I was comforted, and grateful, that they were willing to make room for him on a military plane if emergency evacuations were warranted. This unquestioning attitude of willingness to protect a citizen completely unknown to them, based solely on my telephone call disclosing his passport details, contrasted wildly with the Canadian government's long-standing resistance to the repatriation of child soldier Omar Khadr, who was first held at the American prison in Guantánamo from 2002 to 2011 and subsequently has been incarcerated in Canada—in blatant violation of the optional protocol on child soldiers appended to the 1989 United Nations Convention on the Rights of the Child, a protocol ratified by both the United States and Canada (Amnesty International 2010; UNICEF 2008). The Canadian government's refusal to acknowledge Khadr's right as a citizen to return to Canada struck me as bizarre; it was clearly a reaction to the post-9/11 political climate, but it equally clearly showed a tone-deaf insensitivity to the guarantee, in the Universal Declaration of Human Rights, of a citizen's right to live in his or her country of citizenship and to enter or leave it at will.

Both of these contradictory behaviors are replicated in the news stories that revealed to me the underlying pattern of differential treatment of Canadian citizens. What made these stories comprehensible as part of a pattern, however, is that this time the difference was more visibly linked to race and privilege rather than appearing—as it had with my partner and with Khadr—as arbitrary incommensurability. The first of these objectionable governmental failures to respect the government's own rhetoric concerning its support for citizens overseas[3]—or, at least, the first that impinged on my consciousness—was the deliberate abandonment of Abousfian Abdelrazik in Sudan. Abdelrazik, a naturalized Canadian citizen (like me, like my partner), left Montreal in March 2003 on a Canadian passport to visit his mother in Sudan (People's Commission Network 2009). While there, he was arrested and imprisoned twice between 2003 and 2007, beaten, tortured, and interrogated by officials variously identified as American, Canadian, French, and Sudanese, and released—both times without any criminal charges having been laid at any point. Upon his release, all of his attempts to return home to Montreal were repeatedly blocked; his passport had expired, his name had been placed on a no-fly list by the Bush administration in 2006, and the Canadian government had frozen his assets.[4] In desperation, Abdelrazik went public with his plight and was granted "temporary safe haven" in the Canadian embassy at Khartoum, Sudan's capital, but it took almost two years and the direct order of a Canadian federal judge that the government repatriate him without delay to finally bring Abdelrazik home (in June 2009). Yes, incredibly, it took a ruling from a judge to make the Canadian government issue travel documents and admit Abdelrazik back into the country that is his lawful home.

As the Abdelrazik case was slouching toward its dishonorable resolution—leaving him broke, his reputation besmirched, and his life improved only by virtue of being back home with his children—yet another lapse of Foreign Affairs' stated service standards was taking place. Suaad Hagi Mohamud left Toronto in May 2009, also on a Canadian passport, to visit her mother in Kenya for two weeks. She was prevented from boarding her return flight from Nairobi to Toronto on the grounds that Kenyan immigration officials believed that she did not sufficiently resemble her passport photograph. Despite being able to provide other documents supporting her claim about her identity—including, as I recall from television coverage at the time, a Toronto Public Library card and a receipt from a Toronto-area dry-cleaning store—Mohamud's passport was confiscated and she was thrown into a Kenyan jail for eight days. Released on bail, Mohamud found herself charged

by Kenyan officials with identity theft, on the recommendation of the Canadian High Commissioner in Kenya. "All Canadians who hold passports generally have a picture that is identical in their passport to what they claim to be," declared Foreign Minister Lawrence Cannon in a 24 July press briefing, adding that "there is no tangible proof" that Mohamud is Canadian (CBC News 2009b). Emergency travel documents were issued for Mohamud, permitting her return to Canada, only after a DNA test was performed to show that the scientific probability of her being the biological mother of the Toronto boy she claims is her son is 99.99 percent. In the wake of Mohamud's return on 15 August 2009, the government continued to deflect responsibility for her ordeal, claiming that consular officials believed she was an impostor and had undertaken "extensive investigation" of her documents. The latter claim was disputed by her lawyer, Raoul Boulakia, who cited documentation proving that little was done after the initial assessment in late May. Yes, in Mohamud's case, it took a DNA test to make the Canadian government acknowledge the citizenship of a woman who could pull personal papers out of her purse that suggested a whole life lived in Canada.

Contrast these two experiences with the story of Amanda Lindhout, a young Calgary woman whose freelance journalism took her to Somalia in 2008. She and the Australian photojournalist Nigel Brennan were kidnapped by unidentified gunmen and held for fifteen months, until family and friends paid a ransom that secured their release (Wilton 2009). While the Canadian government stood by its policy of not paying ransoms for abducted citizens, there was no question in this case of difficulties in issuing emergency travel documents; moreover, the government even sent a plane to pick Lindhout up and fly her back to Canada. Considering these three stories together, it is hard for me to see any plausible explanation for such inconsistent behavior other than that race matters to the protection one gets as a citizen. Lindhout—white and Christian—got the full benefit of the service standards that the Department of Foreign Affairs promises on its website; Abdelrazik and Mohamud—both black and Muslim—did not.

The reason for this differential treatment is a social context grounded in white privilege, in white people's ability to marshal the sense of entitlement that cows other people into acceding to their demands. And because the capacity to credibly exercise that entitlement is simultaneously the source *and* the outcome of social privilege, this means a social context in which some of us are arrogant and others of us are abject. Certainly, it is a system far removed from the ideal of equal rights for all that is enshrined in the

Universal Declaration of Human Rights, a document that Canada helped draft but apparently no longer lives by.

My nagging fear about the inequity of citizenship that I have sketched here—the icy little worry that runs alongside my anger at the injustice of it all—is that this widespread, undiscussed choice to carry on with our privilege framework extends beyond the government's treatment of citizens, to Canadians' view of other people in other nations. We spend, in my view, an inordinate amount of time and energy obsessing about our relations with the "white money" power structure that rules the United States and, at the same time, display a disgraceful apathy in the face of the ongoing Afghan detainee scandal. The Canadian Forces' practice of rounding up suspects and handing them over to Afghan police forces without bothering to gain assurances that they will not be tortured is one that diplomat Richard Colvin apprised the Canadian Forces' chain of command and Foreign Affairs officials of for three years before he finally went public in late 2009, describing it as "contrary to Canada's values, contrary to Canada's interests, contrary to Canada's official policies and also contrary to international law" (CBC News 2009a). It is indeed a clear violation of the third Geneva Convention, the one governing treatment of prisoners and specifically conferring upon states responsibility for protecting detained individuals from violence, mutilation, and other forms of inhumane treatment. Article 12 stipulates, "Prisoners of war may only be transferred by the Detaining Power to a Power which is a party to the Convention and after the Detaining Power has satisfied itself of the willingness and ability of such transferee Power to apply the Convention" (ICRC 1949). As Colvin's own inquiries convinced him that "all detainees transferred by Canadians to Afghan prisons were likely tortured by Afghan officials," there is good reason to raise concerns about a breach of international law—especially in light of the interpretation of the Department of National Defence that "Canada has a positive duty" to educate soldiers about the Geneva Conventions and ensure that they are upheld in all conflicts to which Canada is a party (Government of Canada, National Defence 2005, 40). We have for some time now been in breach of our duty to care for prisoners of war—that is, we are in violation of international law—and the public is showing no signs of moral outrage.

This disturbing moral apathy on our part was noted by the late journalist and political commentator Jim Travers in a CTV *Question Period* retrospective, aired on 2 January 2011, of the top ten newsworthy scandals of 2010. His analysis of the Conservative government's handling of the Afghan detainee

scandal and the Official Opposition's response centered on the undeniable observation that Canadians don't care about how (so-called) Taliban detainees are being treated. Travers contended that effective opposition to the government would have focused on the paper trail suggesting a cover-up within the government and the military (the lies they told a parliamentary committee in an attempt to discredit Colvin's testimony), instead of the Geneva violations, which appear to concern very few Canadian voters.

Placid acceptance of a privilege-based system and concomitant disregard for the framework of human rights that institutions such as the United Nations, Amnesty International, and the International Committee of the Red Cross have worked so hard to develop alarms me because it obscures one of the two things I know about how privilege functions. In addition to the ease with which it is deployed—an aspect that Peggy McIntosh has done so much to critique, both here in this volume and in her other work—I am keenly aware of the ease with which privilege can be taken away. Failing to care about our responsibility for the suffering of nameless brown-skinned Afghani torture victims really does hurt us all in the long run, just as failing to care that Abdelrazik and Mohamud are not valued as citizens to the same extent as Lindhout hurts us. Our response to privilege—moral *and* pragmatic—must be to reject it, to turn away from its lure and build a system of rights that is as impregnable as we can possibly make it. That way, the next time someone comes for trade unionists, or any despised other of the moment, perhaps we can all be standing together.

Notes

1. Or a Latino youth, like Honduran-Canadian Fredy Villanueva, who was shot twice by an officer of the Montreal police force, Service de police de la ville de Montréal, who broke up a game of dice Fredy was playing with his brother Dany and three friends in a Montréal-Nord parking lot on the evening of 9 August 2008. See Martin 2010.

2. "Coup-napping" is former Haitian president Jean-Bertrand Aristide's own term for the removal from office and country forced upon him by the collusion of members of the Canadian, American, and French governments with right-wing paramilitaries and hostile homegrown elites. It marks the second time that Aristide has been removed from the presidency by small, powerful groups unwilling to respect the outcomes of the international observer–certified elections that put him in power (in 1990 and again in 2000). See Farmer 2004.

3. "The Consular Services Bureau of Foreign Affairs and International Trade Canada is committed to provide to all Canadians effective and efficient service throughout the world. Our commitment is for service characterized at all times by sensitivity, empathy,

courtesy, speed, accuracy and fairness." Canadian Department of Foreign Affairs, Trade and Development 2009.

4. All of this despite the fact that no evidence of criminal or terrorist links has ever been produced, that the Sudanese government has formally exonerated him, and that his only involvement with terrorist investigations prior to returning to Sudan in 2003 was his testimony in 2000, *for* the prosecution, *against* millennium bomber Ahmed Ressam.

References

Amnesty International. 2010. U.S.A. must address Omar Khadr rights violations following plea deal. 25 October. http://www.amnesty.org/en/news-and-updates /usa-must-address-omar-khadr-rights-violations-following-plea-deal-2010–10–25.

Canadian Department of Foreign Affairs, Trade and Development. 2009. Consular services: Service standards. 13 October. www.voyage.gc.ca/about_a-propos/ standards-services-normes-eng.asp.

CBC News. 2009a. All Afghan detainees likely tortured: diplomat. 18 November. http://www.cbc.ca/news/canada/story/2009/11/18/diplomat-afghan -detainees.html.

———. 2009b. Suaad Hagi Mohamud's detention in Kenya. 12 August. http://www .cbc.ca/news/world/story/2009/08/12/f-haji-mohamud-timeline.html.

Farmer, Paul. 2004. Who removed Aristide? *London Review of Books*, 15 April, 28–31.

Government of Canada, National Defence. 2005. Leadership and the law. In *Leadership in the Canadian Forces: Conceptual foundations*, 35–44. 2 September. http:// publications.gc.ca/collections/collection_2013/dn-nd/D2-313-2-2005-eng.pdf.

ICRC (International Committee of the Red Cross). 1949. Convention (III) relative to the treatment of prisoners of war. 12 August. http://www.icrc.org/ihl.nsf/FULL /375?OpenDocument.

Martin, Megan. 2010. Protestors march on anniversary of Fredy Villanueva's death. *Montreal Gazette*, 9 August.

People's Commission Network. 2009. Abousfian Abdelrazik: Project fly home. http://www.peoplescommission.org/en/abdelrazik/summary.php.

UNICEF (United Nations Children's Fund). 2008. Convention on the rights of the child. 26 August. http://www.unicef.org/crc/.

United Nations. Universal declaration of human rights. 1948. http://www.un.org/en /documents/udhr/.

Wilton, Suzanne. 2009. Freed journalist Lindhout returning to Canada. *Calgary Herald*, 6 December.

13

Rethinking Ethical Feminism Through uBuntu

Drucilla Cornell

Transnational feminism, as both an ethical ideal and an actual struggle to form political alliances, raises some of the most difficult and burning issues of what it means to challenge profound Eurocentric biases that have often stood in the way of such a coalition. In this chapter, I attempt to address how and why such a transnational alliance actually demands of us that we open ourselves to rethinking some of our most cherished feminist ideas, such as freedom and equality, without, of course, giving up on those ideals. That is, in a profound sense, the challenge of how we rethink the feminist project, without in any way conceding anything to the horrific oppression women suffer under global apartheid (Hardt and Negri 2004, 160–67). The complexities of this challenge have led me to rethink what I long ago called "ethical feminism," and indeed to deepen my understanding of ethical feminism through an engagement with the works of Judith Butler and Gayatri Spivak. Sometimes, when the issues are so big, they can best be examined by looking at a specific case, and in this case an alternative non-Western (South African) ethic: uBuntu. The ethic of uBuntu, as we will see, raises questions about some Anglo-American assumptions about freedom and equality, specifically freedom and obligation. Part of the reason why I turn to uBuntu is autobiographical, because I have been working in South Africa for nine years. But I turn to uBuntu more generally to try to address what it might mean for us to respect a non-Western ethic that does not justify itself through an appeal to its indigenous roots, but instead through a claim to universality.

Rethinking Ethical Feminism

In the mid-1990s, I argued that feminism must involve an apotropaic gesture against the incessant fading of the diversification and differentiation of
the feminine within sexual and cultural representations (Benhabib et al.
1995). This gesture not only operates against simplistic notions of what
women supposedly are; it also brings to light how reigning definitions of the
feminine undergird notions of civilization and a philosophically bloated conception of man. Thus feminism was for me then, and is now, ethical in three
senses. First, it challenges the close connection between morality and conceptions of man, as these are rooted not only in a narrow Eurocentric view of
"men" but also in a conception of civilization that in its very premises has
become both gendered and whitened. Gayatri Spivak has emphasized over
and over again how so-called ideals of civilization have been used to prop up
notions of the human that not only exclude certain women from the field of
meaning and representability but are also used as justifications for the worst
kinds of violence (Spivak 2010b). Thus feminist struggles are not only against
the subordination of women, although of course feminism must fight against
that subordination, but more broadly construed, feminism is both a political
and an ethical struggle against hegemonic meanings and institutions that
deny the being of anyone as fully human. This expands the reach of feminism to fight alongside all others who are dropped below the bar of humanity
by this pumped-up notion of man as the civilized as well as the civilizer. This
is the second sense in which feminism is ethical, in that it fights against a
process of othering that drops human beings below the bar of what purportedly constitutes "our" humanity. In this second sense of what I am now
defining as ethical feminism, there is no feminist struggle without the battle
against racism, neocolonialism, and continuing forms of privilege and imperial domination. We need to remember this integral connection, because
even the most sophisticated psychoanalytic justifications for why civilization
demands that woman be barred from full humanity are inseparable from the
idea that "man" must reign (Lacan 1985). Here, "man" is the very definition
of what it means to be human and thus civilized. As Frantz Fanon and so
many others have reminded us, that "man" is always imagined as white
(Fanon 1991). So-called civilization then sets up a bar against others, who
make man what he purportedly stands for, precisely by marking his difference from these others. Thus feminism is always against this "othering,"
which takes some beyond the reach of humanity and registers them as less
than human. As Gayatri Spivak writes, "Why have I written largely of women

to launch the question of the recognition of ceaselessly shifting collectivities in our disciplinary practice? Because women are not a special case, but can represent the human, with the asymmetries attendant upon any such representation. As simple as that" (Spivak 2003, 70). Thus ethical feminism expands the reach of feminist politics and integrally connects it to antiracist struggles, as well as to the worldwide politics against global apartheid.

The second aspect of ethical feminism was based on a defense of an aspiration to a nonviolent relationship to the other and to otherness in the widest possible sense of the word. I deliberately used a broad brush in defining the ethical relationship, although I also clearly meant to evoke the spirit of Emmanuel Levinas. Crucial to this aspiration is the responsibility to struggle against the appropriation of the other into any preconceived meaning of her difference and her singularity, a precarious undertaking indeed, as Spivak reminds us in her rightfully renowned essay, "Can the Subaltern Speak?" (Spivak 2010a). I am using the word "precarious" deliberately, because in a profound sense the struggle for a nonviolent relationship to the other—and it is a struggle—must come to terms with what Judith Butler has recently called "precarious life" (Butler 2004). For Butler, this precariousness has at least two aspects. The first is a fearless confrontation with our shared corporeal vulnerability that demands nothing less than that we put down our defenses that keep us from facing that we, too, can be violated, harmed, and indeed killed:

> Negotiating a sudden and unprecedented vulnerability—what are the options? What are the long-term strategies? Women know this question well, have known it in nearly all times, and nothing about the triumph of colonial powers has made our exposure to this kind of violence any less clear. There is the possibility of appearing impermeable, of repudiating vulnerability itself. Nothing about being socially constituted as women restrains us from simply becoming violent ourselves. And then there is the other age-old option, the possibility of wishing for death or becoming dead, as a vain effort to preempt or deflect the next blow. But perhaps there is some other way to live such that one becomes neither affectively dead nor mimetically violent, a way out of the circle of violence altogether. This possibility has to do with demanding a world in which bodily vulnerability is protected without therefore being eradicated and with insisting on the line that must be walked between the two. (2004, 42)

The second aspect, related to the first, deepens and extends the Levinasian mandate, with its biblical roots, "Thou shalt not kill." For Butler—and I am in agreement with her—human beings can be violated by a force so great, whether through indeterminate detention, poverty, or other sources of cruelty and oppression, that they are "derealized," to use her phrase, as human beings long before they actually die: "What is real? Whose lives are real? How might reality be remade? Those who are unreal have, in a sense, already suffered the violence of derealization. What, then, is the relation between violence and those lives considered as 'unreal'? Does violence effect that unreality? Does violence take place on the condition of that unreality?" (2004, 33). Thus I think we need to deepen our understanding of what is required to even aspire to a nonviolent relationship to the other through the evocation of precarious life.

And this leads me to the third aspect of ethical feminism. For many years now, Butler has argued powerfully that the incompleteness of any appeal to the universal, which must necessarily be caught in the particularity of language and culture always demands that we engage in the ethical task of mutual translation (Butler 2000). So, of course, has Spivak in her careful suturing of any human rights discourse to an ethics of responsibility (Spivak 2004; cf. Cornell 2010). Both authors emphasize that the appeal to universality *must* include the demand for translation, in order to push against both the silencing that pushes women in the global South below the bar of representability, and what Butler has called the violence of the "derealization" of a human life. The work of both Spivak and Butler has never been more important, in that both continue to advocate for a nonviolent ethic, and in Spivak's case, explicitly, for a complex Marxist project of global transformation. The aspiration to a nonviolent ethic, and with it the struggle for global transformation, has itself become controversial, in that some thinkers have argued that it is a form of bad utopianism that either runs up against some ontology of the human and social relations as inevitably violent, or, worse yet, refuses the fundamental violence that inevitably defines the political (Ashforth 2005; see also Mouffe 1999). Sometimes the insistence on the connection between politics as necessarily violent and the ethical rupture or relationship as madness allies itself with the Left, and even with the project of global transformation (Žižek 2008). Nothing, however, in the aspiration to a nonviolent relationship to the other necessarily implies pacifism or the complete abdication of the use of violence in all circumstances. If we are to take the struggle against global apartheid seriously, then it may well

be necessary at times to turn to certain kinds of violence (Negri 2008, 90–91). But what kinds? And must they involve a violation in any of the senses defined by Butler and Spivak? These are two questions that must be raised if we are to aspire to a nonviolent ethic. So, while I stand behind the three aspects of ethical feminism I defended long ago, we also need to deepen the understanding of ethical feminism through the recent work of Butler and Spivak.

Further—and this is the central issue of this chapter—the call for translation must not only be made; it must be heeded. What follows is, in a very real sense, such an effort at translation through an engagement with the South African notion of uBuntu, and an attempt to understand what this ethic might teach us about different notions of freedom and obligation that inspire feminists to action. There are again two aspects of the call to comprehend universality as carrying within it an ethical demand for translation. The first is to take seriously the idea that other intellectual heritages do offer us competing notions of freedom and obligation. The second is that these heritages do not—or at least frequently do not—base their advocacy of an ethic on the particularity of a language and culture—i.e., that it is "indigenous"— although those particularities may well be why an ethic is compelling to those who live within this heritage. Such counterviewpoints, values, or ideals are often defended as universal in their reach, which in turn means that we should not only take them seriously but should seriously consider them as a possibly more integrative way of thinking about freedom, obligation, and equality than those offered to us in even the best philosophical traditions of European and Anglo-American constructions of those ideals. It is the second step that is too rarely taken. Thus the call for translation is also a call to judgment, including a call to judgment about the value of Anglo-American traditions of freedom and equality. But this call to judgment should not be mistaken for either a simpleminded moralism or the romanticism of going native ("they have it right, we have it wrong"). Rather, the call to judgment recognizes that there is a complex terrain of competing universals, that if we actually engage in that terrain, assuming the notational equality of other intellectual heritages, then we may be called to change and revise our own ideals, as we engage with the universals of "others" and with other universals. Only then are we taking seriously the idea that other cultures, or what I am calling "intellectual heritages," offer universal justifications that put a demand on us both to translate them and to engage them in such a way that we are open to a shift and a challenge to the hegemony and privilege of Eurocentric philosophy.

More specifically, in this chapter I examine how uBuntu offers us a notion of freedom that is certainly different from the main definitions of freedom that feminists in the West have often taken for granted, and yet still is an ethic of freedom. Saba Mahmood poses the following question:

> How does one rethink the question of individual freedom in a context where the distinction between the subject's own desires and socially prescribed performances cannot be so easily presumed, and where submission to certain forms of (external) authority is a condition for the self to achieve its potentiality? What kind of politics would be deemed desirable and viable in discursive traditions that regard conventions (socially prescribed performances) as necessary to the self's realization? (2004, 149)

uBuntu does indeed take certain socially prescribed performances as necessary to self-realization. To draw out the relationship between an uBuntu relationship between freedom and obligation, let us examine an actual and controversial case that came before the South African Constitutional Court—the Bhe case (see *Bhe and Others v. Magistrate* 2005; see also Cornell and Muvangua 2011).

uBuntu, Obligation, and Succession: The Bhe Case

Bhe actually involves three cases: Bhe, Shibi, and an application for direct access to the Constitutional Court by the South African Human Rights Commission and the Women's Legal Center Trust. I now offer a short summary of these cases, beginning with Bhe. Ms. Bhe and the deceased had lived together as husband and wife for twelve years. They had two children, girls, both of whom were minors at the time of their father's death. The deceased died without a will, and during the couple's life together as husband and wife, they had acquired immovable property in Khayelitsha (a township of Cape Town), in which they lived together, and in which Ms. Bhe and her daughters continued to live after her husband's death. After his son's death, the father of Ms. Bhe's partner claimed that he was the administrator and sole heir of the estate under African customary law, because there were no sons born in the marriage. Further, he wanted to sell the property in order to cover the expenses of his son's funeral, even though Ms. Bhe and the daughters were still in residence. The magistrate of Khayelitsha appointed the father

administrator and sole heir of the property. The magistrate arrived at this judgment through an appeal to the Black Administration Act (BAA), a notorious piece of legislation passed during the apartheid era, which gave recognition to the principle of male primogeniture.

In the Shibi case, the applicant's brother had also died without a will, had no children, and was not survived by parents or grandparents. Because the applicant was a female, she was excluded from inheriting under the BAA, and her brother's estate passed to his closest male cousin. Both the South African Human Rights Commission and the Women's Legal Center Trust applied for direct access to the Constitutional Court, acting in their own and in the public interest. They sought to strike down the whole of section 23 of the BAA—which deals with succession and inheritance of deceased African people—as unconstitutional because of its inconsistency with section 9 (the equality clause), section 10 (the dignity clause), and section 28 (which guarantees the rights of children). The two issues before the Constitutional Court, then, were the validity of section 23 of the BAA and the question whether the rule of primogeniture was constitutional, as it was codified not only in the BAA but in other sources of the written customary law.

The high court declared section 23 of the BAA fundamentally unconstitutional and against the spirit of uBuntu because the rule of primogeniture denied women their full humanity. The high court also found section 23 of the BAA racist and fundamentally against the constitution. Moreover, Justice Langa, writing for the majority, found that not only was the BAA against the spirit of uBuntu but that the rule of primogeniture in the written customary law—which would replace section 23 once it was struck down—was against uBuntu as well. The Constitutional Court also held that section 3 of the BAA was fundamentally unconstitutional and in violation of a number of sections of the constitution. The Constitutional Court further held that the exclusion of women and extramarital children from the status of heir under the principle of primogeniture in the written customary law violated the equality clause (section 9), as well as the dignity clause (section 10). It ruled further that the Intestate Succession Act, as altered to make provision for polygamous unions, should replace the impugned section 23 of the BAA until Parliament had a chance to act.

In a dissenting opinion, Justice Ngcobo, although he firmly agreed that section 23 of the BAA was one of the pillars of the apartheid legal order and that it should be struck down, argued that until Parliament could act, the rule of primogeniture should be developed and not simply invalidated. Under section 39 of the constitution, the courts have a mandate to develop both the

customary and the common law in accordance with the purpose and the spirit of the constitution. Thus Justice Ngcobo argued strongly that the Constitutional Court should develop customary law rather than strike it down, so as to give recognition to the customary law. Furthermore, the constitution places customary law on a par with English common law and the Roman-Dutch private law in the new dispensation. He also held, against the majority, that minor children could justifiably be refused the status of heir under the limitations clause (section 36). In the South African constitution, no right remains supreme. To quote section 36:

> 1) The rights in the Bill of Rights may be limited only in terms of law of general application to the extent that the limitation is reasonable and justifiable in an open and democratic society based on human dignity, equality and freedom, taking into account all relevant factors, including: a) the nature of the right; b) the importance of the purpose of the limitation; c) the nature and extent of the limitation; d) the relation between the limitation and its purpose; and e) less restrictive means to achieve the purpose. 2) Except as provided in subsection 1) or in any other provision of the Constitution, no law may limit any right entrenched in the Bill of Rights.

I will return shortly to Justice Ngcobo's limitations analysis in more detail. For now, let me stress that for Ngcobo, the limitations of the rights of children could be justified in this way, precisely because the family's successor had to be old enough to fulfill the requisite obligations, including caring for his or her entire family. But what lies at the heart of this seemingly small legal issue—whether or not the Intestate Succession Act should stand until Parliament could act—actually implies a huge ethical question. Justice Ngcobo wrote in his dissent,

> A sense of community prevailed from which developed an elaborate system of reciprocal duties and obligations among the family members. This is manifest in the concept of *uBuntu—umuntu ngumuntu ngabantu*—a dominant value in African traditional culture. This concept encapsulates communality and the interdependence of the members of a community. As Langa DCJ put it, it is a culture which "regulates the exercise of rights by the emphasis that it lays on sharing and co-responsibility and the mutual enjoyment of rights." It is this system of reciprocal duties and obligations that ensured that every family

member had access to basic necessities of life such as food, clothing, shelter, and healthcare. (*Bhe and Others v. Magistrate* 2005, par. 163)

As Justice Ngcobo argued, inheritance and succession under African customary law are completely different rationalities in terms of the division of estates. In African customary law, the primary issue is not the division of the property of the deceased. In agricultural societies, succession had as its primary goal the maintenance of the family, and the one who succeeded the deceased did not inherit *property*, which was often owned in common; he inherited the responsibility to take care of all of his family and to make sure that their well-being was maintained. As Ngcobo put it, "The concept of succession in indigenous law must be understood in the context of indigenous law itself. When dealing with indigenous law every attempt should be made to avoid the tendency of construing indigenous law concepts in the light of common law concepts or concepts foreign to indigenous law. There are obvious dangers in such an approach. These two systems of law developed in two different situations, under different cultures and in response to different conditions" (ibid., par. 156). Formerly, in an agricultural society, the demand that the head of the household remain in the family homestead prevented women from holding the status of successors, as women were thought to leave the family homestead when they married. Whatever the reasons for justifying primogeniture in agricultural societies, those reasons are no longer applicable to "modern" rural or urban societies. This inapplicability is due both to the fact that, under apartheid, women were forced into the workplace, and to the struggle for the rights of women. Thus Ngcobo argued powerfully that the living customary law should be developed so as to remove the defect of male primogeniture. To quote Ngcobo again, "The defect in the rule of male primogeniture is that it excludes women from being considered for succession to the deceased family head. In this regard it deviates from section 9(3) of the Constitution. It needs to be developed so as to bring it in line with our Bill of Rights. This can be achieved by removing the reference to a male so as to allow an eldest daughter to succeed to the deceased's estate" (ibid., par. 222).

The ethical significance of Justice Ngcobo's dissent is twofold. First, he insisted that indigenous law has a very different notion of community than the one represented in the Intestate Succession Act. That notion of community in the living customary law must be respected and therefore developed, rather than simply struck down and replaced by a system of inheritance that is completely foreign to indigenous law. Second, the living customary law (as

opposed to the law written down by foreign officials) is dynamic and indeed has been transforming itself in accordance with the constitutional demand for respect for the dignity and equality of women. Thus it needs to be developed to respect its very dynamism. Some feminists received the majority judgment as a great victory, but many black women on the ground objected strenuously that it was a violent imposition on the dynamic system of living customary law, that it completely failed to grapple with the difference between inheritance and succession, and that, with its different understanding of the relation between succession and inheritance, the court failed to grasp the relationship between freedom and obligation in the living customary law (Himonga 2005). Indeed, the view of the indigenous practice that upheld the inheritance of the eldest male son, with all of the obligations that came with it, as the rule of primogeniture was itself criticized as a misunderstanding of this practice. Primogeniture was a narrow English rule about inheritance, not obligation, and aimed primarily to maintain as much land as possible in the hands of the chief heir. The English rule of primogeniture was designed to protect property rights and said nothing about family members' obligation to one another; thus to conflate it with indigenous customary law was a mistake.

More important, significant evidence suggests that changes are being made in the practice of succession, so that South African women can in fact succeed to all of the obligations of their families. In like manner, women can now receive *lobola*, which is a wealth exchange at marriage, whereas in preconstitutional times only the father or senior male relative could receive *lobola* for the woman. Justice Ngcobo argued that indigenous law should be respected and should be allowed to correct the defect of gender inequality, or that the Constitutional Court itself should develop that law. That there were resources within the law to allow this is demonstrated by the high court decision, in which the law of primogeniture was challenged as contrary to uBuntu because it violated the full humanity of women and of extramarital children.

Both Justice Ngcobo in his dissent and Justice Langa in his majority opinion referred to uBuntu as one of the most important values underlying the idea of familial obligation, inseparable from the idea of succession. Let us turn now to the meaning of uBuntu as an important resource for correcting the defect of gender inequality in the indigenous law. In uBuntu, to paraphrase Justice Ngcobo, human beings are intertwined in a world of ethical relations and obligations from the time they are born. This inscription is part of our finitude. We are born into a language, a kinship group, a tribe, a nation, a family. But this inscription cannot simply be reduced to a social fact. We come into the

world obligated to others, and these others are obligated to us, to support us in finding our way to becoming a unique and singular person. Thus it is a profound misunderstanding of uBuntu to confuse it with Anglo-American concepts of communitarianism. It is only through the engagement and support of others that we are able to realize our true individuality and rise above our merely biological distinctiveness.

How to Think About the Ethic of uBuntu

Famously, at birth in the Xhosa and Zulu traditions, the baby's umbilical cord is buried, and the place of burial marks the beginning of one's journey to becoming a person. This achievement of singularity is always a project that is inseparable from the ethical obligations to which one is tethered in one form or another from the beginning of life. We could say that the person is ethically intertwined by others from the beginning. But this intertwining does not constitute who we are or who we might become. Instead, we must find a way to realize our singularity as a unique person. In that singularity, we become someone who will define our own ethical responsibilities as we grow into our personhood. If a community, then, is committed to individuation and the achievement of a unique destiny for each person (often reflected in the individual's name but not determined by the name), then the person in turn is obligated to enhance the community that supports him or her, not simply as an abstract duty correlated with a right but as a form of participation that allows the community to strive for fidelity to difference and singularity— what D. A. Masolo (2004) has called "participatory difference." For Masolo, this participatory difference recognizes that each one of us is indeed different from all others. But part of this difference is that we are also called to make a difference, by contributing to the creation and sustenance of a humane and ethical community.

For the great African philosopher Kwasi Wiredu, participatory difference includes the principle of sympathetic impartiality, as we seek to imagine ourselves and others as uniquely singular beings. Sympathetic impartiality in this unique meaning calls us not to seek likeness but to imagine others in their difference from us and in their singularity. For Wiredu, this principle can only develop in association with others and as part of our ethical and moral training in our journey to becoming a person. The problem of how we develop such a connection to otherness is explained in part because we

are always already ethically entwined with others, and they are in a profound sense a part of ourselves. Critics of uBuntu, including critics who conflate uBuntu with outdated modes of social cohesion and hierarchy, make the mistake of reducing uBuntu to an ethical ontology of a purportedly shared world. What this criticism misses is precisely the activism that is inherent in participatory difference. uBuntu clearly has an aspirational and an ideal edge. There is no end to the struggle to bring about a humane world, and to become a person in that humane world who makes a difference in it.

Professor Mogobo Moore brings together different aspects of uBuntu in his own profound yet succinct definition: in one sense, uBuntu is a philosophical concept forming the basis of relationships, especially ethical behavior. In another sense, it is a traditional politico-ideological concept referring to sociopolitical action. As a moral or ethical concept, it is a point of view according to which moral practices are founded exclusively on consideration and enhancement of human well-being. It says that what is morally good is what brings dignity, respect, contentment, and prosperity to others, to the self, and to the community at large. uBuntu is a demand for respect for persons, no matter what their circumstances may be. In its politico-ideological sense, it is a principle for all forms of social or political relationship. It promotes peace and social harmony by encouraging the practice of sharing in all forms of communal existence (Wiredu 2004, 17).

As an ethical as well as a politico-ideological concept, then, uBuntu always entails a social bond, but one that is always in the course of being reshaped by the ethical demands it puts on its participants. uBuntu in a profound sense encapsulates the moral obligations for human beings who must live together. It implies a fundamental moralization of social relationships, and this moralization of social relationships is the one unchanging aspect of uBuntu, instructing us that we can never escape from this ethical world that we share together. But the actual demands of uBuntu must change, since uBuntu is inseparable from a relationship between human beings but is also connected to how we are always changing in those relations and our need to change with them. The aspirational aspect of uBuntu holds that we must strive together to achieve the public good in a shared world so that we can both survive and flourish, each one of us in our singularity. It is uBuntu's embeddedness in our relationships that makes it a transformative concept at its core, but this transformation can never be taken away from the moralization of social relationships. It would have been absurd if uBuntu had demanded access to electricity five hundred years ago, since there was no

access to electricity at all. Now, however, it is not at all absurd to make such a demand, because electricity is integral to securing a human life in modern society.

Thus it is not surprising that uBuntu is often hailed in the new counter-hegemonic movements that are challenging the neoliberal policies of the African National Congress in their demand for an ethical politics. It has been a commonplace since the path-breaking work of V. Y. Mudimbe (1988) that Africa has been invented, but it has been invented through actual and philosophical struggles over what Africa can or should be in modernity. It would be a mistake, in the context of Mudimbe's idea of invention, to argue that there is no such thing as Africa, or African social thought, and I have been suggesting that uBuntu is certainly part of South African social and political philosophy as well as part of its law.

Although it is beyond the scope of this chapter to address Achille Mbembe's argument, I do want to stress here that uBuntu is a principle of Afro-modernity and can best be understood as the African principle of transcendence for the individual and for the law of the social bond. Thus it would be a serious mistake to reduce uBuntu to the crypto-radicalism or naïve nativism that Mbembe characterizes as a primary mode of African self-writing that is unable to ascend to the status of universality:

> The emphasis on establishing an "African interpretation" of things, on creating one's own schemata of self-mastery, of understanding oneself and the universe, of producing endogenous knowledge have all led to demands for an "African science," and "African democracy," and "African language." This urge to make Africa unique is presented as a moral and political problem, the re-conquest of the power to narrate one's own story—and therefore identity—seeming to be necessarily constitutive of any subjectivity. Ultimately, it is no longer a matter of claiming the status of alter ego for Africans in the world, but rather of asserting loudly and forcefully their alterity. (Mbembe 2002, 255)

There are two important general points to make in relation to dominant Western notions of the social contract as they differ from uBuntu. Feminists have criticized neoliberal notions of freedom as well as Kant's notion of equality, and yet, as Saba Mahmood points out, we remain dangerously ensnared in these notions. The notion of freedom as lack of restraint can only accept the social bond, and a legal system, because without law we would exist in a world of horrific violence and brutality. Thus for Thomas

Hobbes, for example, we can yield authority to the Leviathan, so long as it protects our basic rights and provides us with basic security and stability, so that we can know what to expect.

In Kant, of course, because it is at least a practical possibility that human beings can postulate themselves as autonomous, in that they can lay down a law unto themselves, we might be able to represent ourselves as free from the pull of the day-to-day desires that drive us and indeed knock us about like bits of flotsam and jetsam. The relationship between the realm of internal freedom, or morality, and the realm of external freedom of right has long been debated in Kantian scholarship (Wood 2007). But clearly there must be a connection between the two realms. If there were no connection, then there would be no ground for the realm of external freedom, in which we can imagine how we can coordinate our ends with one another in a way that is consistent with each person's freedom. Kant's hypothetical experiment in the imagination, by which we can configure the conditions in which human beings aspire to the great ideal of the kingdom of ends, turns on the possibility that as creatures of practical reason, we can harmonize our interests and do so in accordance with our freedom (Kant 2012).

The dignity of human beings, for Kant, is to be found precisely in the possibility offered to us by our practical reason: to aspire to live together, guided by the ideal of the kingdom of ends. But even the Kantian hypothetical experiment of the imagination in which we configure the ideal conditions of a social contract, rooted in the respect for the freedom of other human beings, still begins with imagined individuals, even if moral individuals. It is still individuals who agree to accept some degree of coercion, even if rooted in the basic understanding of Kant's notion of right, which holds that individuals are allowed the greatest possible space for their freedom as long as it allows for the freedom of others within the social contract. As Mahmood points out, as different as these European conceptions are, they both root freedom in the individual. Thus he or she succumbs to the greater interest of security, or, alternatively, transcends her day-to-day desires. But in uBuntu the social bond does not proceed from our personal life through an imaginary social contract. Nor is our freedom separable from the ethical relationships in which we are interpellated but which at the same time support us in the ethical journey to becoming a person.

As Mogobo Moore emphasizes, uBuntu is not only an ethical concept but also an ideological and a political one that insists that democracy should not be understood primarily as an engagement with the representational apparatus of the state but is instead found in face-to-face participation. Therefore

uBuntu underwrites a political ethic, which, for example, has been echoed in the word adopted by the Shantydwellers—"Abahlalism," which means "the people together" (uBuntu Township Project n.d.). There is clearly no split in uBuntu between the phenomenal and the noumenal, as there is in Kant, and thus uBuntu is not in the strict Kantian sense a regulative ideal, even if it has an aspirational edge.

uBuntu is materialized in ethical actions, which has often led to the charge that it is vague. More specifically, it is materialized in the struggles of individuals in conflict. This enactment of uBuntu materializes a more humane world. There are several philosophical points important to the debates in Anglo-American and Western European feminism here, in that care and dignity or care and justice are not separable. Some Western feminists have contrasted the two conceptions, while others have argued that they are not incompatible (Held 1995). In uBuntu, however, they are integral to each other. First, to respect the dignity of a person is to respect her in her singularity, and in her material existence, not simply respecting her in her abstract equality. This respect will change its demands with regard to the circumstances. Second, feminists have criticized the notion of the independent individual whose freedom is an individual attribute, whether ideal or otherwise (Nussbaum 2003). As Mahmood reminds us, we need to ask how we can think about freedom as other than these two conceptions (and I would add, as she does, the Foucauldian notion of freedom as resistance). Then it would no longer be a matter of thinking freedom either as the basis of an abstract morality, as lack of restraint, or as resistance to hegemonic norms, but instead as an activist ethic that can only be realized in and through ethical relations to other people. Thus it is freedom through obligation, even if it includes the freedom to be oneself, through the support of others rather than against that support. uBuntu emphasizes freedom through other people, which is undoubtedly why it has become the basis of constitutional justifications by the South African Constitutional Court of socioeconomic rights in the name of freedom for all.

It is precisely this idea of freedom through others that Justice Ngcobo underscored in his dissenting argument in the Bhe case. In living African customary law, no one has the freedom to take the money and run. Instead, the successor is in a profound sense the guarantor of the well-being, and in that sense of the freedom to flourish, of all those in his or her family. Let me stress here that it is a serious error to designate the living customary law as premodern. It is as modern as the other sources of law in South Africa, such as British common law and Roman-Dutch law. The anthropologists John and

Jean Comaroff have argued that the living customary law is best understood as vernacular law, in order to avoid the mistake of contrasting it as a premodern form of law to other forms of law (Comaroff and Comaroff 2004).[1] What is significant in South Africa is that all other sources of law, including the living customary law, have to be rendered consistent with the constitution. At stake in this debate is the question of how the customary law should be developed, and not whether it was modern and a valid source of law.

Misinterpretations of the Living Customary Law

I stress the modernity of the living customary law to make a further point, which, as I said at the outset, is underscored by Judith Butler in her call for translating universals. In his powerful, hard-hitting book, *First as Tragedy, Then as Farce*, Slavoj Žižek reminds us that we must be thoroughly modern.[2] He uses the example of how the slaves in Haiti sang the Marseillaise, and by so doing enacted universality as a political category, and also profoundly shook the soldiers who were fighting against them, making them wonder if they were on the wrong side. Žižek rightly warns us against any kind of facile notion of "multiversality," or even multiple modernities. He suggests that colonial powers often engage with delight in singing the fight songs of the colonized. Of course, this would mean that the colonizers had actually mastered the languages of the colonized, and at least in South Africa a miniscule number of whites speak any language other than English and Afrikaans, while the black majority frequently speaks both English and Afrikaans in addition to other languages. Žižek's point is well taken, however, that at crucial moments in an emancipatory struggle, taking up what is best in the European tradition does indeed shift that tradition. My point is that it can also go the other way, in which the mobilization of non-European intellectual heritages, and even the battle over language, can also enact a political universality. Think, for example, of the Soweto uprising, which is commemorated on "Youth Day," when hundreds of thousands of children refused to be educated in Afrikaans, the language of the group that they saw as the primary oppressor. This uprising did indeed enact a political universality, in which the particularity claiming to be the language of education was challenged, not simply by arguing that Xhosa should be the name of education for Xhosa speakers, but in the name of freedom of education, and of the struggle against the institutions of apartheid more generally.

So, although we need to worry about a simplistic language of tolerance and facile notions of diversity, we also have to follow Butler in recognizing that the incompleteness of universality means that political universality can be enacted in different struggles through appeals to non-European values and ideals as much as to European ones. Both will have the effect of changing the intellectual heritages that are being mobilized in the direction of changing those heritages towards political universality. So my argument for uBuntu—and I have made this argument extensively elsewhere[3]—is not simply that it is African but that it claims a universality that should be taken seriously in the development of any nonviolent ethic and the political alliances of transnational feminism.

Obviously, uBuntu implies a very different way of thinking about freedom and obligation even from that offered by Kant, in which freedom and obligation are integrally tied together. Am I advocating that we entirely replace notions of Kantian freedom, or indeed the project of freedom more widely defended in German idealism and, later, in the writing of Karl Marx? Obviously not, since I myself remain a socialist and take very seriously the idea of rethinking communism. But what I *am* advocating, in accordance with some of the most searing insights of Butler and Spivak, is that we allow ourselves to engage with competing ideals of freedom, and indeed open ourselves to their significance, so that we may actually be able to form transnational alliances that can accept that there are competing universals concerning the most important ideals. uBuntu is one such ethic, and, as we have seen, it is often integrally tied to struggles for social and economic transformation.[4] We have to risk this openness that demands that we drop our defenses, so as to allow for a truly contested terrain of different meanings of such great ideals as freedom. Only by dropping our defenses and privileges can we hope to enter a transnational feminist coalition that does not fall into the kind of violence about which Gayatri Spivak constantly warns us, in which poor women of the global South are reduced to objects of our imposed meanings.

Notes

1. The Comaroffs have repeatedly made this argument in the uBuntu workshop on the naming and status of customary law, which was held at the University of Cape Town between 2007 and 2009.
2. I thoroughly agree with Žižek that the time has come to take communism seriously as a practical and philosophical task.

3. See Cornell, "The Recognition of uBuntu," introduction to Cornell and Muvangua 2012. See also uBuntu Project n.d., especially the interviews with social movements such as the Shantydwellers.

4. Cf. uBuntu Project n.d., interview with S'Bu Zikode, the current president of the Shantydwellers Movement.

References

Ashforth, Adam. 2005. *Witchcraft and democracy in South Africa*. Chicago: University of Chicago Press.
Benhabib, Seyla, Judith Butler, Drucilla Cornell, and Nancy Fraser. 1995. *Feminist contentions: A philosophical exchange*. New York: Routledge.
Bhe and Others v. Magistrate, Khayelitsha and Others; Shibi v. Sithole and Others; SA Human Rights Commission and Another v. President of the RSA and Another. 2005. BCLR 1 (CC) and 2004 (1) BCLR 27 (C). Selections in *uBuntu and the law: African ideals and postapartheid jurisprudence*, ed. Drucilla Cornell and Nyoko Muvangua, 222–32. New York: Fordham University Press.
Butler, Judith. 2000. Restaging the universal: Hegemony and the limits of formalism. In *Contingency, hegemony, universality: Contemporary dialogues on the left*, ed. Judith Butler, Ernesto Laclau, and Slavoj Žižek, 11–43. London: Verso.
———. 2004. *Precarious life: The powers of mourning and violence*. London: Verso.
Comaroff, John, and Jean Comaroff. 2004. Criminal justice, cultural justice: The limits of liberalism and the pragmatics of difference in the new South Africa. *American Ethnologist* 31, no. 2: 188–204.
Cornell, Drucilla. 2010. The ethical affirmation of human rights: Gayatri Spivak's intervention. In *Can the subaltern speak? Reflections on the history of an idea*, ed. Rosalind C. Morris, 100–116. New York: Columbia University Press.
———. 2014. *Law and revolution in South Africa: uBuntu, dignity, and the struggle for constitutional transformation*. New York: Fordham University Press.
Cornell, Drucilla, and Nyoko Muvangua, eds. 2011. *uBuntu and the law: African ideals and postapartheid jurisprudence*. New York: Fordham University Press.
Fanon, Frantz. 1991. *Black skin, white masks*. Trans. Constance Farrington. New York: Grove Press.
Hardt, Michael, and Antonio Negri. 2004. *Multitude: War and democracy in the age of empire*. New York: Penguin.
Held, Virginia. 1995. *Justice and care*. Boulder, Colo.: Westview Press.
Himonga, Chuma. 2005. African customary law in South Africa: The many faces of *Bhe v Magistrate, Khayelitsha. Recht in Afrika* 2:163–83.
Hobbes, Thomas. 1997. *Leviathan*. New York: W. W. Norton.
Kant, Immanuel. 2012. *Groundwork of the metaphysics of morals*. Trans. Mary Gregor. Cambridge: Cambridge University Press.
Lacan, Jacques. 1985. *Feminine sexuality: Jacques Lacan and the École freudienne*. Ed. Juliet Mitchell and Jacqueline Rose. Trans. Jacqueline Rose. New York: W. W. Norton.
Mahmood, Saba. 2004. *Politics of piety: The Islamic revival and the feminist subject*. Princeton: Princeton University Press.

Masolo, D. A. 2004. Western and African communitarianism: A comparison. In *A companion to African philosophy*, ed. Kwasi Wiredu, 483–98. New York: Wiley-Blackwell.

Mbembe, Achille. 2002. African modes of self-writing. Trans. Steven Rendall. *Public Culture* 4, no. 1: 239–73.

Mouffe, Chantal. 1999. *The challenge of Carl Schmitt*. London: Verso.

Mudimbe, V. Y. 1988. *The invention of Africa: Gnosis, philosophy, and the order of knowledge*. Bloomington: Indiana University Press.

Negri, Antonio. 2008. *Goodbye Mr. Socialism: Radical politics in the twenty-first century*. New York: Seven Stories Press.

Nussbaum, Martha. 2003. Capabilities as fundamental entitlements: Sen and social justice. *Feminist Economics* 9, no. 2: 33–59.

Spivak, Gayatri Chakravorty. 2003. *Death of a discipline*. New York: Columbia University Press.

———. 2004. Righting wrongs. *South Atlantic Quarterly* 103, nos. 2–3: 523–81.

———. 2010a. Can the subaltern speak? In *Can the subaltern speak? Reflections on the history of an idea*, ed. Rosalind C. Morris, 237–92. New York: Columbia University Press.

———. 2010b. In response: Looking back, looking forward. In *Can the subaltern speak? Reflections on the history of an idea*, ed. Rosalind C. Morris, 227–36. New York: Columbia University Press.

uBuntu Township Project. N.d. *uBuntu in Everyday Life*. http://www.yumpu.com/en/document/view/6910294/ubuntu-in-everyday-life-in-everyday-life-in-everyday-life.

Wiredu, Kwasi, ed. 2004. *A companion to African philosophy*. New York: Wiley-Blackwell.

Wood, Allen W. 2007. *Kantian ethics*. Cambridge: Cambridge University Press.

Žižek, Slavoj. 2008. *In defense of lost causes*. London: Verso.

———. 2009. *First as tragedy, then as farce*. London: Verso.

14

The Afrocentrist Critique of Eurocentrism: The Decolonization of Knowledge

Ernest-Marie Mbonda

Translated by Chris Bourne and Bettina Bergo

The concept of Afrocentrism can be attributed to Molefi Kete Asante (1980), a professor at Temple University in the United States. Afrocentrism opposes Eurocentrism in that it affirms the importance of African history, civilizations, and discoveries, as well as the necessity for Africans, both from the continent and from the diaspora, to make these their point of departure (on the cultural level generally, as on the academic one) for their relationship to the world, to events, and to others. In the domain of the social sciences and of philosophy in particular, Afrocentrism takes the form of a manifesto against the Western monopoly on rationality and the epistemological imperialism through which it is translated. Afrocentrism's response has been a plea for the "decolonization of knowledge," or, more concretely, for the right to invent, in Africa, rationality criteria that are both specific and universally acceptable.

I wish to analyze the significance of the Afrocentrist project, with the goal of illuminating both its motivating ambition and the paradox that fundamentally undermines it. Both my own subjective experience and the attempts to free knowledge from the methodological hegemony of Western science lead me to conclude that the "decolonization of knowledge," while providing the assurance of a relative epistemological identity/autonomy, paradoxically contributes to a reinforcement of white privilege rather than calling it into question. Whether it is presented as a claim to the right to resemblance or a claim

to the right to difference, it consecrates and confirms the hegemony of others (l'hégémonie des autres). This hypothesis is stuck in an initial power struggle that irrevocably prevents it from asserting itself without having to measure itself (whether through rejection or acceptance) against a model defined by other people.

Samba Diallo at the School of Philosophy

Students who reach their seventh year of study in Cameroonian secondary school have no doubt experienced the jubilation of discovering a new discipline called "philosophy," and a certain intellectual joy in the study of modes of argumentation that allow one to establish or refute particular theses.[1] I particularly remember a chapter entitled "Nature and Culture" in one of my philosophy textbooks. After a presentation of the different definitions of the concept of culture, we discussed, on the one hand, the relation between culture (human) and nature (to determine whether, in a particular case, the relation is one of opposition or interweaving) and, on the other hand, the relations between different cultures (ethnocentrism, cultural relativism, etc.). My enthusiasm was tempered by a certain anxiety as I discovered that certain "philosophical" questions were related to what we could fairly call "white privilege," in particular with regard to notions such as ethnocentrism.

To be sure, I was no stranger to problems of race and racial differentiation. Since my birth, I have had the chance to understand that, even without living "au pays des Blancs," or even with them, in the eyes of Africans, whites incarnate in a certain way perfection, knowledge, intelligence, and so on. I had also already discovered, through literature, notably through the "Négritude" of Aimé Césaire and of Léopold Sédar Senghor, and the work of Albert Memmi ([1966] 2002) and Frantz Fanon ([1952] 2006, 1961), a certain way of living and talking about this privilege. Thus I did not discover white privilege in philosophy class.

What was relatively new to me in studying this chapter on nature and culture was that the question of white privilege was not only part of the popular representations, among both blacks and whites, but that it also gave rise to "scholarly" theorizations and legitimations on the part of anthropologists and even philosophers such as Hegel, Lucien Lévy-Bruhl, and Arthur de Gobineau. Of course, the text on nature and culture demonstrated the falseness of these constructions and supported the idea that skin color, or even different ways of thinking, feeling, and acting, were merely different modes

of existence for an identical humanity (une humanité identique). The chapter concluded by inviting the reader to consider racism and ethnocentrism as the products of errors in judgment, theories from another age in human culture.

No sooner had I finished with that debate than I entered a new arena in which I again encountered the "philosophical" question of white privilege, this time in a way even more troubling because it more directly concerned the very discipline of philosophy in which I had resolved to engage. The question of white privilege emerged in the section of the course on African philosophy. Rather than being an opportunity to study the philosophical ideas that were developed in Africa, this section raised the question whether an African philosophy could even be said to exist. This question might initially seem quite innocent, as it might signify the simple difficulty, from a descriptive or factual point of view, of finding, in the manuals of the philosophy program, texts by African authors engaging the great questions of philosophy. The question becomes more serious, however, when it refers not only to the claim maintaining the nonexistence of such a philosophy but, above all, to the very negation of its possibility.

This question brought me back to the initial debate, where I found essentially the same protagonists: Hegel, Lévy-Bruhl, Gobineau, et al. When they did not argue directly against the possibility of African philosophy, they did intimate that the predominance of mysticism and irrationality in Africa precluded any sort of development of philosophy. Rationality is Greek, that is to say, Western; emotion is *nègre* (Senghor). Rationality is an element of Western privilege. Blacks are irremediably excluded from this privilege, owing, as Hegel argued, to a congenital deformation of their pelvis.

But the debate over the existence of African philosophy does not end there. Here too, as with relations between cultures, comforting positions are not lacking. For example, *Bantu Philosophy*, a work by Father Placide Tempels, a Belgian missionary posted in the Congo (now the Democratic Republic of the Congo), is one of the first texts that recognizes the existence of African philosophy. This text does not question the superiority of Western civilization over African civilization. Its stated objective is to provide recipes for a successful "civilizing" mission. But, for Tempels, the success of such a mission is predicated on the recognition of a system of metaphysics upon which African cultures are built—an unformulated system, to be sure, but no less real, and capable of being reconstructed by Westerners: "We do not claim that the Bantus might be capable of presenting us with a philosophical treatise articulated in an adequate language. Our intellectual education enables us to systematically develop it. It is we who can tell them, in a precise

manner, what the content of their conception of entities is in such a way that they will understand, and acquiesce, saying, 'you understand us; now you know us completely, you "know" in the way that we "know"'" (Tempels 1945, 24). White privilege is not called into question here, as blacks have been said, up to now, to be merely the Monsieur Jourdain of philosophy,[2] and it is up to whites to bring to light the (Western) philosophical concepts that have heretofore existed as a jumble of confused thoughts.

Despite Tempels's breathtaking condescension, his work is seductive. Alioune Diop, the founder of the journal (and also the publishing house) *Présence Africaine*, helped popularize Tempels's work by republishing it in 1949 (the first francophone edition, translated from the Dutch, dates from 1945), not without honoring it with an elegiac preface filled with gratitude: "Here is an essential book for the Black, to his consciousness, to his desire to situate himself in relation to Europe. . . . For me, this little book is the most important of those I have read on Africa. . . . We thank R. P. Tempels for having given us this book, a monument to the humility, sensitivity, and integrity which marked his relations with Blacks" (preface to the 1949 edition, 5–6).

The work has likewise been subject to severe critiques in both Europe and Africa (Eboussi Boulaga 1968). Nonetheless, *Bantu Philosophy* seemed to herald the end of an exclusive privilege, because what had previously been the purview of a single people was henceforth accepted as a sort of shared heritage of humanity. The end of this privilege was even accompanied by the recognition of "past ethnological errors" committed by Europeans with regard to African peoples. This was the start of what Pascal Bruckner has called "the tears of the white man" and "the tyranny of guilt" (Bruckner 1986, 2010).[3] We can see therein a certain anticipation of the Afrocentrist critique of Eurocentrism, but also the beginning of the ambiguous adventure of the decolonization of knowledge.

Afrocentrism and the "Ambiguous Adventure" of the Decolonization of Knowledge

Is Afrocentrism condemned to be defined only in relation to Eurocentrism, at the risk of negating itself in the very process of its self-definition, and, still more paradoxically, to endlessly bring about the rebirth of that Eurocentrism whose end it prepared? Molefi Kete Asante's *The Painful Demise of Eurocentrism* (2000) might be merely an illusion, a ruse on the part of Eurocentrist reason, which, rather than subsist in the form of an overt or brutal manifes-

tation of itself, gets metamorphosed into its opposite in the name of decolonization, and finds its whole substance and energy anew in that very act of self-negation.

This subtlety, this ruse, is apparent in those African authors who trumpet the recognition of an African philosophy: it is located in the assertion of resemblance by way of difference. The argument is roughly that we (Africans) *also* have our own philosophies, *just as you* (Westerners) have yours, even if our philosophies are not like yours. Yours are to be found in systematic treatises, while ours are to be found in folktales, myths, and proverbs. This is where the difference resides. But this difference is merely accidental, because what is essential is to have philosophies, and to be capable of rationality or philosophy *like you*. This is what is *identical* to the two groups. It signifies that we need not refer only to Western models in order to do philosophy. In this, we can see a certain power struggle: in the apparently simple affirmation of this "also" lies a muffled contestation of white privilege. In reality, there is no privilege when what we consider the sole prerogative of a people can also be found elsewhere, albeit in a different form. But it is in that same "also" that this Afrocentrism radically fails to emancipate itself from the hegemony of the other, because the "also" always presupposes a model or paradigm relative to which we situate ourselves. Only that which does not diverge, at least in principle, from the paradigm can be considered an "also." In this Afrocentrism, one starts from the rationality of Western thought to defend the possibility of a plurality of rationalities (Hountondji 2007). One redefines the categories or criteria of rationality only to reintroduce what the defenders of a narrow conception of rationality had excluded from it.

The partisans of this position are all the more comforted in their approach given that, even in Western culture itself, there was not always only one conception of rationality. Beside the abstract and "monological" rationalism of Descartes or Kant, there is indeed a "dialogical," communicational rationalism (e.g., Habermas). One could also call on those authors who challenged rationalism itself in a more or less radical way (Nietzsche, Bergson, Heidegger, Kierkegaard, Foucault, Sartre, etc.), in order to show that the critique of dogmatic and monist rationalism is already well under way in Western culture itself. To respond to the objections that might be raised by proponents of classical rationalism, it is enough to refer them to these authors, observing that their distance relative to rationalism never kept them from being considered philosophers.

We can see this line of defense clearly in the work of the Cameroonian philosopher Pierre Meinrad Hebga, author of works as renowned as they are

controversial, such as *Afrique de la raison, Afrique de la foi* (1995) and *La ratio-nalité d'un discours africain sur les phénomènes paranormaux* (1998). We find in most of this author's works an illustration of rational pluralism within the history of Western philosophy, with as many examples from ancient philoso-phy (Gorgias, Parmenides, Plato, Aristotle) as from modern and contempo-rary philosophy (Descartes, Kant, Hegel, Bergson, Einstein). This reading of the history of philosophy leads Hebga to argue, "*Rationality is necessarily par-ticularistic and therefore plural*. I wish to establish this incontrovertible truth through facts patent in the philosophical works of well-known Westerners, and in the essays of African thinkers. I do this not to isolate *African rational-ity* from all the others, but to show, on the contrary, that African rationality is qualified to encounter the other forms, and that the others *must recognize it* [emphasis added], discerning therein what they find in themselves" (Hebga 2007, 37).

The other thesis that Hebga defends with comparable vigor is that of the particular character of each philosophy and its tie to the specific culture that nourishes it, in which we find elements both mythical and concrete, just as in Plato and Heidegger. "More than two millennia after Plato," writes Hebga, "Heidegger, to cite only him, believed he could start from German poetry and folklore to construct metaphysical developments of *universal* signifi-cance" (37).

The Congolese philosopher Marcel Tshiamalenga Ntumba adopted the same method to defend the recourse to myth in African philosophy. If we can consider, without a second thought, the meditations of Marcus Aurelius or the maxims of La Rochefoucauld as belonging to philosophy, then we hardly see why African folktales should not find their place in the same discipline. Nothing, in either the form or the content, makes the thoughts of these authors more "philosophical" than the same genres in Africa. To establish this thesis, Ntumba constructs the following syllogism:

> If the epistemological status of a part of traditional black-African thought (A) is identical to the epistemological status of a part of pre-Socratic philosophy and similar thought (B), and if the epistemological status of the same pre-Socratic thought is philosophical (C), then it follows that the epistemological status of that part of traditional black-African thought (A) is philosophy (C). (1977, 37)

What is remarkable in both Hebga and Ntumba is that the philosophical dignity of African thought is only established by a line of argumentation that

involves finding identical traits in Western thought. There is certainly an effort to refer to norms that might be labeled universal, relative to which some thought can be considered philosophical. But these "universal" norms actually emerge from working on one particular form of thought, that is, the Western form. For Hebga, this work shows us that in Western thought, rationality appears plural. From this conclusion emerges a "universal" datum, that of the plurality of rationality. And from this datum one establishes a norm for the integration of particular forms of African thought (myths, legends, etc.) into rationality. Paradoxically, the same procedure that detaches Western rationality from its privilege as a model consecrates its paradigmatic character. Privilege is reestablished as soon as it is challenged; it is reestablished by the very procedure that contests it.

The Language of the Colonizer as the Language of "Decolonized" Knowledge

Can we decolonize knowledge, and philosophical knowledge in particular, without inventing a new language (or several new languages) of philosophy in Africa? A language is never a simple system of words; the words of a language and the particular way in which they are employed to express an idea are always imbued with a set of meanings for which it is difficult to find exact equivalents in another language. It should be added that the language of each text we read sends us back to the particularity of the culture that gives it meaning, and that this language contributes to the signification or expression of the culture itself. The language in which we choose to write either compels us to think within the particular cultural framework in which that language has meaning—insofar as this is possible—or it leads us to apply to our own context words and concepts that can only explain, in a deficient way, the realities of that context. These problems are posed in a general way in the translation, communication, and transmission of knowledge. We already encounter them in the relation between the Greek and Latin languages, when, for example, Latin authors attempt to make Greek philosophy their own (see, for example, Flamant 1992; Michel 1992). Every translator knows that "all translation is treason."

In the case of African philosophy, however, the problem is not simply a technical one. A specific difficulty arises in the degree to which the languages of knowledge are linked to domination, and with respect to the necessity of expressing oneself solely in these languages, which looks like the acceptance

or, worse, the consecration of this domination. To be sure, certain authors experience the mastery of these languages as a veritable privilege. But when it comes to analyzing the African reality itself, and to developing an African philosophy, it becomes difficult not to feel a certain amount of "shame" (in Aristotle's sense of shame at lacking the ability to use speech—see *Rhetoric* 1.1.1355b) in having to do so in another language—and, what is more, in the language of the society from which we want to emancipate ourselves culturally. As Ngugi wa Thiong'o affirmed, it is impossible to express true African sensibility in European languages, "with the baggage of their imperialist, colonialist, and racist vision of the world" (quoted in Tiyambe Zeleza 1997, 51).

The languages of African philosophy in the era of the "decolonization of knowledge" are French, English, Portuguese, German, Latin, and Arabic. It is through these languages that African authors either explain, which is to say "translate," thoughts one finds in oral literature, or expound their own thoughts constructed from more contemporary concerns. Henry Odera Oruka, who conducted a survey of several Kenyan sages, presents their thought in English in a work entitled *Sage Philosophy: Indigenous Thinkers and Modern Debate on African Philosophy* (1990).

How can we understand this quasi-exclusive recourse to European languages by authors who are clearly aware of the stakes involved, and who believe that it is important that African philosophies (at least those of African authors) express themselves in African languages? The Czech philosopher Alena Rettova advances several arguments in an attempt to explain the non-use of African languages by African philosophers: the possibility of reaching a wider audience, particularly of texts written in English; the difficulty of promoting African languages in a context of underdevelopment; the prestige attached to the mastery of Western languages; and, finally, the difficulty of selecting one among the multiplicity of African languages (Rettova 2002, 129–30).

The most serious difficulty is the very strong influence of the categories of Western thought in the very attempts to analyze African thought through recourse to words from African languages. The Rwandan philosopher Alexis Kagame begins, in his *La philosophie bantu comparée* (*Comparative Bantu Philosophy*), with the postulate that to speak of an authentic African philosophy, it is necessary to "adopt a specific cultural zone and to identify the philosophical elements contained within its language and institutions, in its folktales, stories, and proverbs" (1976, 7). He analyzes nearly 180 Bantu languages to reveal the metaphysical systems they express; his book is a

veritable magnum opus of African philosophy. We should note, nevertheless, that the analytic model that guides his study is that of Aristotle. Indeed, he attempts to construct the categories of being for the Bantu by opposing them to Aristotle's ten categories (see Rettova 2002, 140). But Aristotle's model is so integral to Kagame's analyses that we could consider it a sort of translation of Aristotelianism into Bantu thought.

Kwasi Wiredu (1998), even more motivated by the concern over "conceptual decolonization" in Africa, also focuses his attention on the question of languages, and proposes as a solution that African philosophers think in their own languages: "The main antidote to that impediment, as far as I can see, is for African philosophers to try and think philosophically in their own vernaculars, even if they still have to expound their results in some Western language" (Wiredu 2002, 56–57). But Wiredu cannot fail to observe immediately that such a strategy is not simple, because these African philosophers received their education only in Western languages. He does relativize this difficulty when he asserts that "we are not prisoners to language" (57), before adding that all philosophers must be able to achieve a certain critical distance from every language, including their own. Wiredu suggests, moreover, that conceptual decolonization must lead to a negation of itself as a motivation for African philosophers, in order to give way to a more open, more "trans-African" approach, in which one could just as well combine the elements of local languages as those of Western tongues.

Can we interpret this position as dictated by resignation? It is as if one decided to come to terms with an "adversary" because one could not get rid of him, and then justified this position by lauding the virtues of conciliation. I admit that this is a matter of conjecture, which ventures rather far into the twists and turns of individuals' intentions and motivations. However, the difficulty of sheltering oneself from the influence of a dominant system of thought makes the hypothesis of resignation altogether plausible, unless we made a dialectical conjecture that envisions the possibility of appropriating a dominant system of thought—an appropriation that would, to be sure, confirm its domination—which at the same time might allow us to banish it.

Notes

1. Samba Diallo is the name Cheikh Hamidou Kane gives the hero in his celebrated novel *L'aventure ambiguë*. I believe that there is a parallel between my discovery of white privilege in philosophy and the adventures of Samba Diallo.

2. In Molière's *Le bourgeois gentilhomme*, Monsieur Jourdain is a naïf and a buffoon, attempting to join the aristocracy. The play turns around his attempts to learn the art of "gentlemanship." (Editors' note.)

3. Bruckner's two works were first published, respectively, in 1983 and 2006.

References

Asante, Molefi Kete. 1980. *Afrocentricity: The theory of social change.* Trenton, N.J.: Africa World Press.

———. 2000. *The painful demise of Eurocentrism: An Afrocentric response to critics.* Trenton, N.J.: Africa World Press.

Bruckner, Pascal. 1986. *The tears of the white man: Compassion as contempt.* Trans. William R. Beer. New York: Free Press.

———. 2010. *The tyranny of guilt: An essay on Western masochism.* Trans. Steven Rendall. Princeton: Princeton University Press.

Eboussi Boulaga, Fabien. 1968. Le Bantou problématique. *Présence Africaine* 66:4–40.

Fanon, Frantz. [1952] 2006. *Peau noire, masques blancs.* Paris: Le Seuil.

———. 1961. *Les damnés de la terre.* Paris: Maspéro.

———. 1965. *The wretched of the earth.* Trans. Constance Farrington. New York: Grove Press.

———. 2008. *Black skin, white masks.* New York: Grove Press.

Flamant, Jacques. 1992. Macrobe: Une langue philosophique? In *La langue latine, langue de la philosophie: Actes du colloque de Rome (17–19 mai 1990),* 219–32. Rome: Publications de l'École Française de Rome. http://www.persee.fr/web/ouvrages/home/prescript/article/efr_0000-0000_1992_act_161_1_4276.

Hebga, Pierre Meinrad. 1995. *Afrique de la raison, Afrique de la foi.* Paris: Karthala.

———. 1998. *La rationalité d'un discours africain sur les phénomènes paranormaux.* Paris: L'Harmattan.

———. 2007. Pour une rationalité ouverte: Universalisation de particuliers culturels. In *La rationalité, une ou plurielle?,* ed. Paulin Hountondji, 31–44. Dakar: Codesria.

Hountondji, Paulin, ed. 2007. *La rationalité, une ou plurielle?* Dakar: Codesria.

Kagame, Alexis. 1976. *La philosophie bantu comparée.* Paris: Présence Africaine.

Memmi, Albert. [1966] 2002. *Portrait du colonisé, précédé du portrait du colonisateur.* Paris: Gallimard.

Michel, Alain. 1992. Cicéron et la langue philosophique: Problèmes d'éthique et d'esthétique. In *La langue latine, langue de la philosophie: Actes du colloque de Rome (17–19 mai 1990),* 77–89. Rome: Publications de l'École Française de Rome. http://www.persee.fr/web/ouvrages/home/prescript/article/efr_0000-0000_1992_act_161_1_4265.

Ntumba, Marcel Tshiamalenga. 1977. Qu'est-ce que la philosophie africaine? In *La philosophie africaine: Actes de la première semaine philosophique de Kinshasa,* 33–46. Kinshasa: Faculté de Théologie Catholique de Kinshasa.

Odera Oruka, Henry. 1990. *Sage philosophy: Indigenous thinkers and modern debate on African philosophy.* Leiden: Brill.

Rettova, Alena. 2002. The role of African languages in African philosophy. In *Philosophies africaines: Traversées des expériences,* ed. Jean-Godefroy Bidima, 129–50. Paris: Presses Universitaires de France.

Tempels, Placide. 1945. *La philosophie Bantoue.* Élisabethville, Congo: Lovania.

———. 1969. *Bantu philosophy.* Paris: Présence Africaine.

Tiyambe Zeleza, Paul. 1997. *Manufacturing African studies and crisis.* Dakar: Codesria.

Wiredu, Kwasi. 1998. The concept of truth in the Akan language. In *African philosophy: An anthology,* ed. Emmanuel Chukwudi Eze, 176–80. Oxford: Blackwell.

———. 2002. Conceptual decolonization as an imperative in contemporary African philosophy: Some personal reflections. *Rue Descartes* 2, no. 36: 53–64.

Contributors

Professor of philosophy (Université de Montréal) **Bettina Bergo** is the author of *Levinas Between Ethics and Politics* and co-editor of several collections, notably *Levinas and Nietzsche: After the Death of a Certain God* (2008); *Trauma: Reflections on Experience and Its Other* (2009); and *Levinas's Contribution to Contemporary Thought* (1999). She translated three works of Emmanuel Levinas, Jean-Luc Nancy's *Dis-Enclosure: Deconstruction of Christianity* (2008), and Didier Franck's *Nietzsche and the Shadow of God* (2012), among other works. She is the author of numerous articles on ethics, phenomenology, critical race theory, and feminist questions.

Eula Biss is the author of *On Immunity: An Inoculation, Notes from No Man's Land: American Essays*, and *The Balloonists*. She holds a BA in nonfiction writing from Hampshire College and an MFA in nonfiction writing from the University of Iowa. Her second book, Notes from No Man's Land, received the Graywolf Press Nonfiction Prize and the National Book Critics Circle Award for criticism. Her work has also been recognized be a Pushcart Prize, a Jaffe Writers' Award, a 21st Century Award from the Chicago Public Library, a Guggenheim Fellowship, a Howard Foundation Fellowship, and an NEA Literature Fellowship. Her essays have recently appeared in *The Best American Nonrequired Reading, The Best Creative Nonfiction*, and *Touchstone Anthology of Contemporary Creative Nonfiction*, as well as in *The Believer, Gulf Coast, Columbia, Ninth Letter, North American Review, Bellingham Review, Seneca Review*, and *Harper's*.

Eduardo Bonilla-Silva is professor and chair of the Sociology Department at Duke University. He is the author of five books, most notably *White Supremacy and Racism in the Post–Civil Rights Era* (2001); *Racism Without Racists* (4th ed., 2013); and *White Logic, White Methods* (with Tukufu Zuberi). The author of many articles, he has recently published "'Si me permiten hablar': Limitations of the Human Rights Tradition to Address Racial Inequality," in *Societies Without Borders* (2009); "When Whites Love a Black Leader: Race Matters in Obamerica," in the *Journal of African American Studies* (2009);

"The Sweet Enchantment of Color-Blind Racism in Obamerica," in the *Annals of the American Academy of Political and Social Science* (2011); and "The Invisible Weight of Whiteness: The Racial Grammar of Everyday Life in America," in *Ethnic and Racial Studies* (2011). Professor Bonilla-Silva has received various book awards, including the 2007 Lewis A. Coser Award for Theoretical Agenda Setting, given by the American Sociological Association Theory Section, and, in 2011, the American Sociological Association Cox-Johnson Award for his foundational work on racial and ethnic issues.

Christopher Bourne is professor of political science at Dawson College (Montreal). He is faculty advisor to the award-winning Dawson College Model United Nations Club and co-founded the Montreal United Nations Conference. He earned his master's degree in public policy and administration from Concordia University. He is also an accomplished editor and translator.

Nyla R. Branscombe is professor of psychology at the University of Kansas. Her research has addressed basic issues of intergroup relations from the perspectives of both disadvantaged and privileged groups. An important emphasis in her research has been the role of group history and its implications for emotional reactions to group-relevant outcomes in the present. She is the co-editor of *Collective Guilt: International Perspectives* (2004); *Commemorating "Brown": The Social Psychology of Racism and Discrimination* (2008); and *The Handbook of Gender and Psychology* (2013). Her research has benefited from a Canadian Institute for Advanced Research Fellowship—Social Interactions, Identity, and Well-Being Program.

Drucilla Cornell is Professor of Political Science, Women's and Gender Studies, and Comparative Literature at Rutgers University. She also teaches at Birkbeck College, University of London and the University of Pretoria in South Africa. Her most recent books are *uBuntu and the Law: African Ideals and Postapartheid Jurisprudence* and *The Dignity Jurisprudence of the Constitutional Court of South Africa: Cases and Materials*, Volumes I and II.

Hermenegildo Galeana is general director, dancer, and choreographer at the Ballet Mexicain de Montreal. He studied administration at the Instituto tecnológico de Acapulco from 1988 to 1992. He was choreographer and principal dancer at the Ballet Folklórico de Mexico (Mexico City), touring the world with this company as its artistic coordinator (1993–2004). He worked at the Heidelberg-Mexico Company as commercial supervisor and translator. He works with Rideau Inc. as accounts coordinator for Latin American and

North American clients. As an independent researcher, he translates literary and social science texts.

Lewis R. Gordon is professor of philosophy, Africana studies, and Judaic studies at the University of Connecticut at Storrs; Europhilosophy Visiting Professor at Toulouse University, France; and Nelson Mandela Visiting Professor of Politics and International Studies at Rhodes University, South Africa. He is the author of numerous award-winning books and articles, and his work is the subject of articles, books, and doctoral dissertations across the globe. His website is http://lewisrgordon.com.

Paget Henry is professor of sociology and Africana studies, specializing in dependency theory, Caribbean political economy, sociology of religion, sociology of art and literature, Africana philosophy and religion, race and ethnic relations, poststructuralism, and critical theory. He has served on the faculties of SUNY, Stony Brook, the University of the West Indies (Antigua), and the University of Virginia. He is the author of *Caliban's Reason: Introducing Afro-Caribbean Philosophy* (2000) and *Peripheral Capitalism and Underdevelopment in Antigua* (1985), and the co-editor of *C. L. R. James's Caribbean* (1992) and *New Caribbean: Decolonization, Democracy, and Development* (1983). His more than fifty articles, essays, and reviews have appeared in such journals, newspapers, and magazines as *Caribbean Quarterly, Social and Economic Studies, Cornell Journal of Social Relations, Encyclopedia of the Left, Sociological Forum, Studies in Comparative International Development, American Journal of Sociology, Antigua and Barbuda Forum, Third World Affairs, Bulletin of Eastern Caribbean Affairs*, and *Blackworld*. Henry is the editor of the *C. L. R. James Journal* and co-editor of the Routledge series *Africana Thought*. His fellowships include research fellow at the Bildner Center for Western Hemispheric Studies and research fellow at the Center for Inter-American Relations, and he is the recipient of a Ford Foundation grant.

Ernest-Marie Mbonda is professor of philosophy at the Université Catholique d'Afrique Centrale, Faculté de Philosophie, Yaoundé, Cameroon. He teaches moral and political philosophy and philosophy of law. His research focuses on questions of social and political justice in multiethnic societies, questions of economic and global justice, humanitarian intervention, and human rights. Among Mbonda's publications are *La philosophie africaine, hier et aujourd'hui* (2013); *Justice ethnique: Identités ethniques, reconnaissance et représentation politique* (2009); *John Rawls: Droits de l'homme et justice politique* (2008); *L'action humanitaire en Afrique: Lieux et enjeux* (2008); and *La justice globale et le droit*

d'être migrant (2005). In 2014, he published *Cosmopolitisme et universalité des droits humains. A partir de Rawls, Emboussi et Panikkar* (Québec: Presses universitaires de Laval).

Peggy McIntosh is associate director of the Wellesley Centers for Women at Wellesley College in Massachusetts. She is the founder and Senior Associate of the Seeking Educational Equity and Diversity (SEED) Project on Inclusive Curriculum at Wellesley. She consults widely in the United States and throughout the world with college and school faculty who are creating more gender-fair and multicultural curricula. In 1988, she published the groundbreaking article "White Privilege and Male Privilege: A Personal Account of Coming to See Correspondences Through Work in Women's Studies." This analysis and its shorter form, "White Privilege: Unpacking the Invisible Knapsack" (1989), have been instrumental in putting the dimension of privilege into discussions of gender, race, and sexuality in the United States. McIntosh has taught at the Brearley School, Harvard University, Trinity College (Washington, D.C.), the University of Denver, the University of Durham (England), and Wellesley College. She is co-founder of the Rocky Mountain Women's Institute and has been consulting editor to *Sage: A Scholarly Journal on Black Women*. In addition to having four honorary degrees, she is the recipient of the Klingenstein Award for Distinguished Educational Leadership from Columbia Teachers College.

Mark McMorris is the author of *Entrepôt*, a book of poetry (2010). His other books include *The Black Reeds* (1997), winner of the Contemporary Poetry Series Prize from the University of Georgia Press; *The Blaze of the Poui* (2003), a finalist for the Lenore Marshall Prize; and *The Café at Light* (2004), a text of lyric dialogue and prose. His poetry is widely published and anthologized in volumes such as *Black Nature: Four Centuries of African American Nature Poetry* (2009), *American Hybrid: A New Norton Anthology of Poetry* (2009), and *Postmodern American Poetry: A Norton Anthology* (2013). He founded and directed the Lannan Center for Poetics and Social Practice at Georgetown University, where he is currently professor of poetry in the English Department. In 2005 he was the Roberta C. Holloway Visiting Professor of Poetry at the University of California, Berkeley. Born in Kingston, Jamaica, McMorris has lived in the United States since 1979.

Tracey Nicholls is associate professor of philosophy and co-director of the Women's Studies Program at Lewis University. She received her BA in philosophy from the University of British Columbia in Vancouver, and her PhD

in philosophy from McGill University in Montreal. She works in the intersection of aesthetics and political philosophy, primarily on questions of how to build more responsive and democratic communities. Her recent publications include *An Ethics of Improvisation: Aesthetic Possibilities for a Political Future* (2012) and *Fanon and the Decolonization of Philosophy*, co-edited with Elizabeth Hoppe (2010). In addition to aesthetics and decolonization theory, Nicholls also publishes in peace studies, feminist theory, critical race theory, and the political implications of social marginalization.

Marilyn Nissim-Sabat is professor emerita of the Department of Philosophy, Lewis University (Chicago). The author of numerous essays in philosophy, psychoanalysis, feminism, and critical race theory, Nissim-Sabat has published "Where Do We Go from Here? Relational Analysis and the Struggle Against Positivism," in *Relational and Intersubjective Perspectives in Psychotherapy* (2004); "Toward a Visionary Politics: Phenomenology, Feminism, and Transcendence," in *Philosophy, Feminism, and Faith* (2003); and "Culture and Race," in *The Oxford Companion to Philosophy and Psychiatry* (2004). Currently a psychodynamic psychotherapist in private practice, Nissim-Sabat also published *Neither Victim nor Survivor: Thinking Toward a New Humanity* in 2009. Her most recent publication is "Race and Gender in Philosophy of Psychiatry: Science, Relativism, and Phenomenology," in *The Oxford Handbook of Philosophy and Psychiatry* (2013).

Victor Ray received his PhD from the Sociology Department at Duke University in 2014. His dissertation, "Collateral Damage: Race, Gender, and the Post-Combat Transition," was co-directed by Eduardo Bonilla-Silva and Linda Burton. Ray is a minority fellow of the American Sociological Association; his research interests include race and ethnicity, gender, stratification, sociological theory, and qualitative methods. Ray became an assistant professor at the University of Tennessee at Knoxville in September 2014. He recently published "Coming Home to Friendly Fire," in *Contexts* (2013), and "Scholarship: Humanities (Post-structuralism)," in *The Encyclopedia of Race and Racism* (2nd ed., 2013).

Lilia Moritz Schwarcz is full professor of anthropology at the Universidade de São Paolo. She has published on the history of race and racism in Brazil, social markers and codes of difference, the history of the Brazilian Empire and the Velha Republic, as well as the history of art and symbolic and iconic representations. Schwarcz is the author of *O espectáculo das raças* (1993, English translation, Harvard University Press, 1999); *Racismo no Brasil* (2001);

As barbas do Imperador: D. Pedro II, um monarca nos trópicos (2004), awarded the Jabuti Prize for Book of the Year; *The Sun of Brazil: Nicolas-Antoine Taunay and the French artists in Brazil* (2008, Jabuti Prize); and *The Avay Battle* (2013, Prize of the Brazilian Academy of Letters). Schwarcz has also edited several essay collections and presently directs the six-volume collection *History of The Brazilian Nation* (recipient of three Jabuti prizes to date). She was visiting professor at Oxford University, the University of Leiden, Brown, Columbia, Princeton, and L'école des hautes études en sciences sociales in Paris. A fellow of the Guggenheim Foundation (2006–7) and at the John Carter Brown Library (2007), she has been a Global Scholar at Princeton University since 2011.

Louise Seamster is a PhD candidate in sociology at Duke University, with an MA in liberal studies from the New School for Social Research. Her work focuses on new forms of economic and political exclusion in the twenty-first century, particularly in the areas of race, urban development, privatization, and citizenship. She has written extensively with Eduardo Bonilla-Silva on the racial and political implications of Barack Obama's election, including a co-edited special issue of *Political Power and Social Theory* on the meaning of Obama's election (2011). Her dissertation investigates the racial politics of emergency management and economic development in a small Michigan city.

Tracie L. Stewart is associate professor of psychology at Kennesaw State University. In her research program, she is concerned with elucidating the mechanisms through which intergroup biases are perpetuated and identifying effective strategies for reducing these biases. In much of her work, she examines the constraints under which collective guilt either facilitates or inhibits the reduction of prejudice. Her intergroup relations research has been published in such journals as the *Journal of Personality and Social Psychology*, the *Journal of Experimental Social Psychology*, the *Journal of Social Issues*, and *Psychological Science*. She serves on the editorial board of *Basic and Applied Social Psychology* and recently completed a three-year term as an associate editor for the *British Journal of Social Psychology*. Her research has been supported by a Russell Sage Foundation Cultural Contact Award and a Wayne F. Placek Award. She is a consultant on implicit bias for the U.S. Social Security Administration.

George Yancy is professor of philosophy at Duquesne University. He received his BA (with honors) in philosophy at the University of Pittsburgh, his first master's degree from Yale University in philosophy, and his second master's

degree, in Africana studies, from New York University, where he received a distinguished fellowship. He earned his PhD (with distinction) in philosophy from Duquesne University. His work focuses primarily on the critical philosophy of race, critical white studies, and the philosophy of the black experience. He has written, edited, or co-edited seventeen books and numerous academic articles. His first book, *Black Bodies, White Gazes: The Continuing Significance of Race* (2008), received an honorable mention from the Gustavus Myers Center for the Study of Bigotry and Human Rights. Three of his edited books have received *Choice* Outstanding Academic Book Awards. He has twice won the Duquesne University McAnulty College and Graduate School of Liberal Arts Faculty Award for Excellence in Scholarship. He has just completed a new edited book, *White Self-Criticality Beyond Anti-Racism: How Does It Feel to be a White Problem?* Yancy is the editor of Lexington Books' Series "Philosophy of Race."

Heidi A. Zetzer is the director of the Hosford Counseling and Psychological Services Clinic and a lecturer in the Department of Counseling, Clinical, and School Psychology at the University of California, Santa Barbara. She holds a master's degree and PhD in counseling psychology. Zetzer teaches practicum and supervision courses, supervises student clinicians, and provides psychotherapy to community clients. She has served as president of the Santa Barbara County Psychological Association and is currently the Santa Barbara County chapter representative to the California Psychological Association. Zetzer was a core faculty member in the graduate psychology program at Antioch University, Santa Barbara, from 1996 to 2006. Zetzer co-authored a handbook called *Build the Field and They Will Come: Multicultural Organizational Development for Mental Health Agencies* (2005) and is the author of "White Out: Privilege and Its Problems," in *Explorations in Diversity: Examining Privilege and Oppression in a Multicultural Society* (2nd ed., 2011).

Index

Bear Stearns, and financial crisis of 2008, 187–88
Beckford, George, 179
Beinart, Peter, 155
Bergo, Bettina, 53–67
Bergson, Henri, 233
Berkeley, Busby, 61
Bernanke, Ben, 188
Best, Lloyd, 172, 179
Bhe and Others v. Magistrate (South Africa, 2005)
　and inheritance *vs.* succession, 216, 218–19
　issues at stake in, 215–16
　majority opinion in, 216, 219
　Ngcobo's minority opinion in, 216–18, 219, 224
Birth of a Nation (1915 film), 65
Biss, Eula, 8
black achievement
　undervaluing of, 27
　white objection to, 34
Black Administration Act (South Africa), 215
Black Bodies, White Gazes (Yancy), 114
black bourgeoisie, Frazier's study on, 181
black communities, economies of
　and Africana political economy, importance of, 195
　as distinct from larger white economy, 195–97
　greater impact of crisis of 2008 on, 193, 195
　inability to escape from racialized economic patterns, 182, 195
　ongoing economic dependence on white economy, 197–98
　sectors of, 196–97
　white withdrawal of surplus value from, 196, 197
black countries
　criminalization of blackness in, 32, 36n12
　postcolonial, inability to escape from racialized economic patterns, 182, 195
black crime, and criminalization of a people, 31–32
Black Death, and origin of European whiteness, 176
blackface, in U.S. movies, 65–66
black leaders, perpetuation of white privilege despite election of, 33–34
Black Marxism (Robinson), 174
black power movement, and development of Africana political economy, 179

black radical tradition, Africana phenomenology and political economy as subfields of, 170
Black Reconstruction in America (Du Bois), 178
blacks
　rise within U.S. system, as incorporation within the machinery of oppression, 147, 148, 149, 151–52, 158–59
　sensation of being, 95–96, 96–98
　subjugation of, as part of larger U.S. racist imperialism, 147
black unemployment, as challenge to American capitalism, 191–92
Boggs, James, 179
Bolivarian Alliance for the Americas (ALBA), 156
Bolivia, and Obama foreign policy, 156, 157
Bonilla-Silva, Eduardo, 122, 146–59, 192
bourgeoisie
　black, Frazier's study on, 181
　Robinson on rise of, 175
braided narrative
　advantages of using, 1, 6, 8–9, 15
　in Biss, 8
　as restoration of voice, 6
Branscombe, Nyla R., 135–43
Brazil
　colonial characterizations of Indian natives of, 77–78
　color as contextually-dependent characteristic in, 75–76, 83–85
　color designations, stereotypes underlying, 83
　emphasis on color rather than race in, 70, 71, 74–75, 82
　festa do Flor, 73
　flexibility of color designations, 70, 74–75, 76, 81–82
　hierarchical social order of: and camouflaging of black population, 84; history of, 77–80; and miscegenation, evolution of views on, 78–79; ongoing existence of, 79–80, 86; *Pretos contra Brancos* annual football game as dramatization of, 76; and social whiteness, naturalization of, 76–77, 78–79, 80, 83; whiteness as indication of status in, 70; and whiteness as social aspiration rather than color, 83, 85–86
　Maroon societies of, 171, 177
　and mixed race individuals, advantages of, 76

customary law of South Africa
  courts' power to develop, 216–17, 218–19,
    225
  as dynamic, 218–19
  and inheritance law, 216–19
  modernity of, 225
  status of *vs.* English and Dutch law, 217,
    224–25
  succession in: changes to practice of, 219;
    vs. inheritance, as issue, 216, 218–19
  understanding of community in, 218

Davidson, Basil, 98
Davis, Adrienne D., 111
Davis, Angela, 147
Davis, Mike, 157–58
Debs, Eugene Victor, 45
decolonization of knowledge
  as goal of Afrocentrism, 229
  paradoxical reinforcement of white privi-
    lege by, 229–30
  recognition of African philosophy and, 232
Department of Homeland Security, U.S.
  coddling of homegrown white terrorists
    by, 153
  report on right-wing extremism (2009),
    153
derealization of human life, Butler on, 213
deregulation, and financial crisis of 2008,
    185
Descartes, René, and Western rationality,
    233
de Sousa Santos, Boaventura, 30, 33
despair, as response to identification of privi-
    lege, 4
Dewey, John, 22
Dickinson, Emily, 15
dictatorship of labor, during Reconstruction,
    178
Diet for a Small Planet (Lappé), 22–23
differend(s)
  in complaints about privilege, 5
  in debates with Holocaust deniers, 5–6
  witnessing against, 5
Diop, Alioune, 232
Diop, Cheikh Anta, 98
disaffirmative action, as de facto U.S. policy,
    30
disciplinary decadence
  defined, 48n2
  Gordon on, 7, 43
dispossession, whites as sites of, 111–13

diversity training
  feel-good *vs.* guilt-based approaches to,
    140–43
  increased awareness of white privilege as
    goal of, 135
Dodd-Frank Wall Street Reform and Con-
    sumer Protection Act (2010), 188
Dollfuss, Engelbert, 57–58
Douglass, Frederick, 171
do Valle e Silva, Nelson, 85
drones, U.S. use of
  in immigration enforcement, 157–58
  as indiscriminate, 154
  under Obama, 152, 153–54
  political blowback from, 154
Du Bois, W. E. B.
  and Africana phenomenology and politi-
    cal economy, 170, 171
  Black Reconstruction in America, 178
  and development of Africana political
    economy, 179
  and "negro laborer" concept, 180–81
  opposition to World War I, 158
  on Reconstruction, 178
  "The Soul of White Folks," 148, 158
  on U.S. as world policeman, 154
  on white imperialism, 146, 148, 159, 172
  and white privilege, identification of, 16

East Asia, Obama foreign policy in, 155–56
Eastern Europe
  and collapse of Soviet Union, 182
  turn toward state capitalism, 189
Easton, Hosea, 171
economics of scarcity, as justification for
    white privilege, 45–46
Ecuador, and Obama foreign policy, 156
educational disparities, as product of white
    privilege, 135
Egypt, and Arab Spring, 155
elevator effect, 53–54, 105–6
embedded conception of white racism,
    white unwillingness to accept, 106–10,
    110–13
Emigranten film industry, 57
Empowerment Zone projects, 197, 198
Enron, 184
Ephraim, Charles
  and Africana phenomenology and politi-
    cal economy, 170
  on whiteness, formation of concept,
    173–74, 176

health care, and economics of scarcity as justification for white privilege, 45–46

health care disparities, as product of white privilege, 135

Hebga, Pierre Mienrad, 233–34, 234–35

Hegel, G. W. F., 230, 231

hegemonic meanings and institutions, ethical feminism as struggle against, 211

Heidegger, Martin, and Western rationality, 233, 234

Helms, Janet E., 125–26

Henry, Paget, 169–98

Herrenvolk formulation, Robinson on, 175

Hilaire (saint), 84

Histoire Naturelle (Buffon), 78

historical inequality
current society as shaped by, 4–5
necessity of rectifying, 135
and unequal distribution of resources, 135

Hobbes, Thomas, 222–23

Hofstadter, Richard, 192

Holder, Eric, 152

Hollywood, German and Austrian filmmakers in
and B films system, creation of, 57, 65
disenchantment with U.S., 66
escapist dreams of, 58
and film noir, 58, 65, 66
flight to U.S. in 1930s, 57, 58
and frontier-saga individualism, 59
haute culture and communist-leaning branches of, 64–65
influence on U.S. film, 58–59, 65
innovative techniques of, 61
range of films by, 64
U.S. racial attitudes and, 65–66
white transcendentals of, 58

Hollywood collaboration with Austrian studios, in 1920s, 58

Holme, Ingrid, 64, 67

Holocaust deniers, differends in debates with, 5

Homo sapiens, earliest, as dark-skinned, 40, 43–44

Honduras, and Obama foreign policy, 156–57

hooks, bell, 108

Housing Rights Act of 1968, 149

Howard, John, 139

Howard University, founding of, 178

human exchange value
measures of in racial capitalism, 180, 181

rise of nonwhite economic powers and, 190

human rights
Canadian disregard for, 204–5, 206–7, 208
conceptual link of privilege to, 8
incompatibility of white privilege with, 206–7
vs. privilege, Gordon on, 8, 27, 41–42, 44
value of strong system for, 208

Hundred Years' War, and origin of European whiteness, 176

Huntington, Samuel, 183

Husserl, Edmund, 55–56

hypocognition, 22

IAT. *See* Implicit Associations Test

IBGE. *See* Instituto Brasileiro de Geografia e Estatistica

identification of privilege, negative consequences of, 4

identity
vs. appearance, tension between, 90, 91
experience of through reaction of others, 92

ideology
as myth, 55
as perceived motive for study of privilege, 2, 3, 5
real force stemming from, 55

Ignatieff, Michael, 155

Immelt, Jeffrey, 189

Immigration and Customs Enforcement (ICE), and Obama immigration policy, 157

immigration policy, under Obama, 157–58

Implicit Associations Test (IAT), 127

independence movements in Africa and Caribbean, and development of Africana political economy, 179, 180

India, rise of
and global economy, after Great Recession of 2008, 190
as threat to global racial order, 193
weakening of Western influence by, 183

Indian people, racialization of by whites, 172

individual autonomy
as incompatible with privilege concept, 18
and uBuntu, intertwining of self and large society in, 215, 217–18, 219–20, 220–21
white assumptions of, as product of white racist society, 109–10, 111–12, 113

informatic phase of U.S. capitalism
 coming fourth wave of, 189, 193–97
 definition of, 184
 financial crisis of 2008 and, 186, 188, 189
 implications for Africana political economy, 193–97
 planning for within Africana political economy, 197–98
information technology
 financialization of U.S. economy and, 185
 and Great Recession of 2008, 183
 and U.S. efforts to create "new" economy, 184, 185–86
inheritance law, as issue in *Bhe and Others v. Magistrate* (South Africa, 2005), 216–19
institutional bad faith, 27–28
institutional racism, slow progress in dismantling, 42
Instituto Brasileiro de Geografia e Estatistica (IBGE), 82–83
International Committee of the Red Cross, 208
interpellation. *See* racial interpellation
Intestate Succession Act (South Africa), 216
The Invading Socialist Society (James), 193
invisibility of privilege to privileged groups, 2, 9n1. *See also* white privilege, invisibility of
Iraq War, lack of protests against under Obama administration, 151, 155

James, C. L. R., 170, 180, 193–95
James, William, and pragmatism, 14, 15
Japan
 Obama foreign policy in, 155–56
 and post-Great Recession economy, 190
Japanese internment, as part of U.S. racist imperialism, 147
jazz music, unearned white advantage in, 29
The Jazz Singer (1927 film), 65
Jefferson, Thomas, 171
Johns, Michael, 128
Johnson, James Weldon, 28
Jolson, Al, 65, 66
Jones, Claudia, 171
J.P. Morgan Chase, and financial crisis of 2008, 186, 188
Jünger, Ernst, 57, 63

Kagame, Alexis, 236–37
Kane, Cheikh Hamidou, 237n1

Kant, Immanuel
 concept of equality in, ongoing influence of, 222
 freedom in, 223, 226
 and kingdom of ends, 223
 and Western rationality, 233
Karzai, Hamid, 153
Kendall, Frances, 122
Kgame, Alexis, 236
Khadr, Omar, 204
Khel, Renato, 78
Kierkegaard, Søren, and Western rationality, 233
King, Martin Luther, Jr.
 Vietnam War opposition, 158
 white perception of as violent, 31
Knapsack Institute, 17
Koster, Henry, 84–85
Kuti, Fela, 36n12

Lacoue-Labarthe, Philippe, 55
LaGarde, Paul de, 57
Lakoff, George, 22
Lang, Fritz, 64
Langa, Pius, 216, 219
Lappé, Frances Moore, 22–23
Latin America
 Obama foreign policy in, 156–57
 U.S. drone surveillance in, 154
Leclerc, George-Louis, Comte de Buffon, 78
Left wing
 color-blind approach of, 150
 minority politicians from, declining radicalism of, 150
 mistaken assumptions about Obama foreign policy, 152
legal disparities, as product of white privilege, 135
legal profession, obstacles erected to discourage people of color from, 29, 35n7
Lehman Brothers, and financial crisis of 2008, 186, 188
Leiter Report, critique of, 26
Leminski, Pablo, 86
Lenin, V. I., 160n2
Leonardo, Zeus, 66, 111
Levinas, Emmanuel, 212, 213
Lévi-Strauss, Claude, 72
Lévy-Bruhl, Lucien, 230, 231
Lewis, Arthur, 172, 179
liberal guilt, as perceived motive for study of privilege, 2

and antiwar protests, collapse of, 151, 155,
    158, 159
as example of black incorporation into
    U.S. machinery of oppression, 147, 148,
    152, 159
immigration policy under, 157–58
and multicultural white supremacy, 151
as new "shell" covering ongoing racist,
    imperialist U.S. policy, 146, 148, 150–51,
    152–58
perpetuation of white privilege despite,
    33–34
obligation
principles of in other cultures, willingness
    to take seriously, 214–15
in traditional African culture, 217–18, 220
    (*see also* uBuntu); and inheritance *vs.*
    succession, 216, 218–19
obstacles to black achievement, artificial,
    Gordon on, 28–29
Occupy movement, McIntosh on, 18
offensive behavior, unconscious, 121
opaque conception of white racism, 113–16
O'Reilly, Bill, and white privilege, 122–23,
    123–24
Oruka, Henry Odera, 236
Orwell, George, 4
the Other
characterization of, in Germany and
    Austrian white transcendentals of
    1930s, 63–64
nonviolent relationship to: as aspiration of
    ethical feminism, 212–14; critiques of,
    213; and inevitable violence of the politi-
    cal, 213–14; and problem of "precarious
    life," 212–13
othering of human beings, ethical feminism
    as struggle against, 211–12

Padmore, George, 180
The Painful Demise of Eurocentrism (Asante),
    232–33
Pakistan, and U.S. foreign policy, 153, 154,
    160n5
paranoid style in American politics, Obama
    and, 192–93
pardo, as racial term, 70–71, 76, 82
participation, foreclosures of by white privi-
    lege, 5
participatory difference, in Ubuntu,
    220–21
Pasternak, Joe, 58
Paul III (pope), 78

Paulson, Hank, 188
Pauw, Cornelius de, 78
Payne, Charles, 149
Pearson, Lester B., 200
Pereira, Senhor Ze Lauro, 74
Petersen, Steven E., 126
phenomenology, and sedimented images,
    56
Philosophical research on Americans (Pauw),
    78
La philosophie batu comparée (Kagame),
    236–37
philosophy
culturally-bound elements in, 235–36
Eurocentric, principles of other cultures
    as challenge to, 214–15
limited area of inquiry in, 13–14, 19
more-open conception of, potential bene-
    fits of, 14–15, 19–23
shaping of by white male privilege, 19,
    20, 21
study of in Cameroonian secondary
    school, 230
philosophy, African
definition of in terms of Western norms,
    233–35
possibility of, while using Western lan-
    guages, 235–37
recourse to myth in, as issue, 233, 234
Western characterizations of as inchoate,
    231–32
Western debate on possibility of existence
    of, 231
pieza, as measure of human exchange value,
    180, 181
plantation system, Africana political econ-
    omy and, 178
Plato, 20, 234
police, experiences with, variation by race,
    202–4
Pommer, Erich, 64
popular culture, influence of privilege con-
    cept on, 18–19
popular uprising, potential for, 198
populist movement in U.S., McIntosh on,
    18–19
Portraits of White Racism (Wellman), 16
positive psychology, in white racial identity
    development, 130
Posner, Michael I., 126
postcolonial black nations, inability to
    escape from racialized economic pat-
    terns, 182, 195

and extraction of surplus value from
   working classes, 194, 195
James' theory on, 193–95
State Capitalism and World Revolution
   (James), 193
State of Black America (National Urban
   League), 191
stereotypes of black males
   McMorris on, 90
   Yancy on, 104–5
stereotype threat, impact on attention, 127–28
Stevens, Thaddeus, 178
Stewart, Maria, 171
Stewart, Tracie L., 135–43
study of privilege
   as activism, 19
   bravery required for, 19
   comparative, interdisciplinary approach
      to, 6–9, 15
   impact of: in academia, 16–17, 22; in
      larger society, 17–18; methods of
      extending, 18–19
   as insufficient response to privilege, 4
   metaposition for, as point of contention, 2
   as still-new discipline, 16
   synthetic, issues in, 1–6
   widening of to include class, gender and
      sexual orientation, 17
Style, Emily, 19–20
subprime mortgages, and financial crisis of
   2008, 187
succession, in South Africa customary law
   changes to practice of, 219
   vs. inheritance, as issue in *Bhe and Others
      v. Magistrate* (South Africa, 2005), 216,
      218–19
Sue, Derald Wing, 120, 123, 126
supports of privilege, factitious quality of, 6
Swain, Carol, 192
sympathetic impartiality, in uBuntu, 220–21
Syria, Arab Spring in, 155

TARP (Troubled Assets Relief Program), 188
Taylor, John Russell, 64
Tea Party, as part of larger strategy of
   oppression, 149
Tempels, Placide, 231–32
Thatcher, Margaret, 33
Theweleit, Klaus, 54, 59, 61, 63
Thiong'o, Ngugi wa, 236
Third World debt crisis of 1980s, and West-
   ern economic dominance, 182

Thomas, Clarence, 149
Thomas, Clive, 172, 179
Tillotson, Michael, 33
Tobis-Sascha film studio, 58
torture
   Canada and, 200, 207–8
   by U.S., 152, 153
Toussaint Louverture, François-Dominique,
   178
transcendentals. *See* false transcendentals;
   white transcendentals
translation, call for inherent in ethical femi-
   nism, 213, 214
TransPacific Partnership, 156
Travers, Jim, 207–8
Trepagnier, Barbara, 113
trope of white privilege, Gordon's critique of,
   8, 27, 41–44
Troubled Assets Relief Program (TARP), 188
Turner, Victor, 71

uBuntu, 220–25
   as authentic African social thought, 222
   and call for translation inherent in appeal
      to universals, 214
   community-based concept of self-realiza-
      tion in, 220, 221–22
   community in, *vs.* Western social contract
      model, 222–25
   concept of freedom in, *vs.* West, 210, 215,
      224, 226
   critiques of, 221, 224
   intertwining of self and large society in,
      215, 217–18, 219–20, 220–21
   moralization of social relationships in,
      221
   participatory difference in, 220–21
   potential influence of in liberation strug-
      gles, 226
   respect for others in, 224
   South African inheritance law and, 216,
      219
   sympathetic impartiality in, 220–21
   universality of, 222, 226
Ulmer, Edgar, 58, 64
unconscious biases, sedimented images
   and, 53–54, 55–56
"uncontrollable" women and minorities,
   Gordon on exclusion of, 28
underprivileged persons, effectiveness of
   focus on, *vs.* focus on white privilege,
   136–37, 141–42

white anger, as stage in white racial identity development, Zetzer, 124
white antiracism
as stage in white development of racial awareness, 124
Yancy on, 116
white assumptions of individual autonomy, as product of white racist society, 109–10, 111–12, 113
white color-blindness
and ambush experience, 114–15
claims of, as anterior processes of subject formation, 114
white complicity in white racist society
Applebaum on, 103
importance of confronting, 107–8
painful process of confronting, 135
white reluctance to accept, 106–10, 110–13
white distancing strategies, 104. See also color-blindness; psychological strategies for minimizing white guilt; racism, white denials of
white distress, as stage in white racial identity development, 124
white embedded self, as transitive, 112
white empathy with black suffering, as erasure of race, 108–9
white guilt
barriers to development of, 136, 138–40
benefits of, 140–43
conditions necessary for experience of, 139
as goal of increasing white awareness of privilege, 135–36
Gordon on, 27
necessity of for rectifying past inequalities, 135–36, 138
psychological strategies for minimizing, 138–40
as stage in white racial identity development, 124
strength of, perceived likelihood of effective action and, 142
Yancy on, 106
white hope, Yancy on, 105, 106–7
white mediocrity in academia
cognitive incapacity to see, 27–28
Lewis on, 25–28, 35n3
white moral superiority, as incompatible with privilege concept, 18
whiteness
development of concept: Africana phenomenology on, 173, 176–77; Africana

political economy on, 172; as compulsive drive for global domination, 172; as effort to compensate for feelings of lack of full determinacy, 173, 176–77; Ephraim on, 173–74, 176; Gordon on, 173, 174, 176; historical context of, 172; as response to life-threatening events faced by Europeans, 173, 176–77; Robinson on, 174–76
as site of terror, 2, 108–9
as socially-constructed category, 7, 42–43
as transcendental purity, in films of 1930s Germany, 54
whiteness studies, and changing phenotype of racism, 159
white privilege. See also psychology of white privilege
as analogous to private laws, 3
blocking of productive multicultural relationships by, 47–48, 121
definition of, 122
economics of scarcity as justification for, 45–46
efforts to counteract in social situations, 39–40, 47
experiences of, Nicholls on, 200–201, 201–4
incompatibility with Universal Declaration of Human Rights, 206–7
increased white awareness of: benefits of, 136, 140–43; feel-good vs. guilt-based approaches to, 139–40, 140–43; obstacles to, 136–38; as unpleasant experience, 135, 138; white guilt as goal of, 135–36
individual, focus on as distraction from institutions of oppression, 147–48
invisibility of, 120–21, 135, 136, 137
as Marxist alienation of consciousness, 46
motivation for combating, perceived likelihood of success and, 140, 141–42
muddy boots metaphor for, 120–21
as mythological category, 7
opposition of to traditional American values, 18
O'Reilly interview of Obama and, 122–23, 123–24
and privileging of white worldview, 127
psychological dilemma for people of color created by, 120–21, 123
psychological strategies for minimizing personal responsibility for, 138–40